China as the World Factory

Few countries have integrated into the world economy as fast – or as dramatically – as China has since 1978. Within the next decade, China will become the largest exporting nation; this will have an effect not only on the global economy but also on individual people.

China as the World Factory brings together a team of leading international scholars to provide an analytical framework for assessing the potential and prospects of China as a world factory. They present the latest development of Chinese industrial competitiveness in the global market, and examine the policy implications of China as the world factory. This book provides a rigorous analysis of pertinent issues such as: the evolution of China's integration into the world economy; the dynamic development of China's manufacturing sector and exports; the determinants of China's global competitiveness; the role of foreign capital; and the opportunities and challenges facing China's industries after entering the WTO.

This book will prove essential reading for economists as well as all those who are interested in Chinese economic developments.

Kevin Honglin Zhang is an economics professor at Illinois State University, USA.

Routledge studies in the growth economies of Asia

China as the World Factory

Edited by Kevin Honglin Zhang

Routledge
Taylor & Francis Group

LONDON AND NEW YORK

First published 2006
by Routledge
2 Park Square, Milton Park, Abingdon, Oxon OX14 4RN

Simultaneously published in the USA and Canada
by Routledge
270 Madison Ave, New York, NY 10016

Routledge is an imprint of the Taylor & Francis Group, an informa business

© 2006 editorial matter and selection, Kevin Honglin Zhang;
individual chapters, the contributors

Typeset in Times by Wearset Ltd, Boldon, Tyne and Wear
Printed and bound in Great Britain by TJI Digital, Padstow, Cornwall

British Library Cataloguing in Publication Data
A catalogue record for this book is available from the British Library

Library of Congress Cataloging in Publication Data
A catalog record for this book has been requested

ISBN10: 0-415-70126-0 (hbk)
ISBN10: 0-203-79952-6 (ebk)

ISBN13: 978-0-415-70126-6 (hbk)
ISBN13: 978-0-203-79952-9 (ebk)

To my parents, Xuan Zhang and Suying Yang

Contents

Illustrations

Figures

Tables

Contributors

Editor

Kevin Honglin Zhang, associate professor of economics at Illinois State University, received his PhD from the University of Colorado and was a post-doctoral fellow at Harvard University and consultant with the Harvard Institute of International Development. Dr Zhang's research field is foreign direct investment (FDI), international trade, the Chinese economy, economic growth and urban economics. In addition to five books on the Chinese economy, he has published over 70 articles and book chapters in leading journals such as *Journal of Development Economics*, *Economic Development and Cultural Change*, *Journal of Development Studies*, *International Economics*, and *Urban Studies*. Dr Zhang is associate editor of *The Chinese Economy* (published by M.E. Sharpe of New York), is in the editorial board of the *International Trade Journal* (a leading academic journal in China), and was vice president of the Chinese Economists Society for two terms (2000–2001 and 2002–2003).

Contributors

Ramesh B. Adhikari is Principal Economist at the Asian Development Bank (ADB). He is currently the head of country programs and economics in Vietnam at ADB's Vietnam Resident Mission. Previously, from July 1999–July 2000, Dr Adhikari worked with the ADB Institute in Tokyo as a Senior Capacity Building Specialist in the area of development research and training; and from 1996 to 1999 he worked with ADB's economics department. Before joining ADB, he worked with Maxwell Stamp PLC, economics consultants, in London and taught at the University of Bradford, UK.

Thomas F. Cargill is professor of economics at the University of Nevada, Reno. He has written extensively on financial and monetary issues in Japan and the US and has been a visiting scholar at a number of policy-making institutions including the Bank of Japan and the Federal

Reserve Bank of San Francisco. He has also written on Korean issues, has been a visiting scholar at the Bank of Korea and is a member of the advisory council for the Korea Economic Institute, Washington, DC.

Chen Chen is a graduate student of economics at the University of International Business and Economics, Beijing, China.

Federico Guerrero is assistant professor of economics at the University of Nevada, Reno. He has been a visiting economist at both the Infrastructure and Financial Markets Division of the Inter-American Development Bank and a visiting professor at the Universidad del CEMA. He has also held positions at the University of Buenos Aires and the Universidad de San Andres. He completed his PhD at the University of Maryland, College Park.

Jie Li received his doctoral degree in economics from Lingnan (University) College, Sun Yat-Sen University in June, 2004 and is now a lecturer there. His main research interests are transitional economics, industrial organization, and international trade.

Zijie Li is associate professor of management, University of International Business and Economics (UIBE), Beijing, China. Currently he serves as executive dean of Haier Business School. He received his PhD in economics from UIBE. Dr Li's main research fields include international management and operating, enterprise and corporate theories, and industrial property. He has published regularly in top academic journals in China.

Liu Liu is currently a PhD student in economics at Fordham University, USA. Her research interests include China's foreign direct investment, labor reforms, and the financial market.

Minquan Liu is professor of economics and chair of department of environmental, resource and development economics, School of Economics, Peking University, China. He also serves as director of Center for Human and Economic Development Studies (CHEDS) in Peking University. Dr Liu was a professor at the Johns Hopkins-Nanjing Center, China, for several years after receiving his PhD in economics from Oxford University. His main research interests over China's agricultural development, credit market, foreign direct investment, and labor reforms.

Elliott Parker is associate professor of economics at the University of Nevada, Reno, and a co-editor of the *China Economic Review*. He studied under Nicholas Lardy at the University of Washington and has taught economics in China for the Johns Hopkins University, the Shanghai Institute of Foreign Trade, and the University Study Abroad Consortium.

Larry D. Qiu received his PhD in economics from the University of British Columbia in 1993. He is now an associate professor at Hong Kong University of Science and Technology. His research covers international trade, industrial organization, and foreign direct investment.

Qunyang Sun received her doctoral degree in economics from Lingnan (University) College, Sun Yat-Sen University in June, 2002 and is now a lecturer there. Her main research interests are industrial organization, transitional economics, and game theory.

Xinquan Tu, is assistant professor of economics and assistant director of China Institute for WTO Studies, University of International Business and Economics (UIBE), Beijing. He received his PhD in the field of international trade from UIBE. His expertise focuses on the World Trade Organization and Chinese foreign trade policy. Dr Tu conducted his research on US–China trade relations as a postdoctoral visiting fellow at the School of Advanced International Studies (SAIS), Johns Hopkins University.

Chen-yuan Tung is assistant professor at the Sun Yat-Sen Graduate Institute of Social Sciences and Humanities, National Chengchi University (Taiwan), director of China Economic Analysis project of the Cross-Strait Interflow Prospect Foundation, adjunct assistant professor at the Graduate Institute of National Development, National Taiwan University, and adjunct assistant professor at the Department of Economics, National Taipei University. He received his PhD degree majoring in international affairs from the School of Advanced International Studies (SAIS), Johns Hopkins University. His expertise focuses on economic relations between Taiwan and China, Chinese economic development, Taiwan–US–China relations, and international economics.

Yanling Wang is assistant professor in the Norman Paterson School of International Affairs in Carleton University. Before she joined Carleton University in 2003, she worked as a consultant in the World Bank from 2001 to 2003 focusing on trade-related technology spillovers from the north to the south. She holds a PhD in economics from Georgetown University, and a Master's from the People's University of China. Before her PhD, she worked as a researcher from 1995 to 1997 in the State & Trade Commission, PRC, addressing issues of China's ongoing economic reforms.

Yuqing Xing is associate professor of economics at the Graduate School of International Relations of the International University of Japan. He obtained his PhD in economics from the University of Illinois at Urbana-Champaign. He has been a visiting research fellow at the World Institute for Development Economics Research and the Institute of Advanced Studies of the United Nations University, among others.

He has also been a visiting professor of Japan's National Graduate Institute for Policy Studies. His research interests focus on trade, FDI, and exchange rates. He has substantial publications on the nexus of FDI and exchange rates in the context of Japanese FDI in China and other Asian countries.

Bin Xu is associate professor of economics and finance at the China Europe International Business School, and associate professor of economics at the University of Florida. He received his PhD in economics from Columbia University. His research focuses on international trade, international technology diffusion, and economic development. He has published in the *Economic Journal*, the *Journal of Development Economics*, and the *Journal of International Economics*, among others.

Luodan Xu is professor of economics at Lingnan College, Sun Yat-Sen University, China. She received her PhD at the University of Lapland in Finland. Dr Xu has been vice president of Lingnan College since 1996. Her current research and publications address FDI in China, focusing on the impact of FDI's linkage, technological spillover, and labor standards.

Yongzheng Yang is Senior Economist in the African Department at the International Monetary Fund. Before joining the IMF, he was senior lecturer at The Australian National University, where he taught international economics. Dr Yang's main research interests include international trade and the Chinese economy. He is co-editor of the book *China's Agriculture at the Crossroads* (Yongzheng Yang and Weiming Tian, eds, Macmillan, Houndmills, 2000).

Introduction

Kevin Honglin Zhang

The Chinese century

Few countries have integrated into the world economy as fast, or as dramatically, as China has since 1978, when it started opening up from almost isolation. The world's most populous country is emerging as the world factory through turning into an exporting machine. A visit to a department store will reveal that many of today's consumer goods are made in China. Export volume increased over 60-fold in 26 years, from $9.8 billion in 1978 to $593.4 billion in 2004. As a result China is now the world's third largest exporting nation, accounting for over 6 percent of world merchandise exports. It is virtually certain that China will become even more important in the near future because of its size, dynamic economic growth, and continuing policy reforms. Many analysts predict that in a few years China will become the second largest exporting nation in the world, after the US, and its share in world exports will be more than 10 percent, making it the world factory.

While these numbers are impressive, there is less understanding of fundamental issues about China's export miracle, ranging from determinants of its industrial competitiveness to the potential of China as the world factory. China's real distinction is its huge size and enormous population. The combination of its rapid economic growth, export expansions, and its large country size raises a host of interesting questions as follows: Is China's miracle real? How has China achieved an export boom, and is it sustainable for another decade?

China as the emerging world factory has immense implications for the world economy as well as the Chinese economy. A study of the prospect of the change and the factors behind the process should be of importance to both policy makers and academia. The expertise of the authors makes this book a most timely contribution to our understanding of Chinese exports, industrial competitiveness in the global market, and prospects after its entry into the World Trade Organization (WTO).

Structure of the book

The book consists of 13 chapters, which are organized into four parts. Part I presents a comprehensive investigation of China's foreign trade, especially exports, which symbolized the emergence of China as the world factory. The four chapters in Part II address the most important aspects of China's export boom, such as the role of foreign direct investment (FDI), industrial competitiveness and the rise of China as the major exporter of information industry products. Part III deals with the issues related to China's rise as the world factory in a broad perspective, including the impact on the rest of the world, the role of China in the WTO, China's financial and exchange rate system, and FDI-labor market reform linkages. Finally in Part IV, summary and concluding remarks are provided.

Chapter 1 by Kevin Zhang discusses China's foreign trade and export boom over the period of 1978–2004. His analysis focuses on the following questions: Is China's trade miracle real? How did China achieve the trade expansion, and is it sustainable for another decade? What are the main characteristics of China's trade? The basic conclusions from the study are as follows. China's achievement in foreign trade is real, but not as great as it appears or what is suggested by the raw numbers. The emergence of China as a trading nation may be explained by the rapid growth of the domestic economy, large FDI inflows, liberalized trade institutions and policies, and the devaluation in China's real official exchange rate. Along with the trade boom, five features about China's trade can be identified: the critical role of processing trade and FDI, improving trade structure of products, concentrated exporting and importing markets, concentrated sources of trade surplus and deficits, and the coastal region as trade leaders within China. China's trade boom is likely to continue for another 10–15 years because of its strong manufacturing capability, huge labor supply, and rising domestic demand.

In Chapter 2 Qunyang Sun, Larry Qiu, and Jie Li document as well as analyze how the Pearl River Delta (PRD) has become a world workshop. Since 1979, the economic reform and open-door policies in China have brought changes everywhere in the country. The economic development of PRD has been most spectacular. It has been the fastest growing region in the world for a long period of time. In addition, it is a world's workshop for products such as electrical appliances and sports wear. Why? In this chapter the authors argue that among others, the reform policies, the geographic advantage, the connection with Hong Kong, foreign trade and foreign direct investment and domestic labor mobility all are factors that contribute to the PRD's world workshop status. Moreover, local governments and enterprises (state-owned and private) are able to capitalize on these advantages and position themselves well. We provide a historical review, an analysis of recent economic data, and various economic theories (including international trade theory and economic geographic theory) to uncover the secrets to PRD's success.

China is no longer only about labor-intensive products such as toys and no longer uses foreign brand names only for exports. China is a major player in product lines that are still mass produced in industrialized countries, such as home appliances. The Chinese manufacturers have started exporting under their own brand name and set up for production on US soil, just like Haier Group in the past years. The successful story of Haier not only attracts much attention in business circles, but also raises interest in political and academic circles. How did Haier grow so fast as China's most powerful multinational company? What key strategies did CEO Zhang design at different stages of development? Why did Haier go international with the target of developed markets first? What competitive advantages does Haier have in global markets? Zijie Li and Chen Chen attempt to provide answers to these questions in Chapter 3.

In Chapter 4 Yanling Wang analyzes how China's labor structure and its cheap labor cost affect its export capacity. Using the classical Heckscher-Ohlin framework, she shows that China has a comparative advantage in labor-intensive goods compared with its top trading partners, and that China's cheap labor cost is one of the key elements attracting huge amounts of foreign direct investment. By exploring China's historical trade statistics, it shows that China has a large trade surplus in labor-intensive goods and a big trade deficit in capital-intensive goods. Finally, the article analyzes how China can climb the technology ladder by upgrading its products.

Taiwan has been one of the top sources for Mainland China's inward FDI, especially for the information technology (IT) industry. Chen-yuan Tung in Chapter 5 estimates that the increase of every percentage of Taiwan businessmen's production of IT products in China to their overall production in both Taiwan and overseas bases has increased 0.5 percentage of the market share of Taiwan businessmen's IT products in the world. In addition, between 1999 and 2001, Taiwanese businessmen contributed to around 60–70 percent of China's IT hardware products and at least 60–70 percent of China's IT hardware exports. To conclude, "Made by Taiwan but Made in China" would be a new expression to describe the global division of labor across the Taiwan Strait driven by Taiwanese businessmen's direct investment in China.

Japan is one of the top FDI sources for China. Chapter 6 by Yuqing Xing analyzes the trend, structure, and characteristics of Japanese FDI in China from 1981 to 2001. It provides an in-depth analysis on Japanese affiliated manufacturers in China at both industrial and firm levels. He concludes that: (i) Japanese FDI in China's manufacturing was mainly export oriented and using China as a production base for global market dominated the agenda of Japanese multinational corporations; (ii) reverse imports, one of the major factors driving the growth of Sino-Japan trade, represented a major activity of Japanese affiliated manufacturers; and (iii) yuan's cumulative devaluation and pegging yuan to the dollar policy performed a critical role in boosting FDI inflows, and partially explained the shift of Japanese FDI from ASEAN-4 (Indonesia, Malaysia, Philippines and Thailand) to China. The findings suggest that export-oriented FDI from leading manufacturers in Japan deepened the vertical integration between industries in the two economies, and effectively integrated China's domestic industries into fragments of global production chains.

The purpose of Chapter 7 by Bin Xu is to assess the impact of foreign competition on Chinese firms' productivity. Using a sample of 822 non-state-owned Chinese firms, Xu investigates the effects of foreign trade and foreign direct investment on total factor productivity growth of Chinese firms in the period 1998–2000. He finds that exporting firms have higher productivity growth and show evidence that the causality runs from exporting to productivity. The estimates also suggest that majority foreign ownership also enhances productivity growth. These results are robust in a growth regression that controls for factor accumulation, R&D intensity, and unobserved industry and city effects. Exporting exposes firms to international competition; majority foreign ownership facilitates transfer of foreign technology; both have contributed to the productivity growth of Chinese firms.

China's export boom has been accompanied by huge inflows of FDI since its opening up in the late 1970s. As China became the third largest exporting nation ($594 billion) in the world in 2004 from the thirty-second ($18 billion) in 1978, its FDI inflows rose from zero to $61 billion in the same period, with the accumulated FDI being as much as $560 billion by the end of 2004. The exports generated by foreign-invested enterprises in 2004 were $339 billion, comprising 57 percent of China's total exports. What role does FDI play in China's export expansion? How does FDI affect China's export performance? Kevin Zhang attempts to address these questions in Chapter 8. FDI promotes China's exports mainly through labor-intensive processes and component specialization within vertically integrated international industries, in addition to exports through converting import-substituting industries, exports through converting import-substituting industries, and exports of local raw materials processing. FDI enhances exports as well through spillover effects on local firms' exporting activities (demonstration effects, linkages, and diffusions of technology). Moreover, FDI helped in improving China's export commodity structure through expanding exports in manufactures and high- and new-technological products. However, China needs to pay special attention to FDI trade balance and upgrading of the export-oriented production.

China's increasing openness has caused considerable concerns over its impact on other developing countries, especially those in Asia. They fear that competitive manufactures from China will not only flood their markets, but also replace their exports in Third country markets, especially in industrial country markets. As China becomes increasingly attractive to FDI with its WTO accession, these developing countries also fear that FDI will be further diverted away from them. Ramesh Adhikari and Yongzheng Yang in Chapter 9 address these concerns from a broader and long-term perspective. They argue that given China's sheer size, its growing openness is bound to cause dislocation in some developing countries in the short to medium term, but it also provides many opportunities for exports and investment from other developing countries, especially in the long run. To seize upon these opportunities, these countries need to undertake further structural reforms and improve their competitiveness, just as China must continue to do to maintain its current strong growth.

China's WTO accession has substantial implications for both China and the WTO. Many people fear that China may not comply with and may even damage the multilateral trading system by right of its size and power. Chapter 10 by Xinquan Tu analyzes China's current economic and political situation and its history of integrating into the international society. It concludes that China would be willing to and able to play an important role in the WTO because of its increasing power due to rapid economic growth and opening up. China is likely to support, rather than to damage, the existing multilateral trading system since it needs the WTO to increase its own national interests. China would be a vindicator and promoter of the multilateral trade liberalization while impelling the WTO to be more development oriented from its status as a developing member.

China's current situation in both its financial system and its international exchange regime resembles the earlier experiences of Japan and South Korea in many ways. Thomas Cargill, Federico Guerrero, and Elliott Parker in Chapter 11 explore the similar history of these three nations, along with the linkage between the financial and international sectors, and argue that China has fallen into policy traps, both *vicious* and *virtuous*, that make change less likely while simultaneously offering an opportunity for further liberalization. In particular, authors of the chapter explore the undervaluation of the yuan and the effects this is having on Chinese export performance and financial markets, and discuss both the reforms necessary and the difficulties of these reforms.

Labor reforms in China have aimed at two major changes from the pre-reform system: (i) a transition from a highly compressed wage system to a market-governed one reflecting differences in human capital, and (ii) a break-up of the former rigid labor allocation system giving workers more freedom in choice of employment, including inter-regional migration. In China's gradualist market-oriented labor reforms, FDI has acted as an important catalyst for changes, serving as a model of labor reforms for domestic enterprises. Chapter 12 by Minquan Liu, Luodan Xu, and Liu Liu investigates how foreign-invested enterprises (FIEs) affect China's labor markets. New labor practices in FIEs exert a competitive pressure on domestic enterprises, overcoming former geographical and sectoral segmentations, thus helping the formation of a national labor market. Using survey data of 405 FIEs from Guangdong Province of China in 1998, this chapter studies the role of FIEs in promoting labor reforms in China. It is shown that while FDI exerts a positive impact on China's labor reforms in general (as indicated by better labor practices in wholly foreign funded than in non-wholly foreign funded enterprises), this impact in general differs according to source of investment and firms' export orientation.

The final chapter by Kevin Zhang summarizes the main points of the book and offers concluding remarks. Zhang does not merely conclude the preceding chapters but addresses the issues of why China is not the world factory yet and the potential for China to be so in the near future. The analytical framework he uses is the international comparison of industrial competitiveness and export competitiveness based on the latest data. The main reasons for China not currently being the world factory are as follows: (a) more than half of China's exports are not generated by domestic firms but FIE – "made in China" does not mean "made by China"; (b) most of the manufacturing exports are not capital- and techno-logy-intensive but labor-intensive. China is merely a manufacturing center for low-end products; (c) even in exports of labor-intensive products, China's value-added is small. China has a long way to go in building its own brand names and international marketing network. However, the potential exists for China to be the world factory due to three unique advantages: (i) its current industrial capacity and export competitiveness are growing and have already reached impressive levels; (ii) its large size provides China with tremendous bargaining power in global competition and abundant human capital as well as other resources; and (iii) its strong centralized government helps China to efficiently allocate resources in order to achieve industrial upgrading through moving from labor- and low-tech-intensive to capital- and high-tech-intensive production.

Part I
Export competitiveness

1 China's foreign trade and export boom: 1978–2004

Kevin Honglin Zhang

China has been the most dynamic trading nation in the world for two decades since 1978, when it started economic reforms. China's foreign trade experienced a phenomenal growth in volume. A visit to any department store in an industrialized country will reveal that many of today's consumer goods are made in China. In 1978 China's exports and imports accounted for only 10 percent of GDP – one of the lowest nations in the world. Since then China's trade has surged to 75 percent of GDP. As shown in Table 1.1, trade volume increased 56-fold in 26 years, from $21 billion in 1978 to $1,155 billion in 2004. As a result China has become the world's third largest trading nation, accounting for 6.5 percent of world exports. It is virtually certain that China will become even more important in the future because of its size, dynamic economic growth, and continuing policy reforms.

While these numbers are impressive, there is relatively less understanding of some fundamental elements of China's trade miracle, ranging from factors behind the trade boom to the extent of its integration with the global economy.[1] China's real distinction is its huge size and enormous population. The combination of the trade boom and its size raises a host of interesting questions, including how China achieved the success of the trade boom, and is it really as great as it appears?

This chapter addresses these two questions. Since China's emerging as a trading nation has immense implications for the world economy as well as the Chinese economy, a study of the prospect of the change and the factors behind the process should be of interest to policy-makers and in academic circles. The general conclusions of the study are as follows. China's achievement in foreign trade is real, but not as great as it appears or what is suggested by the raw numbers. The emergence of China as a trading nation may be explained by the rapid growth of the domestic economy, large inflows of foreign direct investment, liberalized trade institutions and policies, and the devaluation in China's real official exchange rate. Along with the trade boom, five features about China's trade can be identified: the critical role of processing trade, improving trade structure of products, concentrated exporting and importing markets, geographic

Table 1.1 China's trade and exports, 1978–2004

Year	Total trade			Export		
	Value ($ billion)	Index (1978 = 100)	Growth rate (%)	Value ($ billion)	Index (1978 = 100)	Growth rate (%)
1978	20.640	100	39.40	9.750	100	28.40
1980	38.136	185	30.02	18.119	186	32.64
1985	69.602	337	29.98	27.350	281	4.63
1990	115.437	559	3.37	62.091	637	18.18
1995	280.863	1,361	18.70	148.780	1,526	22.95
2000	474.308	2,298	31.52	249.211	2,556	27.85
2001	509.760	2,470	7.47	266.150	2,730	6.80
2002	620.790	3,008	21.78	325.570	3,339	22.33
2003	851.210	4,124	37.12	438.370	4,496	34.65
2004	1,154.740	5,595	35.70	593.370	6,086	35.40
Average growth rate in 1978–2004:		16.74		Average growth rate in 1978–2004:	17.12	

Sources: Computed from *China Foreign Economic Statistic Yearbook* (SSB, 1978–2004), and website of the Ministry of Commerce, China (www.mofcom.gov.cn).

concentration in trade surplus and deficits, and coastal regions of China as trade leaders.

Some cautious explanations are needed, however, for China's trade miracle. First, China's openness index (defined as trade to GDP ratio) is somewhat deceptive because of underestimated GDP and devaluations of China's real exchange rate. Second, the booming trade is misleading since most of the trade growth does not come from the ordinary trade, but the processing trade, which has little effect on the domestic economy. Third, China's trade structure of commodity is a typical inter-industry trade, in which China exports labor-intensive goods and imports capital-intensive products. The raw statistics do not indicate this clearly but suggest a dominance of intra-industry trade in manufacturing products.

Causes of trade growth: a theory

There are two basic reasons for countries to engage in international trade: comparative advantages and economies of scale (Krugman and Obsfeld, 2003). Countries differ from each other because of either factor endowments or technology. The differences thus result in lower opportunity costs for a country to produce particular goods relative to other countries. The country therefore has comparative advantage in these goods in the international markets. Countries would be better off if they produced and exported goods that have comparative advantages. International trade can also be caused by economies of scale (or increasing returns) that make each country better off by specializing in the production of only a limited range of goods.

Correspondingly, two types of trade can be identified: inter-industry and intra-industry trade. Inter-industry trade (e.g. manufactures for food) reflects comparative advantage, in which a labor-abundant country (e.g. China) exports labor-intensive goods and imports capital-intensive products, and vice versa for a capital-abundant country (e.g. the US). Intra-industry trade (e.g. manufactures for manufactures) reflects economies of scale, in which countries with a similar capital–labor ratio would specialize in a limited range of differentiated goods and trade for foreign goods for greater variety of consumption. The relative importance of inter- and intra-industry trade depends on how similar or different countries are. Countries that are similar in factor endowments and technology will not have much inter-industry trade, however, inter-industry trade will be dominant for countries that are very different. In practice, the trade between developed and developing countries is basically inter-industry trade, while the majority of the trade between developed countries is intra-industry trade.

Trade volume of a country increases with the country's economic size. As the domestic economy grows, capacity of production increases and therefore its exports expand. Demand for both domestic foreign goods becomes larger too due to economic growth. In sum, the larger the GDP for a country is, the greater trade volume. From an autarky to an open economy, liberalizing trade policy can also stimulate trade volume. Trade (especially exports) may rise when a country devaluates domestic currency relative to foreign currencies.

The pattern of trade: 1978–2004

China's opening to the outside world was probably the most visible of its economic reforms since 1978. Staring from a position of a near-autarky and an inward-looking nation, China has become one of the major players in world trade. The pattern of China's trade in the past 26 years may be characterized by the following features of this change: the significant expansion of trade volume; the increasing role of processing trade and FDI; improving trade structure of products; and the concentration of exporting and importing markets; concentrated sources of trade surplus and deficits; and coastal regions as China's trade leader.

Sources of trade growth

At the outset of its economic reforms in the late 1970s, China was an insignificant participant in international market for goods and services. Since then China's role in the international economy has been totally transformed. China's trade boom in the past 26 years may be easily seen from several indicators. As shown in Table 1.1, China's foreign trade volume (sum of exports and imports) in 1978–2004 grew by 56 times, with an average annual growth rate of 17 percent, more than double that of world trade (Tables 1.1 and 1.2). Exports increased by 61 times, from $10 billion in 1978 to $593 billion in 2004, at a growth rate of 17 percent. China's faster growth in trade than the world results in a rapid rise in China's ranking and share in the world trade. As shown in Table 1.2, China's exports share in 1977 is only 0.6 percent of world exports, ranked as the thirty-fourth. By 2004 China had become the third largest exporting country in the world, and its share in world exports increased to 6.5 percent. The expansion of China's trade has been faster than that of its gross domestic products (GDP), as indicated in Table 1.3. The ratio of trade to GDP rose from less than 10 percent in 1978 to 75 percent in 2004.

The trade boom is a result of several factors including: (a) the liberalization of trade institutions and policies; (b) the rapid growth of the Chinese economy; (c) the increase in foreign direct investment (FDI) inflows; and (d) devaluations of China's real exchange rate (World Bank, 1994, 1997; Lardy, 1992, 1994; Naughton, 1996; Zhang, 2002; Zhang and Song, 2000). The first two are straightforward. In the 1980s China began trade reforms by moving from monopoly to decentralized system. Special economic zones and open cities led to greater openings for trade. Government direct controls on trade, especially restrictions on imports, have been gradually relaxed. Thus trade reforms as a necessary condition for the trade boom was created over time. According to the theory of international trade, trade volume in a country is positively associated with that country's GDP. China's GDP grew at a rate of near 10 percent in the last 26 years, the highest in the world for that period.

The third source of the trade boom is the emergence of export-oriented foreign-invested enterprises (FIEs) (Zhang and Song, 2000). China had been the largest FDI recipient among the developing countries and globally the second since 1993, and has become the number one in the world since 2002. Most of the inward FDI in China came from Asian newly industrialized economies (NIEs), in particular Hong Kong and Taiwan, based on changing comparative advantages between China and the NIEs. The NIE invested enterprises in China emerge as a result of reallocating production into China due to rising labor costs in their homes. As more FDI flows into China and the export-oriented FIEs are established, their contribution to China's exports and imports increased dramatically. As indicated in Table 1.3, the share of exports by FIEs in total exports was 20 percent in 1992. The share was doubled after four years, and reached almost 50 percent in 2001. In fact, without exports by FIEs, China's export growth would be less than its GDP growth.[2]

The fourth factor contributing to the trade boom is devaluation of the Chinese currency relative to foreign currencies. As shown in Table 1.3, the exchange rate of Chinese currency (denoted by RMB) to US dollar was

Table 1.2 China's export share and ranking in the world, 1977–2004

Year	World exports	China exports	China's share (%)	Ranking
1977	1,126.9	7.6	0.6	34
1978	1,241.8	9.8	0.8	32
1980	1,990.6	18.1	0.9	26
1985	1,927.7	27.4	1.4	17
1990	3,470.0	62.1	1.8	15
1995	5,020.0	148.8	3.0	11
2000	6,358.0	249.2	3.9	7
2001	6,031.1	266.2	4.4	6
2002	6,384.3	325.6	5.1	5
2003	7,503.0	438.4	5.8	4
2004	8,703.5	593.4	6.5	3
Growth Rate (%)				
1977–2004	7.87	17.52		

Sources: Computed from *World Trade Report 2005* (WTO, 2005), *International Financial Statistics Yearbook* (IMF, 1978–2004), *China Foreign Economic Statistic Yearbook* (SSB, 1978–2004), and website of the Ministry of Commerce, China (www.mofcom.gov.cn).

Note
World exports and China's exports are in nominal values of billions US dollars.

Table 1.3 China's trade share in GDP, manufactured trade shares, exports by foreign-invested enterprises (FIEs), and exchange rate, 1980–2004

Year	Trade/GDP	Exports/GDP	Manufactured exports/exports	Manufactured imports/imports	Exports by FIEs/exports	Exchange rate (yuan/$)
1978	9.59	4.53	46.50	74.05		1.6836
1980	12.65	6.00	49.75	65.23	0.05	1.4984
1985	22.80	8.96	49.44	87.48	1.08	2.9367
1990	29.77	16.01	74.41	81.53	12.58	4.7832
1995	40.11	21.25	85.55	81.51	31.51	8.3514
2000	43.92	23.07	89.78	79.23	47.93	8.2784
2001	43.98	22.96	90.10	81.21	50.05	8.2770
2002	49.92	26.20	91.23	83.31	52.21	8.2770
2003	60.43	31.12	92.02	80.25	54.83	8.2770
2004	75.15	38.33	93.17	79.11	57.07	8.2770

Sources: *China Foreign Economic Statisic Yearbook* (SSB, 1978–2004), and website of the Ministry of Commerce, China (www.mofcom.gov.cn).

Note
World exports and China's exports are in nominal values of billions USD.

RMB1.6836 per US dollar in 1978. The rate was devalued gradually in the 1980s to RMB3.7651 in 1989. Then in the following five years, the Chinese government lowered the rate substantially, to the level of RMB8.6187 per US dollar. According to international trade theory China's devaluations would make its products cheaper in the world market and thus would cause its exports to grow. This is especially true, since the increase in the competitiveness of Chinese products in the world market was no as fast as it exports in the last ten years.

Main characteristics of trade

The critical role of processing trade and FDI

The duty-free processing trade in China has two variants in practice: processing imported materials into exports (*lai liao jia gong* in Chinese) and processing imported components into exports (*jin liao jia gong*). The first one, referred to as processing materials, takes place under a contract in which a foreign firm (usually located in Hong Kong) ships materials to domestic factories for processing or assembly and subsequent re-export. The foreign firm retains ownership and pays a processing fee to the domestic factories, which usually play a fairly passive role in such contracts. The domestic factories, often township or village enterprises, account for the bulk (86 percent in 1995) of this type of processing trade (Naughton, 1996). In the second type of processing trade, called processing imports, a factory in China purchases the imported materials and organizes production and exports on its own. Foreign invested firms account for the bulk of trade value under this variant (74 percent in 1995).

As a new form of trade, the processing trade has increased rapidly in China during the past 24 years. The share of exports under processing trade in total exports rose from 18 percent in 1986, to 47 percent in 1992, and to 55 percent in 2004. The share of imports in total imports went up from 16 percent to 41 percent, correspondingly (Table 1.4). At least two factors contribute to the rapidly growing processing trade. First, the export-oriented FDI strategy adopted by the government encourages foreign firms (mainly from Hong Kong and Taiwan) to engage in processing trade. Table 1.5 shows trade by ownership in 2004. FIEs generate 57 percent of total exports and 58 percent of total imports. Most of exports and imports conducted by FIEs are associated with processing trade. Along with China's cheap resources (e.g. labor and land), a variety of incentive policies also play a role in attracting large inflows of foreign investment to exporting production. The role of this kind of FIEs in processing trade increased significantly in the 1990s. The share of the trade by FIEs in total processing trade tripled in ten years from 21 percent in 1988 to 80 percent in 2004. Another factor is related to the classification method of processing trade. Due to growing globalization and international

Table 1.4 Exports by trade mode, 2004 (%)

Exporting mode	2004	1992
Ordinary trade	41.06	51.42
Processing trade	55.28	46.63
Processing and assembling with materials provided abroad	11.56	18.01
Processing with imported materials	43.72	28.62
Others	3.66	1.94
Total	100.00	100.00

Source: Website of the Ministry of Commerce, China (www.mofcom.gov.cn).

Table 1.5 Trade by ownership, 2004

	Exports	Share (%)	Imports	Share (%)
State-owned enterprise	1,535.9	26	1,764.5	31
Foreign-invested enterprise	3,386.1	57	3,245.7	58
Other	1,011.7	17	604.0	11
Total	5,933.7	100	5,614.2	100

Source: Website of the Ministry of Commerce, China (www.mofcom.gov.cn).

specialization of labor, more exports involve imported foreign contents, rather than traditional exports that have complete domestic contents only. Although domestic value-added in exports may constitute a small part in the total, the trade volume increases incredibly as a broad definition of processing trade is used in trade statistics.

Improving commodity structure of trade

Due to industrial upgrading and rapid economic growth, China's exports have being experiencing two shifts: one is from primary to manufacturing products, and the other from labor-intensive to capital-intensive manufacturing products. In 1978, more than half of China's exports (63 percent) were primary products. The share fell to 30 percent in 1988 after ten years, and then continually shrank to 7 percent in 2004, while manufacturing products became dominant in exports (93 percent), as indicated in Table 1.6. Among the manufacturing exports are machinery and electric equipments (45 percent of the total). The exports of machinery and electric equipments (relatively more capital-intensive) increased faster than textiles (relatively more labor-intensive) in the 1990s. In 1990 the share of this item in total exports was 18 percent, rising to 30 percent in 1995, surpassing textiles and becoming the largest item of exports.

Table 1.6 Trade structure by sector, 2004 (%)

Sectors	2004		1988	
	Exports	Imports	Exports	Imports
Primary goods	6.83	20.89	30.30	18.30
Manufactured goods	93.17	79.11	69.70	81.80
Chemicals and related products	4.44	11.71	6.10	16.60
Manufactured goods classified by materials	16.96	13.19	22.10	18.80
Machinery and transport equipment	45.21	45.00	5.80	30.20
Miscellaneous manufactured articles	26.36	8.93	17.40	3.60
Products not classified elsewhere	0.19	0.27	18.30	12.60
Total	100.00	100.00	100.00	100.00

Source: Website of the Ministry of Commerce, China (www.mofcom.gov.cn).

Major markets of exports and imports

China's main export markets are the leading industrialized countries (US, EU, and Japan), but it has also been strengthening its regional trade links, notably with the East Asian newly industrializing economies (NIEs). Table 1.7 reports China's top ten exporting and importing markets in 2004. The US, EU, and Japan together absorb more than half of China's total exports; 17 percent of total exports go to Hong Kong, but most of it is re-exported to the US and other industrialized economies.[3] The top ten export destinations make up nearly 90 percent of the total exports. The importance of the US, EU, and Japan in imports (37 percent) is less than that in exports. While most of the imports from the three are capital- and technological-intensive products, China increased its imports of natural resources and raw materials from Southeast Asia. Asian NIEs (Taiwan, ASEAN, S. Korea, and Hong Kong) are emerging as China's major import sources, constituting 36 percent of total imports. The share of top ten importing markets in 2004 is almost 80 percent.

Geographic distributions of trade surplus and deficits

China has been enjoying a trade surplus for about 15 years since 1990, totaling over $200 billion, with $32 billion of trade surplus in 2004. Geographically China runs trade surpluses with Hong Kong (again as re-exporter), the US, and the EU, and has trade deficits with Asian NIEs (Taiwan. S. Korea, and Malaysia) and Japan (Table 1.8). This pattern is closely associated with the processing trade conducted by FIEs (notably Asian NIEs), in which foreign affiliates import parts and components for processing and assembling, and then export most of the finished products to industrialized markets, notably the US and the EU. For example, China's surplus with US now exceeds that of Japan with the US, becoming the largest source of the US trade deficits.

Top regional exporters and importers within China

The regional distribution of trade within China is extremely biased towards coastal areas. Table 1.9 shows the leading exporters and importers by regions in 2004. While there are 31 provinces and municipalities in China, the top nine in the table generated 90 percent of total exports and 92 percent of total imports. Guangdong Province alone contributed 32 percent of exports and 30 percent of imports. It is noted that all of the nine provinces and municipalities are located in the coastal area. Such a regional bias is associated with regional disparities of FDI, income, industrial structure, and factor endowments. For example, the correlation between regional inward FDI and exports is reported as high (Zhang and Song, 2000). The export share of Guangdong is consistent with its FDI

Table 1.7 China's top 10 markets of exports and imports, 2004 (US$ billion)

Rank	Exports			Imports		
	Country/region	Value ($ billion)	Share (%)	Country/region	Value ($ billion)	Share (%)
1	US	124.95	21.1	Japan	94.37	16.8
2	EU	107.16	18.1	EU	70.12	12.5
3	Hong Kong	100.88	17.0	Taiwan	64.78	11.5
4	Japan	73.51	12.4	ASEAN	62.98	11.2
5	ASEAN	42.90	7.2	S. Korea	62.25	11.1
6	S. Korea	27.82	4.7	USA	44.68	8.0
7	Taiwan	13.55	2.3	Russia	12.13	2.2
8	Russia	9.10	1.5	Hong Kong	11.80	2.1
9	Australia	8.84	1.5	Australia	11.55	2.1
10	Canada	8.16	1.4	Brazil	8.68	1.5
	Sum of above	516.87	87.2	Sum of above	443.34	79.0
	Total	593.37	100.0	Total	561.42	100.0

Source: Website of the Ministry of Commerce, China (www.mofcom.gov.cn).

Table 1.8 China's top 10 sources of bilateral trade surplus and deficits, 2004 (US$ billion)

Rank	Country/region	Surplus	Country/region	Deficits
1	Hong Kong	89.08	Taiwan	−51.23
2	US	80.27	South Korea	−34.43
3	Netherlands	15.55	Japan	−20.86
4	England	10.21	Malaysia	−10.09
5	United Arab Emirates	5.54	Germany	−6.61
6	Spain	3.73	Thailand	−5.74
7	Mexico	2.83	Brazil	−5.01
8	Italy	2.77	Philippines	−4.79
9	Belgium	2.34	Saudi Arabia	−4.75
10	France	2.26	Angola	−4.52

Source: Website of the Ministry of Commerce, China (www.mofcom.gov.cn).

share (over 30 percent in the total). It is interesting to note that while the six provinces in Table 1.9 run trade surplus, three municipalities (Beijing, Shanghai, and Tianjin) run trade deficits.

Trade performance and prospect after China's accession to WTO

Entry into the WTO in 2001 has brought China both opportunities and challenges to trade. The new exporting opportunities for China are mainly in labor-intensive manufactures and participation in the labor-intensive segments of the production process of high-tech manufactures. As indicated in Table 1.1, China's trade and exports have expanded dramatically since 2001, with a growth rate of over 30 percent on average in 2002–2004. China's ranking in world exports rose from sixth to third in the three years. Table 1.10 presents the top ten exporters and importers in world merchandise trade in 2004. It is very likely that China will surpass the US in exports and Germany in imports in a few years, given China's faster growth that other countries.

The main driving forces behind the export boom after WTO entry are competitive prices in the world market due to cheap labor and infrastructure, rising ability of processing production, and strong global demand in world market. China's outstanding export performance has been associated with a growth in the share of manufactures, mostly labor-intensive, which amounts to over 90 percent of China's total exports. China has also been increasingly involved in the assembly of technology-intensive products (exports of telecommunications equipment and computers now account for a quarter of its total exports). A number of Chinese exports, including travel goods, toys, sporting goods, footwear and non-textile clothing, account for over 20 percent of total world exports of these products (UNCTAD, 2002a).

Table 1.9 Leading exporters and importers by regions within China, 2004

Rank	Exports			Imports		
	Province	Value ($ billion)	Share (%)	Province	Value ($ billion)	Share (%)
1	Guangdong	191.56	32.3	Guangdong	165.57	29.5
2	Jiangsu	87.50	14.7	Shanghai	86.51	15.4
3	Shanghai	73.51	12.4	Jiangsu	83.36	14.8
4	Zhejiang	58.16	9.8	Beijing	74.09	13.2
5	Shangdong	35.85	6.0	Zhejiang	27.07	4.8
6	Fujian	29.40	5.0	Shangdong	24.82	4.4
7	Tianjin	20.86	3.5	Tianjin	21.18	3.8
8	Beijing	20.57	3.5	Fujian	18.15	3.2
9	Liaoning	18.92	3.2	Liaoning	15.52	2.8
	Sum of above	536.32	90.4	Sum of above	516.28	92.0
	Total	593.37	100.0	Total	561.42	100.0

Source: Website of the Ministry of Commerce, China (www.mofcom.gov.cn).

Table 1.10 Top 10 exporters and importers in world merchandise trade, 2004

Rank	Exports				Imports			
	Countries	Value ($ billion)	Share (%)	Growth (%)	Countries ($ billion)	Value (%)	Share (%)	Growth
1	Germany	914.8	10.0	22	US	1,526.4	16.1	17
2	US	819.0	9.0	13	Germany	717.5	7.6	19
3	**China**	**593.4**	**6.5**	**35**	**China**	**561.4**	**5.9**	**36**
4	Japan	565.5	6.2	20	France	464.1	4.9	16
5	France	451.0	4.9	15	UK	462.0	4.9	18
6	Netherlands	358.8	3.9	21	Japan	454.5	4.8	19
7	Italy	346.1	3.8	16	Italy	349.0	3.7	17
8	UK	345.6	3.8	13	Netherlands	319.9	3.4	21
9	Canada	322.0	3.5	18	Belgium	287.2	3.0	22
10	Belgium	308.9	3.4	21	Canada	275.8	2.9	13
	Sum of above	5,025.1	55.0		Sum of above	5,417.8	57.2	
	World	9,123.5	100	21	World	9,458.3	100	21

Source: World Trade Report 2005 (WTO, 2005).

The big opportunity for China after accession to the WTO is the potential it has to develop self-contained, technology-intensive, large-scale manufactures that combine high quality human capital with low labor and infrastructure costs. China also has the market to support large-scale production. Such a process, based on rapid upgrading, can establish mutually reinforcing links between FDI, exports and growth (UNATCD, 2002b).

The risk for China is that if it does not take the above mentioned route, and accession to WTO encourages multinational corporations to use China as an assembly platform for low-value-added exports, the benefits of rising trade could be extremely limited in terms of technological upgrading and industrialization. Moreover, China has not gained significant market access in traditional labor-intensive manufactures, and implicitly it may not realize the expected degree of benefits in terms of export expansion.

Concluding remarks: assessing China's trade miracle

China's foreign trade has become an engine of economic growth and an engine of growth in world trade. Over the period 1978–2004, trade volume grew by 17 percent annually on average. In 1978, China was ranked thirty-second in the world in terms of exports and accounted for only 0.75 percent of total world exports. Within 26 years, it has become the third largest exporting nation and accounts for 6.5 percent.

While China's achievements in expanding trade are real, some indicators or raw figures about trade are somewhat misleading or deceptive. Three aspects are noteworthy: openness index, booming trade volume, and trade structure of commodity.

The high level of China's openness seems misleading

The index of openness, defined as a ratio of a country's trade volume to its GDP, is usually used to measure the degree of the country's economic integration with the outside world. The rapid growth of China's trade pushed the trade to GDP ratio from 10 percent in 1978 to 50 percent in 2002, much higher than that for other large countries, such as the US (21 percent) and Brazil (19 percent). Does the ratio really mean that China has been more open than the US and trade is more important in China? It is a puzzle that China's trade to GDP ratio has already surpassed the global norms and the US, which is definitely more open, since China, by virtue of its size and the diversity of its resources, should rely less on international trade than almost any other country. Is China special in that regard? Answers to this question are frequently related to the size of China's GDP, which is thought to be underestimated. Usually a developing country GDP is underestimated because of the relatively low prices of non-tradables measured by US dollars; this is especially true for China.

The issue can be addressed by using purchasing power parity-adjusted estimates of GDP, which correct for undervaluation of non-tradables. When applied to China, this brings the ratio of trade to GDP down to 9.26 percent, instead of 43.98 percent in 2001.[4] Thus China's high trade to GDP ratio, calculated conventionally, may be overestimating the openness of the economy.

Large trade volume is deceptive

China indeed has been emerging as a trading nation, but the indication of its trade volume does not reflect corresponding benefits from trade. A critical source of China's trade boom is rapid growth in processing trade in which duty-free imports of components and raw materials are imported for use in export industries. Foreign parts and components are brought in, assembled or processed using relatively low-cost Chinese labor, and then exported to world markets. This capitalizes on China's comparative advantage in labor-intensive activities and thus contributes to economic growth to a certain degree. But the value-added from this type of trade has been small relative to ordinary trade. Since 1984 when the Chinese government started to encourage imports processed for exports, processing trade rocketed to half of China's total trade in 2002. By virtue of its features, the processing trade does not create as many gains as the ordinary trade to China, since it has little connection with domestic firms and the domestic economy does not adjust both to accommodate and to benefit from this expanding volume of processing trade. If the figures on trade are adjusted to exclude processing trade, then China's trade volume reduces by half, and therefore do not appear to be quite impressive.

Intra-manufacturing trade structure is false

By 2001, 90 percent of China's exports are manufacturing goods and 81 percent of imports are manufacturing goods as well (Table 1.3). The largest item in both exports and imports is machinery and electric equipments (Table 1.5). Compared with the trade structure in the late 1970s, China indeed has improved its composition of commodities in exports and imports. But the improvement does not suggest that China has shifted its comparative advantage from labor-intensive products to capital-intensive products, nor imply that China has made significant progress in technology. Most of manufacturing goods China exports are either labor intensive, or low value-added processing exports. Almost all imports of manufacturing goods are capital intensive. For example, over 75 percent of exports in machinery and electric equipments are imports processing for exports, which are labor-intensive and low value-added. In sum, China's trade basically is still of the inter-industry, not intra-industry type.

Notes

1 While a lot of work on China's trade has emerged (for example, Lardy, 1992, 1994; World Bank, 1994, 1997; Harrold, 1995; Naughton, 1996; Zhang and Song, 2000; Zhang, 2002), comprehensive analyses on the above two issues have been limited.
2 A comprehensive discussion on the role of FDI in China's exports can be found in Chapter 8.
3 Hong Kong has played a special role as China's window to the world. Hong Kong has been an important "bridge" connecting China with the outside world. Entrepreneurs in Hong Kong have shifted manufacturing facilities to China, attracted by lower labor cost as wages rose rapidly at home. This link has brought not only much-needed capital to China but also new technology, modern management practices, and critical links to the world market. Of $560 billion in cumulative FDI to China through 2001, over 50 percent came from Hong Kong, and most of this investment went to export-oriented joint ventures. A large proportion of export production in coastal provinces (especially Guangdong) is supervised by firms in Hong Kong. Processing activities are also carried out largely in collaboration with Hong Kong partners who supply materials. Many items previously exported by Hong Kong and other Asian NICs are now exported by China, especially toys, clothes, and shoes.
4 China's GDP in terms of purchasing power parity in 2001 is $5,505,714 billion, and GDP without adjustment is $1,159,017 billion in that year (World Bank, 2002). The ratio of the former to the latter is 4.75.

References

Harrold, Peter (1995), "China: foreign trade reform: now for the hard part," *Oxford Review of Economic Policy*, 11, 4, 133–146.

International Monetary Fund (IMF) (1978–2004), *International Financial Statistics Yearbook* 1978–2004, Washington, DC: IMF.

Krugman, Paul and Maurice Obstfeld (2003), *International Economics: Theory and Policy*, 6th edn, Boston, MA: Addition-Wesley.

Lardy, Nicholas R. (1992), "Chinese foreign trade," *The China Quarterly*, 131, 691–720.

Lardy, Nicholas R. (1994), *China in the World Economy*, Washington, DC: Institute for International Economics.

Ministry of Commerce of China, website (www.mofcom.gov.cn).

Naughton, Barry (1996), "China's emergence and prospects as a trading nation," *Brookings Papers on Economic Activity*, 2, 273–344.

State Statistical Bureau (SSB) of China (1978–2004), *China Foreign Economic Statistic Yearbook* (1994, 1996, 198, 1999, and 2000), Beijing: China Statistics Press

United Nations Conference on Trade and Development (UNCTAD) (2002a), *World Investment Report 2002*, New York: United Nations.

United Nations Conference on Trade and Development (UNCTAD) (2002b), *Trade and Development Report 2002*, New York: United Nations.

World Bank (1994), *China: Foreign Trade Reform*, Washington, DC: World Bank.

World Bank (1997), *China Engaged: Integration with the Global Economy*, Washington, DC: World Bank.

World Bank (2002), *World Development Indicators*, Washington, DC: World Bank.

World Trade Organization (WTO) (2005), *World Trade Report 2005*, Geneva: WTO.

Zhang, Kevin H. (2002), "China as a new power in world trade," in Fung, Pei, and Johnson eds, *China's Access to WTO and Global Economy*, Beijing: Yuhang Publishing House, 32–49.

Zhang, Kevin H. and Shunfeng Song (2000), "Promoting exports: the role of inward FDI in China," *China Economic Review*, 11, 385–396.

2 The Pearl River Delta

A world workshop

Qunyang Sun, Larry D. Qiu, and Jie Li

Introduction

The Pearl River Delta (PRD) is a complex of deltas consisting of the West River Delta, the North River Delta and the East River Delta in Guangdong Province, China. The PRD is adjacent to Hong Kong and Macau, covers over 110,000 square kilometers and includes 14 counties.[1] As shown in Figure 2.1, the PRD is located at the mouth of the Pearl River. Partly

Figure 2.1 The PRD.

due to its strategic location, the PRD has become the most rapidly growing economic region in the world since the beginning of China's economic reforms in 1979. In October 1994, the Guangdong provincial government formally proposed to establish the PRD Economic Zone (PRDEZ), aiming to modernize the area. In this chapter, we take a close look at this region. We start with a brief description of the recent history of the PRD. We then analyze the economic development of this region over the past 20 years. Finally, we argue that this region has become the world's workshop for some products.

The rise of the PRD

Earlier history

The PRD is one of the first areas in China that opened up to the world. Dating back to the Ante-Qin Dynasty (before 221 BC), Guangzhou, the capital city of Guangdong Province and the most important part of the PRD, had already formed the rudiments of a port town. After the unification of South China by Emperor Qin Shihuang (in 221 BC), Guangzhou became a foreign trade center in South China. In the Han Dynasty (from 206 BC to AD 220), the PRD already had overseas trade and pioneered the famous Silk Road on the sea. In the Tang (from AD 618 to AD 907) and Song (from AD 960 to AD 1279) Dynasties, foreign trade activities in Guangzhou became very prosperous. In the second half of the Ming Dynasty (from AD 1368 to AD 1644), the PRD experienced a boom in foreign trade. During the Wanli Period in the Ming Dynasty, Guangzhou held foreign trade fairs twice yearly, in the winter and summer, which impacted on the social and economic developments in the PRD. The government of the Qing Dynasty (from AD 1644 to AD 1911) banned maritime trade. In 1757, all ports in Jiangsu, Zhejiang and Fujian Provinces and others were closed down, but the Guangzhou port was kept as China's only port opened to the world. This policy indirectly created a unique advantage for the PRD to further develop its foreign trade. After the Opium Wars (after AD 1840), the UK and Portugal occupied Hong Kong and Macau, successively. The location of the PRD close to these occupied territories gave it a strategic advantage over other parts of China in conducting economic activities related to international trade.

Recent history

In 1978, the Third Plenary Session of the Eleventh Central Committee of the Communist Party of China was held. It was the turning point in the history of China's economic development. Economic reforms and the opening-door policy began in China. In the earlier period of the reform, the central government implemented preferential policies in Guangdong and Fujian Provinces and encouraged them to take bold steps to develop their economies. From then on, the PRD entered a new period of economic development.

As in other parts of China, the PRD began its reforms in the rural sector. By adopting the Household Contract Responsibility System, farmers became independent producers and managers. The PRD was the first area that reformed the purchase and sale system of farm and sideline products in China. All of these reforms brought fundamental changes to the rural areas in the PRD. The most important phenomenon was the birth and growth of township and village enterprises (TVEs). Increases in agricultural productivity released millions of farmers from the land. These surplus laborers stayed in the countryside but started to produce manufacturing products.[2] As a result of economic development in the PRD, the share in GDP of the primary industries dropped from over 30 percent in 1978 to below 6 percent in 2001, and the share in GDP of secondary industries also dropped from nearly 70 percent in 1978 to 49.5 percent in 2002, while the share in GDP of the tertiary industries grew from less than 1 percent in 1978 to 45.2 percent in 2001.[3]

As early as February 1985, the State Council had already ratified the establishment of the PRDEZ. However, there were no concrete plans and policies to develop this region coherently. Local governments of various parts of the PRD lacked coordination. Furthermore, the fiscal decentralization gave them incentives to develop their local economies. There were some unexpected negative effects in the whole economy. First, local governments had strong incentives to protect their localities,[4] this prevented realization of comparative advantages and economies of scale. Second, local governments were competing for foreign direct investments (FDIs) and "processing trade" contracts, especially those from Hong Kong and Macau. This led to vicious competition and redundant industrial structures. Third, without centrally planned coordination, local governments did not take the negative externality of pollution into account when making their economic decisions. As a result, the ecological environment deteriorated seriously. In order to overcome these problems, in 1994, the provincial government of Guangdong decided to establish a formal unified economic zone, called the PRDEZ to be led by Guangzhou and Shenzhen, a newly developed city adjacent to Hong Kong. The economic zone included 12 medium-sized cities, nine small cities and over 420 towns. As a result, the PRD could comprehensively take advantage of the economic radiation effect from Hong Kong and Macau to promote the entire region's economic development in a harmonious way.

As the spearhead of the economic development in the PRD and under the influence of special preferential policies and a flexible management system, Shenzhen has become an economic wonder in the world. The total export volume of Shenzhen has ranked first in the whole country for nine consecutive years since 1993. In 2001, its total exports accounted for

14.1 percent of China's exports, 39.3 percent of Guangdong's exports and 41.3 percent of PRD's exports.[5] With the economic development, Guangzhou as a central city plays an important role in international trade, finance and information, and exhibits a great radiation effect. Led by Shenzhen and Guangzhou, the economy of the whole PRD has achieved rapid development since the 1990s.

Comparison between the PRD and the rest of the country

To better understand the spectacular performance of the PRD, let us examine some macro economic indexes for PRD and the rest of the country. The population of the PRD accounts for less than 2 percent of the national total population (see Figure 2.2). However, its contribution to the national GDP is disproportional. As shown in Figure 2.3, the PRD's share of GDP was above 6 percent in the 1990s. This ratio rose steadily and reached 9 percent in 2001. Consequently, the PRD's per capita GDP is much higher than the country's average. By 2001, its per capita GDP reached 35,792 yuan, 4.76 times the national level. Figure 2.3 shows the comparison of per capita GDP between the PRD and the whole country from 1993 to 2001. In fact, the gap in per capita GDP between the PRD and the country widens over time. This is the result of the more rapid growth of the PRD's economy than the entire country's economy, as indicated in Figure 2.4.

Let us now turn to the structure of the PRD's GDP. The PRD is not rich in natural resource endowments. Decentralization and specialization has resulted in the reduction of the output of the primary industries. The output of the secondary industries increased in the late 1980s and early

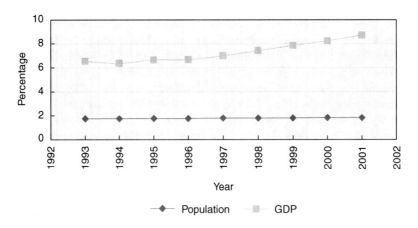

Figure 2.2 Ratio of PRD's population to GDP above national levels (sources: *Guangdong Statistical Yearbook* (1993–2001); *China Statistical Yearbook* (1993–2001)).

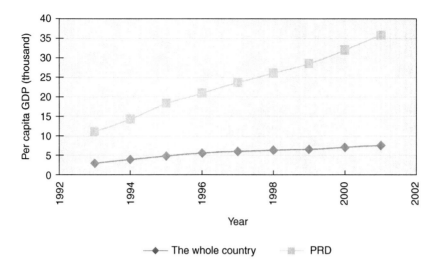

Figure 2.3 Per capita GDP of the PRD and the whole country (source: Guangdong Statistical Yearbook (1993–2001); China Statistical Yearbook (1993–2001)).

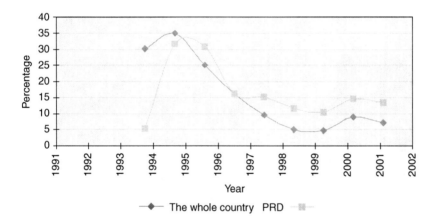

Figure 2.4 Comparison of GDP growth rate between the PRD and the whole country (sources: *Guangdong Statistical Yearbook* (1993–2001); *China Statistical Yearbook* (1993–2001)).

1990s, thanks to the capital and technology influx from abroad, particularly Hong Kong, Taiwan and Macau. However, with the rising labor costs in the PRD, the share of the labor-intensive manufacturing sector in the total GDP declined slightly from its peak level of around 51 percent in 1994 to a steady-state level of around 49 percent after 1996, as indicated in Figure 2.5. In contrast, the output of tertiary industries grew very fast in

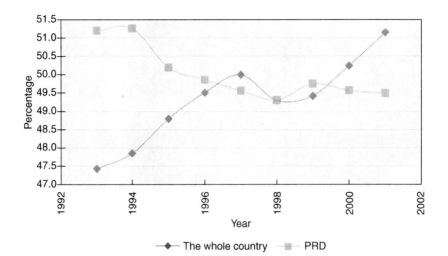

Figure 2.5 Comparison of the share of output from secondary industries in GDP between the PRD and the whole country (sources: *Guangdong Statistical Yearbook* (1993–2001); *China Statistical Yearbook* (1993–2001)).

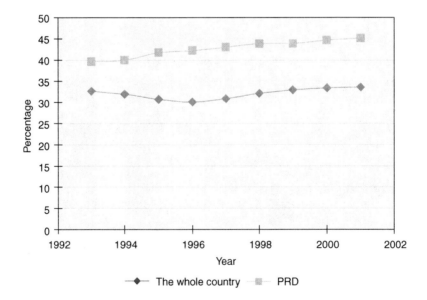

Figure 2.6 Comparison of the share of the output from tertiary industries in GDP between the PRD and the whole country (sources: *Guangdong Statistical Yearbook* (1993–2001); *China Statistical Yearbook* (1993–2001)).

the 1990s. By 2001, the GDP share of the tertiary industries reached 48 percent in the PRD, which is higher than the country's average by ten percentage points, as shown in Figure 2.6.

Economic growth and structure are related to employment growth. Figure 2.7 compares the employment growth rates of the PRD and the nation. During the period 1994–2001, the average rate of employment growth in the PDR was about 3 percent per year while that of the entire country was around 1 percent. Two factors contributed to this continuous high employment growth. First, the long period of GDP growth requires increase numbers of laborers. Second, the industrial structureal change from the resource-intensive primary industries to the labor-intensive secondary and tertiary industries also creates high demand for laborers.

Perhaps the most impressive performance of the PRD economy is its contribution to the country's trade and FDI. Since 1992, the PRD has attracted more than 15 percent of total FDI inflows to China. This share continued to increase and was close to 30 percent by 2001. Figure 2.8 shows the realized FDI inflows to the PRD as a percentage of total FDI in the country.[6] In 2001, total realized FDI in the PRD reached US$14.19 billion. Why is the PRD so attractive for FDI? The most important reason is its proximity to Hong Kong and Macau in terms of geographical location, language, culture, and kinship. Moreover, high productivity and a healthy market environment also encourage foreign investors to choose it as their ideal host location. These factors also make products produced in

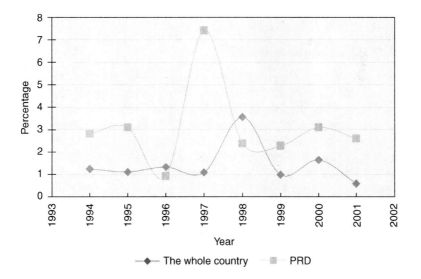

Figure 2.7 Comparison of employment growth rates between the PRD and the whole country (sources: *Guangdong Statistical Yearbook* (1993–2001); *China Statistical Yearbook* (1993–2001)).

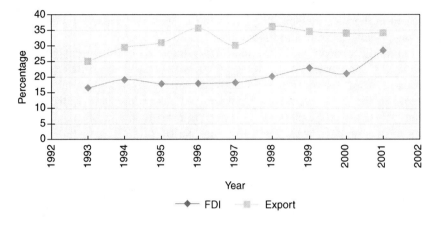

Figure 2.8 Shares of the PRD's FDI and exports in the country (sources: *Guang-dong Statistical Yearbook* (1993–2001); *China Statistical Yearbook* (1993–2001)).

the PRD more competitive in the world markets than those made in the other parts of the country. In addition, most FDIs from Hong Kong are export-oriented. All these factors together enable the PRD to outperform the rest of the country in foreign trade. Figure 2.8 shows that the PRD contributed to more than 30 percent of the country's total exports on average over the period 1993 to 2001. The PRD's export value was US$90.83 billion in 2001.

The PRD as a world workshop

In 2001, Japan's Ministry of International Trade and Industry (MITI) issued a White Paper that mentioned for the first time that China had become the "World's Workshop". Since then, this topic has attracted world attention and serious discussion. The discussion shows that the Chinese economy has been integrated into the global economy and China's economic development in general, and its opening up in particular, has exerted more and more influence on the world economy.

What is a *world workshop*? This term has never been given a clear definition. We are not attempting to provide such a definition here. Rather, we choose to describe two important elements of a world workshop. In general, a world workshop is part of a worldwide economic network that links production to markets. In particular, there is a division of labor between manufacturing industries and market services. A world workshop is a region where large-scale production is concentrated and a substantial world market is supplied by firms located there. However, the term world workshop has different connotations during the industrialization age and the information age, as argued by the Public Policy Group of the Institute of Comprehensive Development and Research, Shenzhen, China (2003). Specifically, during the industrialization age, whether or not a region can become a world workshop depends on the share of its total manufacturing capacity in the world and its share of world exports. In contrast, a world workshop in the information age has a broader definition and is an extension and development of the world workshop in the industrialization age. In the information age, a world workshop must have comprehensive improvements in its manufacturing ability and, more importantly, must be a processing center in the global production network.

In this section, we explore the economic development of the PRD and argue that the PRD is already a world workshop for some manufacturing products. The geographic focus is important because the PRD has been the powerhouse of China's economic growth since the reform and open-door policy began in 1979. If the PRD is not qualified to be a world workshop, then it is difficult to argue that the other parts of the country are world workshops.

FDI from Hong Kong as the means and channel for the PRD to merge into the world economy

How does the PRD engage in the world economy? FDIs, especially those from Hong Kong, are the single most important vehicle. We see this from a comparison on the utilization of FDI between the PRD and the whole country.

Figure 2.9 shows that since 1993, the total amount of utilized FDI invested in the PRD accounts for more than 70 percent of FDI in all of Guangdong Province. In particular, this ratio has been over 80 percent since 1997 and it reached 90 percent in 2001. This figure also shows the importance of FDI inflow to the PRD in the whole country.

Who made FDI in China and in the PRD? There are companies in more than 40 countries and regions that have supplied FDI in Guangdong, but firms from Hong Kong have made the major contributions. During the nine years from 1993 to 2001, the total amount of utilized FDI in Guangdong was equal to US$121.2 billion. Hong Kong was the primary source of foreign capital and its share accounted for 68.2 percent of the total, followed by Taiwan, Japan, and the US, whose shares in Guangdong were 3.8 percent, 3.4 percent and 3 percent, respectively. FDI from Macau and Korea each accounted for 1 percent to 2 percent, and investments from other countries were each less than 1 percent.

It is interesting to make a comparison between the distribution of the FDI sources to Guangdong and that to the whole country. From Figure 2.10 and Figure 2.11, which are based on the cumulative realized FDI from 1993 to 2001, it is easy to observe two things. First, the general distributions are very similar. Hong Kong is the largest source of Guangdong's

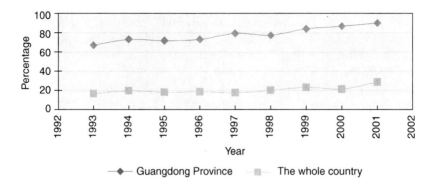

Figure 2.9 FDI and PRD over that in Guangdong Province and the whole country (sources: *Guangdong Statistical Yearbook* (1993–2001); *China Statistical Yearbook* (1993–2001)).

FDI and also the country's FDI and the top ten countries/regions account for most FDI (84.81 percent for Guangdong Province and 82.6 percent for the whole country). Hence, there is a heavy concentration of investment from and dependence on ten countries/regions, especially Hong Kong. Second, although Hong Kong ranks first as a source of foreign capital in Guangdong and in the whole country, its proportion differs dramatically. Hong Kong's investment accounts for 44.7 percent of the country's total FDI inflows, but it contributes 69.2 percent of the FDI in Guangdong. This indicates the relative importance of Hong Kong in affecting the economic development structure of Guangdong and the PRD. It is for this reason that in the following analysis we will focus on the linkage between Hong Kong's economy and the PRD's economy to see how the world workshop in the PRD was formed. Figure 2.10 and Figure 2.11 also reveal some other differences. As a source of foreign capital nationwide, Singapore ranks fifth and France ranks ninth, but they both rank beyond number ten in Guangdong's FDI; Macau ranks the fifth in Guangdong, while it takes the tenth position in the whole country.

FDI from Hong Kong has had a tremendous influence on the industrial development of the PRD. Hong Kong experienced rapid growth in the 1970s, which resulted in significant rises in labor costs. In the 1980s, the traditional labor-intensive manufacturing sectors in Hong Kong, such as textiles and clothing, toys and electronic products, lost their comparative advantages. Naturally, Hong Kong business people started to look for new production locations from which they could still maintain competitive. It was at that time when China began its economic reforms and adopted its open-door policy. Since the Hong Kong manufacturers' markets were in North America, Europe and other overseas countries, it was natural for them to move their production base to the neighboring PRD where it was

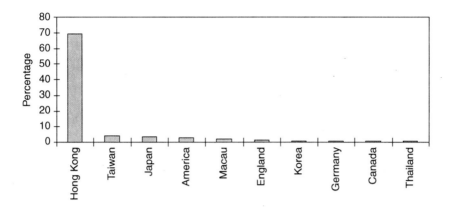

Figure 2.10 Sources of FDI in Guangdong Province (1993–2001) (source: *Guang-dong Statistical Yearbook* (1993–2001)).

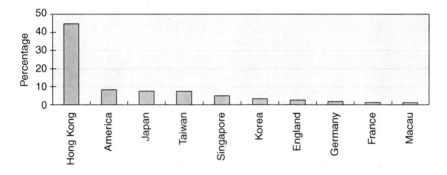

Figure 2.11 Sources of FDI in China (1993–2001) (source: *China Statistical Year-book* (1993–2001)).

easy for them to travel and also it was cost-effective for the products to be exported via Hong Kong. This became a popular mode of production fragmentation: product design, packaging, financing, and marketing were all in Hong Kong, and factory production was in the PRD, which has been called the mode of "shop in the front and factory in the backyard", or SF&FB for short. Ever since, this business mode has been keeping the two economies, Hong Kong and the PRD, in a close relationship. The SF&FB mode, originally innovated by Hong Kong businesses, was later, in the 1990s, imitated by Taiwanese businesses to transfer IT (information technology) production to the PRD. We will further explore this issue later.

The economic linkage and cooperation between Hong Kong and the PRD has been studied by many researchers within China. By comparing the differences between Hong Kong and the PRD in terms of labor cost, capital, technology, and market, Han (1997) argues that the SF&FB mode has real advantage in Southern China's economy. It combines cheap labor of the inland with the modern production technologies from Hong Kong to produce commodities that satisfy world demands. Hu and Sheng (2002) discuss the tendencies of the SF&FB mode by focusing on the changes in industrial structure and development. They believe that new modes of regional cooperation should be adopted and should take the development of high technology as their main focus. Xue (2003) examines the cooperation and development among Hong Kong, Macau and Guangdong since the Chinese reforms began. He argues that the future SF&FB mode should be like the following: the PRD focuses on its comparative advantages in labor and land while Hong Kong and Macau make use of their market experience, management, financial, foreign trade, and other services, to take the advantage of the increasing globalization in general and China's WTO accession in particular. At the same time, he argues that the more than 20 years of effort have built a strong reputation for the "made in China" label in the world. The world workshop has become an international image of Hong Kong, Macau and Guangdong. Feng (2003) thinks the SF&FB mode is not out of date, but needs improvement and extension. The economic cooperation between Guangdong and Hong Kong should be multi-outlet. For example, the cooperative mode should not stay at the level of the SF&FB, unification of shop and factory (US&F for short) is also a feasible cooperative mode. Furthermore, the cooperation should be extended to the service and garment industries. Zhang (1994) reviews the mutual complementarities and mutual dependence of the Hong Kong economy and the PRD economy since the reforms and calls for further increasing the economic cooperation between the two. He argues that considering the future prospect of economic development, cooperation in the tertiary industries, especially the financial industry, should be strengthened to promote adjustments and upgrades of the industrial structure.

In this section, we attempt to provide a more systematic and more rigorous analysis of the world workshop theory applied to the PRD. In particular, we argue that the SF&FB mode, as a unique means of economic cooperation between the PRD and Hong Kong, is still of strategic importance in the era of globalization and China's accession to the WTO. It is still an effective approach to integrating the PRD into the global economy.

First, the economic structures of the two economies (i.e. Guangdong and Hong Kong) are still highly complementary. For example, in 2001, the service sector in Guangdong only accounted for 40 percent of the GDP, while this percentage in Hong Kong was more than 80 percent. This indicates that the PRD still has to rely on Hong Kong to provide the function of the "shop" in the front. On the other hand, manufacturing costs (including rental, labor, and others) are still very high in Hong Kong, which suggests that the PRD can still serve as an efficient backyard factory. This view is supported by recent observations. In 2002, the Industrial Federation of Hong Kong and the University of Hong Kong jointly conducted a survey among local firms in Hong Kong and found that among the 100,000 companies responding to the survey, 60,000 of them had set up manufacturing plants, via foreign direct investment, in the PRD. They employed more than ten million workers in total. Hence, it is safe to say that the SF&FB mode is still strong in this area, a viewpoint also shared by Lin and Zhu (2002).

Second, the SF&FB mode is the primary vehicle for Hong Kong and Guangdong to jointly participate in global production. This can be viewed through the amount of processing trade conducted between Hong Kong and Guangdong. The SF&FB mode is a basic form used by many multinational enterprises (MNEs) to procure their products and distribute them in the world market. The types of the products are mainly light consumables such as textiles and clothing. The features of such industries are that labor cost accounts for most of the total cost. That is, they are highly labor intensive. For these products, it is natural to place the production stage in a low cost country/area, such as the PRD. MNEs such as Nike and Adidas have been using subcontracting to outsource their products. Low production costs and efficient deals are exactly what the MNEs want. The SF&FB mode can provide efficient deals (in the front using the shops) and low production costs (in the backyard using the factories). That is why over the past 20 years, the PRD became the biggest processing and export base in textiles, clothing, shoes, clocks and watches, and toys. We will return to this point later with specific data for further elaboration.

The PRD as the workshop in the international division of labor

In this section, we explore whether or not the PRD satisfies the requirement for a world workshop by examining the economic development of the PRD, with focus on its manufacturing structure, labor costs, and export capacity.

Ever since China began its reforms, the PRD has become the most rapidly developing and richest region in China. The PRD has the highest per capita GDP in the country. After Deng Xiaoping's southern tour in 1992, the PRD economy appears to have an accelerated growing trend. During the period 1993–2001, its average growth rate in per capita GDP was 16.1 percent per annum, much higher than the national average. The per capita GDP of the PRD in 1993 was 11,000 yuan, 3.76 times the country' average; and by 2001, per capita GDP of the PRD reached 35,800 yuan, 4.76 times the country's average.[7]

During the reform period, China's economy achieved great success. Its purchasing power has been greatly improved and the domestic market's potential is enormous. The share of China's GDP over the world increased from 1.79 percent in 1993 to 3.43 percent in 2000.[8] Hence, the domestic market also provides a strong base for the PRD to become a world workshop.

China's manufacturing capability has also improved over time. The value added by the manufacturing sector accounted for 33 percent in China's GDP in 1990, and this share increased to 38 percent in 1999. The increasing rate is faster than the average level of the world. The share held by the Chinese manufacturing industry continues to increase. In 1990 the added value of China's manufacturing industry accounted for 4 percent of the world, and by 1999, it reached 8.8 percent with an annual growth rate at 0.48 percent, which shows that Chinese manufacturing industry is becoming the world production center year by year. In 1990, the total export of Chinese manufacturing products accounted for 1.6 percent of the world's total manufacturing exports, but in 1999, this number increased to 3.3 percent.[9] Notice that the PRD, as one of the main manufacturing production bases in the whole country, is an important contributor to this achievement. Processing trade is the main driving force for the manufacturing activity in the PRD and we shall pay special attention to this mode in the following discussion.

There was almost no processing trade in the beginning of the economic reforms (1979). Then, starting from the middle of the 1980s, processing trade began to blossom in Guangdong. It has become the mainstay of the export-oriented economy of Guangdong. Guangdong's exports increased to US$95.426 billion in 2001 up from only US$1.4 billion in 1978, with an average annual growth rate of 20.9 percent.

From Table 2.1, we can clearly see the growth and importance of the processing trade in Guangdong. The processing trade refers to trade when local firms provide labor service to produce products for exports with materials supplied by foreign firms or samples provided by foreign firms or to assemble parts supplied by foreign firms. This also includes compensation trade. Since the mid-1980s, the proportion of processing trade in total trade has been above 60 percent, and it has been following an increasing trend. This ratio reached 80 percent by 2001. Although we do not have the figures for the PRD alone, it is clear that the ratio in the PRD is higher than the provincial average. The ratio of processing trade to GDP is equally impressive. In recent years, the value of processing trade in Guangdong accounted for more than 60 percent of the province's GDP. This shows the importance in the world market of the PRD's economy and the export-orientation of this economy.

Some sectors make very large contributions to this region's processing trade. By the end of 2001, the output of the electronics and communication equipment manufacturing industries in the PRD amounted to 291.777 billion yuan, accounting for one-third of the national total. The PRD has become one of the largest manufacturing bases for information products not only in China, but also in Asia. In the area of new materials, the

Table 2.1 Two ratios on processing trade

Year	Total processing trade (billion US$)	As a percentage of Guangdong's GDP (%)	As a percentage of Guangdong's total export (%)
1987	6.751	29.68	66.58
1988	9.786	35.53	66.05
1989	12.810	34.92	70.72
1990	16.008	49.12	72.04
1991	20.444	57.47	75.51
1992	25.262	56.23	75.50
1993	29.136	48.92	77.92
1994	36.214	69.10	72.12
1995	42.276	61.57	74.70
1996	47.156	60.14	79.49
1997	.54.831	62.13	73.54
1998	58.361	61.01	74.53
1999	60.377	59.05	77.73
2000	71.782	61.50	78.09
2001	76.505	59.99	80.17

Sources: Guangdong Statistical Bureau, Guangdong Foreign Trade and Economic Cooperation Bureau.

Table 2.2 Sectoral contribution to Guangdong's foreign trade

Year	Total export of electronics and communication equipment (billion US$)	(1) as percentage of Guangdong's total export (%)	High-tech export (billion US$)	(3) as percentage of Guangdong's total export (%)
1999	38.865	50	12.03	15.50
2000	49.980	54	17.02	18.50
2001	55.380	58	22.29	23.35

Source: Guangdong Foreign Trade and Economic Cooperation Bureau.

PRD's output of new ceramics and electronic devices accounts for one-half of the country's total production; its production of synthetic fibers and plastics accounts for one-third of the national total output; and its production of organic silicon accounts for one-quarter of the country's total. In 2001, high-tech products produced in the PRD reached 350 billion yuan, a 43-fold increase over the 1991 level. The proportion of high-tech products to the value of industrial total output increased from 3.3 percent in 1991 to 19.44 percent in 2001. The export of technology products was close to 130 billion yuan, which accounts for 40 percent of nationwide production. Table 2.2 below shows the relative importance of electronics and communication equipment and high-tech products in Guangdong's total export.

We now discuss labor costs and labor productivity. Obviously, China enjoys the advantage of cheap labor costs due to an almost unlimited labor supply. In 2000, the average annual salary of a manufacturing employee in China was 8,750 yuan, equivalent to one-thirtieth of the employee's US counterpart's nominal wage, one-quarter and one-fifth of that of workers in Malaysia and the Philippines, respectively.[10] Due to the low level of urbanization in China, in the coming 20 years, China will still enjoy this labor cost advantage. Although, the PRD has experienced high and sustained economic growth, its labor cost has not increased proportionally. The low-skilled labor force in this region is drawn mainly from the inland regions of China, as the result of the southward "rush of peasant job seekers". According to some scholars' raw estimations (see Wang, 1999), ten years ago, there were about seven million migrant laborers in the PRD and their average salary was around 500 to 600 yuan per month. Now, in the same job market, the average salary remains at a similar level as ten years ago. This indicates that because of the existence of the migrant labor supply, the advantage of low labor cost in the PRD has not faded away.

Of course, low labor cost does not necessarily mean high productivity. We should adjust labor cost using productivity when comparing labor cost advantages across the country. China has low productivity compared with many other countries. Hence, with productivity adjustments, China's labor cost advantage in the labor-intensive sectors should be downward adjusted. In fact, taking the statistics from 1995 to 1999 for example, when measuring the labor cost according to the same value added in the manufacturing industry, the labor cost in the US is just 1.3 times higher than that in China, and the labor costs in the Philippines, Indonesia and Korea are all lower than that in China. Hence, in order to become a real world workshop, China must improve its productivity and efficiency. Since there is high labor mobility (especially for low-skilled labor) in China and in particular in the PRD, we should not examine the labor productivity of the PRD in isolation. Instead, we look at the whole country's labor quality. According to the statistics from the *Chinese Statistical Yearbook* (2001), for every 10,000 people, the enrollment in colleges and universities was 206.3 in 1990 and 719.1 in 2001, the latter being 3.48 times greater than the former and the annual growth rate being 46.62 percent. This is an indicator of improving labor quality.

We now turn to exports. We can divide exports into three categories: domestic exports, processing export and exports by foreign-invested enterprises (FIEs). FIEs are all foreign direct investments in China and they are either Sino-foreign joint ventures or wholly foreign owned enterprises. Processing exports involves little capital investment and is thus not very risky. In the early years of China's reforms, foreign businessmen, including those from Hong Kong, were not confident about China's commitment to reform and so chose the less risky investment activity, i.e., processing exports. With growing confidence in and familiarity with the business environment, foreign investors later began to use FDI to tap the Chinese market. In the 1990s, FDI surpassed processing-trade investments and became the most popular form of foreign capital inflow in Guangdong. In 1993, there were 31,876 FIEs in the PRD and, by the end of 2001, there were 38,679, with an increase of 850 firms per year.[11]

Figures 2.12 and 2.13 illustrate the contributions of processing export and FIEs to the PRD's total exports in recent years. Total exports from the PRD increases every year since 1993. Exports from processing trade

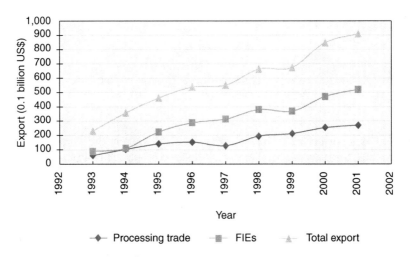

Figure 2.12 Export trends in the PRD (1993–2001) (source: *Guangdong Statistical Yearbook* (1993–2001)).

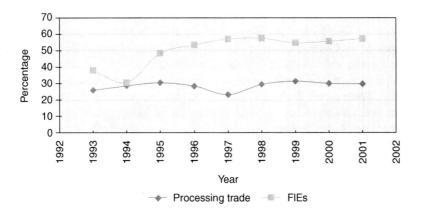

Figure 2.13 Shares of the two types of exports in the PRD (1993–2001) (source: *Guangdong Statistical Yearbook* (1993–2001)).

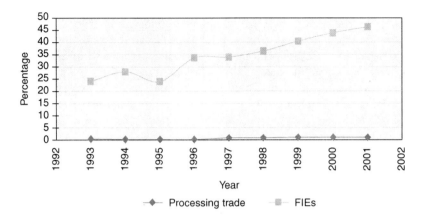

Figure 2.14 Shares of the two types of exports in other regions (source: *China Statistical Yearbook* (1993–2001)).

and FIEs also increase almost every year. However, the contribution of processing trade to the total exports (close to 60 percent) was much higher than that of FIEs (around 30 percent). Notice that processing trade helped the PRD to become a world workshop. Although FDI also contributed to the world workshop status of the PRD, some of the FIEs sold their products to the local market only. The relative importance of processing trade in the PRD can be seen more clearly by comparing its share in the PRD (shown in Figure 2.13) to that in the rest of the country (shown in Figure 2.14).

The development and importance of the information and electronics industries in the PRD, in particular in Shenzhen and Guangzhou, are particularly striking. The two key cities are home to a group of large, high-tech enterprises. Among the top 100 electronics and information enterprises approved by the Ministry of Information Industry in 2001, there are 17 located in Guangzhou and Shenzhen. In 2002, China's total export of software was about US$1.5 billion, of which US$400 million, or more than one-quarter of the total, were contributed by Shenzhen (Guangzhou Tianhe Technology Park, 2003). Moreover, almost half of China's largest 14 mobile communications enterprises made Guangzhou or Shenzhen their home. Partly because of the concentration of these two industries, Guangzhou and Shenzhen contributed half of the whole provincial GDP, and their GDP annual growth rate was over 12 percent from 1993 to 2001, which was 2.5 percent to 3 percent higher than the provincial average.[12] The success of these two cities has stimulated development of high-tech industries across the entire PRD. The IT industrial communities and electrical appliances industrial communities have been set up. The east bank of the Pearl River, which includes Shenzhen, Dongguan, and Huizhou, forms an IT industrial group; while the west bank of the Pearl River, which includes Guangzhou, Foshan, Jiangmen, and Zhuhai, forms an electrical appliances group. These two groups have become an international production base. In particular, the strength of the electrical appliances industry on the west bank of the Pearl River is great. Take the key city of the electrical appliances group, Foshan, as an example. The domestic market share held by Foshan in terms of air conditioners, refrigerators, microwave ovens, and seven other categories of products exceeds 30 percent. The IT industry on the east bank of the Pearl River is equally spectacular. For instance, the volume of computer hard disks made in the PRD accounts for 30 percent of world production and the PRD produces more than 10 percent of the world output in computer chips, floppy disks, keyboards, and CD-ROM drivers. The high-tech industry has made a huge contribution to regional economic growth. In 2001, the value of high-tech products in the PRD reached 350 billion yuan, accounting for 18.6 percent of the provincial industrial output.[13] The PRD has now become the third largest production base of information products in the world, following after the US and Japan. Companies such as HuaWei Group and TCL Group have become the world's top suppliers of information products. Their products have been reaching across the world (Hu and Sheng, 2002).

Dongguan, a city in the PRD and northwest of Shenzhen, is one of the biggest processing bases for electrical products. Its development is noteworthy. Because of its geographical and cultural uniqueness (many Tawainese have relatives in Dongguan), it has close relationships with Taiwanese firms. At present, there are over 4,000 Taiwanese-funded enterprises in the PRD and many of them have rooted in Dongguan. As a result, the economy of Dongguan and that of Taiwan have developed hand-in-hand. Dongguan is the primary production base for many Taiwanese computer firms outside Taiwan. By processing IT products for Taiwanese firms, Dongguan has been able to enter the world market. It is evident that IT products made in Taiwan have enjoyed a good reputation in the international market. Acer, Liteon, Delta, MSI, Giga-Byte, and Primax all are famous brands worldwide. Dongguan has made good use of the "brand name effect" that the Taiwanese firms have brought to the city and has naturally become the principal manufacturing base for IT products in the world. According to statistics released by the Taiwanese Business Association in 2001, among all the Taiwanese-funded enterprises in Dongguan, 53 of them are pure PC manufacturing enterprise, and more than 500 others are also engaged in producing related electronic products. Many other enterprises produce PC products such as rubber, pattern plates, telecommunications cables, and packaging materials. In the past few years, all products related to PCs have grown rapidly. Displays, modems, main boards, and all types of chips and other equipment from Dongguan exceed 10 percent of the world market share. It is expected that the semi-conductor industry and other IT industries from Taiwan will be moved to the mainland. Dongguan is a natural host region for this transformation and will become an even bigger production base for IT products (Tong and Wang, 2001).

From the above analysis, it is clear that the PRD has an attractive comparative advantage in labor costs, location advantages and a good investment environment, which have attracted a great deal of FDI and processing trade activities. All these help make the PRD a world workshop for a range of manufacturing products.

Some theoretical explanations

In this section, we attempt to provide some theoretical explanations for the world workshop phenomenon in the PRD. We make use of the comparative advantage theory, the industry ladder theory, and the Wintelism theory of the economic cluster effect.

More than 150 years ago, David Ricardo introduced the comparative cost theory. The gist of the theory is that productivity differs across countries, which usually results in differences in the comparative cost of production. A country should specialize in producing and therefore should export the products for which it has comparative advantages, and this country should import other products for which it does not have comparative advantages. In the early period of the last century, Heckscher and Ohlin developed an international trade theory based on differences in factor endowments. This theory posited that a country should specialize (not completely) in producing and therefore should export the goods that use the country's relatively abundant resources more intensively (in a relative sense) in their production. In particular, a capital-abundant country should export capital-intensive goods and import labor-intensive goods. In view of these theories, China should export labor-intensive goods and low-tech products. It should be noted that these traditional trade theories define comparative advantage based on given conditions of technologies and natural endowments. They are static in nature.

We are living in a dynamic world, however. On one hand, with increasing globalization, factors of production have become less restrained in international flows. Technologies can be easily transferred from one country to another, while capital movements, via FDI or portfolio investment, increase every year. This reduces differences among countries in technologies and endowments. On the other hand, through investment in human capital, improvement in the quality of the production factors can compensate for the disadvantage in quantity. Hence, comparative advantages bear the characteristics of dynamic change. One implication from this observation is that with capital and technology transfer from Hong Kong, Taiwan, and other regions, and with human capital improvements in China, the PRD can gain comparative advantages in producing some capital- and technology-intensive products.

The traditional comparative advantage theory neglects the existence of increasing returns to scale and imperfect competition. A new trade theory based on increasing returns to scale and imperfect competition emerged in the late 1970s and early 1980s, thanks to Paul Krugman and others. This theory emphasizes that products are differentiated and countries can import and export the same industrial goods, which is the so-called intra-industry trade. Initial comparative advantages do not determine the pattern of trade in these industries. Government intervention and historical events can alter the pattern of trade.

Drawing from the insights of the dynamic comparative advantage theory and the new trade theory mentioned above, we can explain the dynamics of economic development in some regions, such as the PRD. The upgrading of the industrial structure depends on improvements in factor endowments, i.e. an increased share in capital and technology in total factor endowment, and the increasing returns to scale due to fixed investment in capital and technology. At each stage of economic development, dynamic adjustment should be carried out according to the change in the structure of the factor endowments. Meanwhile, the upgrade and transformation of the industrial structure should be carried out in line with changes in international market demand. All of these contribute to building up competitiveness in the international market. The dynamic changes of comparative advantage within a country and across all countries result in the upgrade of industrial structures.

In the beginning of China's reforms, due to the preferential policies, its advantageous geographical location and the existing network of overseas Chinese, the PRD attracted a lot of overseas Chinese, especially from Hong Kong and Macau, to invest in and set up factories there. Relying on Hong Kong and Macau's capital, technology, managerial experience, and international market network, and combining with local and the interior region's cheap labor, the PRD gradually formed the unique economic mode of SF&FB and achieved industrialization in a short period of time. However, in the 1980s, the industrial structure of the PRD mainly focused on traditional manufacturing industries, such as clothing, textiles, plastics, electronic components, and metal and non-metal products. These are by and large labor-intensive products on a relatively low rung on the industry ladder. This industrial structure was an inevitable result of the fact that China's economic development was still in its infancy and also that China had comparative advantage in low-skilled labor in the international division of labor. In this process, Hong Kong played an important role. Due to their own high labor costs, Hong Kong firms chose the PRD to locate their factories to process, assemble, and produce low-skilled, labor-intensive products. At the same time, with Hong Kong a free port and an international financing, shipping, and information center, Hong Kong firms had to keep part of their businesses at home, such as financing, design, marketing, and packaging, to enjoy their own comparative advantage. This is how the SF&FB model was formed.

With the economic developments in the PRD, per capita savings deposits reached 18,730 yuan in 1997 with an annual rate of increase at 34 percent since 1980. Effective supply of capital also became an advantage of the PRD, in addition to low labor costs. Processing and assembling industries achieved sustainable high growth, which in turn led to high demands for infrastructure improvements, such as transportation, electric power, and energy. At the same time, the labor quality has improved, however, cheap labor is no longer the sole factor that boosts the PRD economy. The factor endowment structure has shown substantial changes. Physical capital, technology, and human capital have become more and more important in the PRD's economic development. The economy is ready to transform from relying on labor-intensive industries to relying on capital-intensive, technology-intensive, and even information-intensive industries. Meanwhile, with the arrival of the information age, demand for computer products has increased dramatically. Hence, it has become possible for the PRD to use its accumulated factor advantages to develop the computer and information industries. In the 1990s, the PRD set up policies to encourage development of computer, information, biological engineering, and other high-tech industries. The area aims at further optimizing its industrial structure.

The above discussions offer partial explanations for the PRD's formation of world workshop. The Wintelism theory gives a supplementary explanation for the rapid growth of the manufacturing industry and heavy inflow of foreign capital to the PRD. At the beginning of the 1990s the US economy experienced a rapid recovery due to the birth of the so-called "New Economy." On the one hand, by relying on the prosperous stock market and the effects of asset accumulation the American economy maintained fast growth; on the other in contrast to the past situation in which traditional industries boosted the economy, now the "New Economy" took the information industry as its impetus. Its core is Wintelism, i.e. the US now depends on the Windows operating system and Intel central processors to leverage its control over the computer industry and other information industries in standardization and "soft" technology and on the electronic information industry to drive the growth of the whole economy (Borrus and Zysman, 1997; Tan, 2002). Wintelism provides a persuasive theoretical foundation to explain the economy of clusters with an international division of labor and the composition of transnational corporations. The basic features of this foundation are that technology-advanced top enterprises only control the research and development (R&D) and market standards of the products and they transfer massive manufacturing to other countries. As a consequence, Wintelism motivated the 1990s' reformulation of the division of labor internationally. The wide use of information technology has expanded this mode from the PC industry to other industries.

It is well known that traditional enterprises emphasize all-embracing large enterprises to attain economies of scale and scope. That is the so-called Fordism (McDermott, 1992; Mansfield, 1992). But in IT industry, what is stressed is a new production mode called the economies of cluster. Its emphasis is on cooperation between all component providers. Each enterprise only focuses on production of certain parts or components so as to realize economies of scale; meanwhile, mutual coordination between various enterprises can also create economies of scope. Different from traditional large enterprises, firms in the PC industry are very flexible and therefore they can avoid the malpractice of rigidity in traditional mega-enterprises. We can clearly see that, since the 1990s, industry structures and enterprise organizations in Taiwan have been oriented in this way. In sharp contrast, by following the Fordist mode, the Korean consortia suffered a serious attack during the Asian financial crisis because its pace of adjustment could not keep up with the new development. In fact, in the past 20 years, the PRD experienced fast economic growth and structure changes against this international environment.

Wintelism accelerates industrial upgrades and shortens of product cycles. Under Wintelism, the focus of market competition is not only on maintaining product diversity but also on ensuring the speed of the release of high-tech products into the market. The harsh requirement of speed alters the product life cycle theory in international trade and in international division of labor. Under Wintelism, every two years a new series of products will come out, and the innovating enterprises usually make their profits only in the first three months when the products are introduced into the market. Afterwards, very little profit is made in the local markets, and they have to find new markets to absorb their new products. The most obvious consequence of this trend is that in the middle of the 1990s, America's Silicon Valley, which originates innovations in information products, and Taiwan's Xinzhu, with a large-scale production base, established a direct link. Xinzhu has the capacity for synchronous large-scale production. In turn, since the late 1990s, Taiwanese enterprises transferred part of their production chain to the PRD, which brought on the development of electronic and information manufacturing industries in the PRD.

Under Wintelism, US enterprises have built a new transnational production system. This is a network in which enterprises rely on R&D, product design, purchasing, processing, distribution, and other supportive activities. In the period of Fordism, the economy was driven by direct investment in transnational corporations and successive internal transactions, but it now relies more and more on coordination between enterprises. As far as an enterprise is concerned, the transnational production system includes its subsidiaries, branch offices, subcontractors, suppliers, distribution channels, joint ventures, strategic alliances, and other cooperative deployments. In the past, all these activities were conducted and managed within the transnational corporations vertically. Now, under the impact of the new transnational production system, capital-scarce, small and medium-sized enterprises can be involved in globalization, which was possible only for mega-enterprises in the past. Compared with traditional Fordism, the striking feature of the new transnational corporation system is the cooperation between independent transnational enterprises, through which a large part of value-added is fulfilled outside the leading enterprises, and even the managing function of the whole enterprises can be obtained through outsourcing. Thus, a leading enterprise becomes a virtual one. But due to the impact of Wintelism, leading enterprises control the sales channel and market standards, and the realization of value is still in the hands of America's leading enterprises. On the other hand, after controlling the highest value-added in the market, they are willing to transfer large-scale production to places with the lowest labor cost and sufficient efficiencies. The PRD is one such place.

Due to the prevailing Wintelism and formation of industrial clusters and transnational horizontal division, western enterprises select investment places worldwide. High-quality but low-cost labor and cost advantages in other factors of production in the PRD have a strong appeal to transnational enterprises. In addition, with the support of the reforms and open-door policy, western corporations have transferred their labor-intensive manufacturing bases to the PRD. After China's accession to the WTO and the economy's integration with the international economy, the PRD will become even more attractive. In pursuit of the economic effects caused by clusters, more and more enterprises will move to the PRD, which in turn will help to promote the PRD as a world workshop.

Conclusion

The PRD is an economic phenomenon. It is the region with the fastest growth in the world over the past two decades. It is a region that has become the major supplier for many products in the world market, that is, it is a world workshop for some manufacturing products. Why? In this chapter, we have reviewed the history of the PRD, examined its recent economic developments and tried to provide both evidence as well as theoretical explanations for why and how the PRD has become a world icon of economic development. We argue that, among others, the reform and open-door policies, the geographic advantage, the connection with Hong Kong, foreign trade and foreign direct investment, and domestic labor mobility are all the factors that contribute to the PRD's world workshop status. Moreover, the local governments and enterprises (state owned and private) are able to capitalize on these advantages and position themselves well. They know that they should integrate their regional economy into the world economy and therefore they should specialize in producing certain products and engage in certain stages of the production and service chain. We hope that lessons can be drawn for other regions in China and other countries as well.

The world is still changing and so is China. China has become a new member of the World Trade Organization, which implies that the country is committed to opening its economy further, making and keeping its business practices compatible with the rest of the world, improving its environment, and strengthening intellectual property rights protections. China will continue to change the world's economic landscape. It is conceivable that more world workshops will arise in some other regions in China. The PRD will continue to play an important role in the Chinese economy as well as the world economy as a world workshop.

Acknowledgment

We are thankful for financial support from the Hong Kong government (RGC research grant: HKUST6412/00H), the National Natural Science Foundation of China (NNSFC10131030) and Shichuan Foundation of Sun Yat-Sen University.

Notes

1 The PRD includes the following cities and counties: Guangzhou, Shenzhen, Zhuhai, Foshan, Jiangmen, Dongguan, Zhongshan, Huizhou, Huiyang, Huidong, Boluo, Zhaoqing, Gaoyao, and Sihui.
2 See Zuo (2001) for a discussion and economic analysis of TVEs in China.
3 Industries in China are classified according to the historical sequence of development. The primary industries include extraction of natural resources; secondary industries include processing of primary products; and tertiary industries are services of various kinds for production and consumption. Specifically, primary industries include farming, forestry, animal husbandry, and fishery; secondary industries include construction, mining and quarrying, manufacturing, production and supply of electricity, water, and gas; tertiary industries include all other industries not included as primary or secondary industries.
4 See Li *et al.* (2003) for an analysis of local protection under fiscal decentralization.
5 *China Statistical Yearbook* (2002) and *Guangdong Statistical Yearbook* (2002).
6 In China, there are two statistics for aggregate FDI. One is contracted FDI and the other is realized (or actual) FDI. The former is obtained according to contracts signed by foreign investors and it represents the pledged amount that foreign investors would bring into China. The latter is the actual amount of FDI that foreign investors have already brought into China. Usually the contracted amount is larger than the realized amount.
7 *China Statistical Yearbook* (1994–2002) and *Guangdong Statistical Yearbook* (1994–2002).
8 *International Statistical Yearbook* (2001).
9 *International Statistical Yearbook* (1991–2000).
10 *International Statistical Yearbook* (2001).
11 *Guangdong Statistical Yearbook* (1994–2002).
12 *Guangdong Statistical Yearbook* (2002).
13 *Guangdong Statistical Yearbook* (2002).

References

Borrus, M. and Zysman, J. (1997) "Wintelism and the Changing Terms on Global Competition: Prototype of the future?", Working Paper 96B, BRIE, UC Berkeley.

China Statistical Yearbook (1993–2002) Beijing: China Statistical Bureau.

Feng, X. (2003) "A reconsideration of the mode of shop in the front and factory in the backyard", *Jingji qianyan* 5, (in Chinese).

Guangdong Statistical Yearbook (1993–2002) Guangzhou: Guangdong Statistical Bureau.

Guangzhou Tianhe Hi-tech Park (2003) *Industry Survey of Software in Guangdong Province*, (in Chinese).

Han, Z. (1997) "The strategic advantage of shop in the front and factory in the backyard", *Shangye jingji wenhui 1*, (in Chinese).

Hu, J. and Sheng, J. (2002) "An investigation of industry clusters and hi-tech industry cooperation between Guangdong and Hong Kong", *Jingji qianyan* 12, (in Chinese).

International Statistical Yearbook (1990–2001) Beijing: China Statistical Bureau.

Li, J., Qiu, L.D., and Sun, Q. (2003) "Interregional protection: implications of fiscal decentralization and trade liberalization", *China Economic Review*, pp. 227–245.

Lin, J. and Zhu, W. (2002) *A Study of the Harmonious Development of Hi-tech Industry Park among Dongguan, Hong Kong and Taiwan*, (in Chinese), Working paper (survey), Lingnan University College, Sun Yat-sen University, Guangzhou.

Mansfield, E. (1992) "Flexible manufacturing systems: economic effects in Japan, United States, and Western Europe", *Japan and the World Economy*, vol. 2, pp. 1–16.

McDermott, J. (1992) "History in the present: contemporary debates about capitalism", *Science & Society*, vol. 56, no. 3, pp. 291–323.

Public Policy Group of the Institute of Comprehensive Development and Research (Shenzhen, China) (2003) "China as the potential to be a world bivariate workshop", *Kaifang daobao* 1, (in Chinese).

Tan, Z. (2002) "Product cycle, Wintelism and cross-national production networks", working paper.

Tong, X. and Wang, J. (2001) "The evolution of the local industry cluster of PC related manufacturing industry in Dongguan", *Dilixuebao* 11, (in Chinese).

Wang, J. (1999) "The development stages and prospect of the Pearl River Delta", *Tequ Lilun yu Shijian*, (in Chinese).

Xue, F. (2003) "A solution to the economic transition of Hong Kong, Zhuhai and Macau", *Jingji qianyan* 1, (in Chinese).

Zhang, Z. (1994) "The economic relationship between Hong Kong and the Pearl River Delta", *Zhongshan daxue xuebao* 2, (in Chinese).

Zuo, Z. (2001) "A study of historical traditions and new progress for the economic development in the PRD", *Jinan xuebao* 11, (in Chinese).

3 Developing global competitiveness

The case of Haier Group

Zijie Li and Chen Chen

China is no longer only about labor-intensive products such as toys, and using foreign brand names for exports; China is a major player in product lines that are still mass produced in industrialized countries, such as home appliances. Chinese manufacturers have started exporting under their own brand name and have set up production on US soil, just like the Haier Group did in the past. Formally called Qingdao General Refrigerator Factory (located in the east coastal city, Qingdao, Shandong Province), the firm had less than 800 workers and was more than $10 million in debt in 1984, when Haier's CEO Zhang Ruimin aged 35 years, joined the company. By 2004 Haier Group had become one of the worlds' top five producers of household appliances, with 30,000 employees and more than $12 billion in revenue. Haier grew overseas the hard way. It first entered developed markets, such as Germany and the US, where it began selling refrigerators under its own brand name in 1999. In 2000, the company built a $40 million industrial park in Camden, South Carolina. In 2002, Haier purchased a landmark building in Manhattan for its US headquarters, and later it built an office outside Wal-Mart's Bentonville, Arkansas, base. The achievements are attributed to CEO Zhang's goal of creating a global brand. "Now even the government is paying attention to developing China's own famous brand," says Zhang. "It is not whether you want to or not. It is a must for Chinese companies, because we feel the pressure from the market." In a recent issue of *Newsweek* (9 May 2005), Zhang was called the Jack Welch of China.

The successful story of Haier not only attracts attention in the business circle, but also raises a lot of interesting questions in policy and academic circles. How did Haier grow so fast as China's most powerful multinational company? What key strategies did CEO Zhang design at different stages of development? Why did Haier go international targetting the developed markets first? What competitive advantages does Haier have in global markets? This chapter attempts to investigate these issues.

According to conventional theory of multinational corporations, a firm must possess certain intangible asset (mainly technological advantage, or called ownership advantage in the framework of ownership–location–

internalization) before it begins its international operation (Dunning, 1993). Obviously, enterprises in developing countries lack these advantages. They are short of unique and superior technology, they own few global brands in the real sense, and moreover, they don't have global marketing expertise and network (Lall, 1998. 2000; United Nations, 1993). The rise of Haier in international production has prompted questions about how well traditional theories of multinational corporations explain the emergence of Haier (from developing China) and what its competitive advantages are. We intend to provide some analyses on these questions.

A brief history

The Haier Group was set up at the base of Qingdao General Refrigerator Factory, which was once a small, nearly bankrupt collective enterprise. The company was developed after its successful adoption of refrigerator manufacturing technology of Liebherr (a German company). In 20 years Haier transformed into a multinational firm under the leadership of CEO Zhang Ruimin.

The following figures are witness to Haier's achievements. In 2003 global sales reached $9.7 billion, 22,988 times that of 1984, and the average growth rate in the past 20 years is as incredible 70 percent (Figures 3.1 and 3.2). In 1984 Haier only produced one type of refrigerator. Now Haier manufactures a wide range of household appliances (96 kinds of products with over 15,100 specifications, especially in the sectors of white goods, black goods, and home integration) and exports its products to more than 160 countries and regions.

Haier's products win more and more consumers for their high quality and unique design. Haier's four main products – refrigerators, freezers, air-conditioners, washing machines – occupy a steady 30 percent domestic

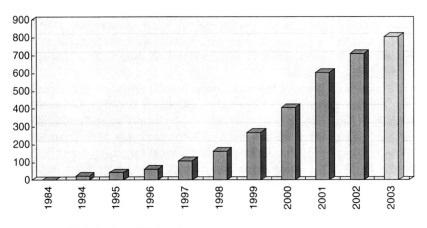

Figure 3.1 Global sales of Haier Group.

Billion of US$

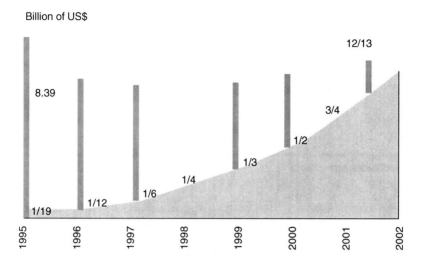

Figure 3.2 The gap between Haier and Fortune 500 (source: Haier Group).

market share (see Table 3.4). In the overseas market, according to a Euromonitor survey (2002), Haier ranked fourth on sales and jumped to second on brand sales among global white goods manufacturers (Tables 3.1 and 3.2). Haier has the largest world market brand share for refrigerators.

Haier persists in its pursuit for creating a world-class brand. It established global networks for design, production, distribution, and after-services. As shown in Figure 3.3, Haier has established 18 design centers (15 in foreign countries), ten industrial parks (two overseas parks: one in the US, one in Pakistan; five out of eight domestic parks are located in Qingdao, the other three are located in Hefei, Dalian and Wuhan), and 22 overseas manufacturing facilities. The total numbers of market outlets and after-services stations are 58,800 and 11,976, respectively. Haier's products are marketed in 12 out of 15 European chain supermarkets and nine out of

Table 3.1 Global market share ranking of white goods manufacturers

Rank	Firms	Market share (%)	
		Year 2002	*Year 2001*
1	Whirlpool	5.23	5.17
2	Haier	3.79	3.24
3	GE	3.79	3.68
4	Siemens	2.81	2.83
5	LG	2.64	2.35

Source: Euromonitor, 2002.

Table 3.2 Global sales ranking of household appliance manufacturers

Rank	Firms	Sales (billion in US$)	
		Year 2002	*Year 2001*
1	Whirlpool	11.02	10.34
2	Merloni	9.76	8.94
3	Panasonic	9.40	10.83
4	Haier	8.59	7.27
5	GE	6.07	5.81

Source: Euromonitor, 2002.

the top ten in America. Haier's design, production, and sales facilities in the US and Europe are staffed by local employees. The largest overseas Haier industrial park, located in South Carolina, US, started to produce and supply the domestic market in March 2003. All Haier overseas factories are in good operation.

Haier's exports in 2003 are $530 million, an increase of 20 percent from 2002. Haier ranks number one in household appliances industry for its contribution to China's foreign exchange reserve. Take refrigerator as an example, Haier's export-generated foreign currency is about 27 percent of the total Chinese refrigerator export outcome (Table 3.3). On 31 January

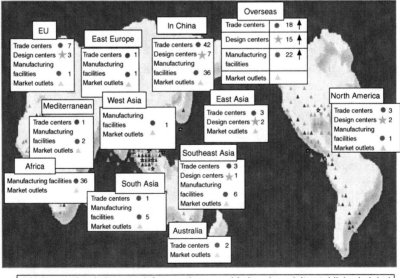

● Haier persists in its pursuit for creating a world-class brand. It established global networks for design, production, distribution and after-services.

Figure 3.3 Global operations of Haier Group (source: Haier Group).

Table 3.3 Top 10 Chinese refrigerator exporters in China

Firm	Brand	Export sales (US$ 10,000	Percentage in China's total export	Export volume (set)
Haier	Haier	13,088.00	0.2671	1,605,734
Kelon	Kelon, Rongsheng	9,706.00	0.1981	1,199,269
Samsung (Suzhou)	Samsung	6,227.00	0.1271	680,058
Hualin	Hualin	3,400.00	0.0694	428,966
Xinfei	Xinfei	2,953.00	0.0603	325,788
Meilin	Meilin	2,645.90	0.0540	312,561
Sharp (Shanghai)	Sharp	2,353.00	0.0480	219,880
Xingxing	Xingxing	2,237.20	0.0457	240,152
Whitesnow (Jiangsu)	Whitesnow	2,109.58	0.0431	204,317
Huayi	Huayi	1,160.00	0.0237	141,000
Total		48,995.49		5,996,909

Source: CHEAA Report 2004.

2004, Haier, the only Chinese brand, was named ninety-fifth of the world's most recognizable brands in the Global Name Brand List edited by the World Brand Laboratory, one of five world brand evaluation agencies.[1] CEO Zhang Ruimin was placed nineteenth on the list of the World's 25 Most Powerful People in Business in *Fortune*, August 2003 issue.

Developing strategies of Haier

Three strategic phases can be identified for the development of Haier as follows.

Phase one: brand development (1984–1991)

In 1984, two small failing workshops were merged to form Qingdao General Refrigerator Factory headed by Zhang Ruimin. At that time, there were more than 100 enterprises competing in Chinese refrigerator market with various brands and specifications. Zhang was convinced that the core of an enterprise was its human resource and he aimed to change his workers' attitude. One of the widespread stories about Zhang was that in early 1985, when he found 76 refrigerators that had come off the line flawed, he made the workers responsible for that batch of products smash the refrigerators instead of repairing them. The move shocked every Haier employee not only by the huge financial losses but by Zhang's determination to build high-quality goods. From then on, a brand new quality management mode was introduced into the company and gradually boosted Haier to one of the most welcomed white goods market players in China. Zhang's words, "Haier offers no second-class but only first-class products.

Flawed products are nothing but a waste," have become the promising image of Haier.

Another cornerstone of Haier's growth was its cooperation with foreign partners. After careful evaluation and assessment of technical information from more than 30 foreign manufacturers, Zhang decided to introduce the technology and equipment from Liebherr of West Germany into Haier. In 1985, Haier's new generation refrigerator type, "Qingdao-Liebherr" made its debut in China, quickly winning the title of "most welcomed refrigerator" of that year for its high-tech features and assured quality.

During this phase, while other companies focusing on quantity, Haier was busy improving its quality and control mechanism. Working on only one refrigerator product in seven years built a solid foundation for Haier's future development. "OEC" is one of the methods Haier used to consolidate its daily management. OEC (Overall Every Control and Clear) implies a detailed performance inspection of every employee, every day, and every task to insure overall high efficiency. In other words, there was always somebody assigned to supervise a specific task and to guarantee that the task was accomplished as planned. At the end of each day personnel would discuss and compare rates of progress according to the schedule before moving on.

Phase two: pluralistic development (1992–1998)

Since 1992, Haier started its pluralistic expansion by intruding other related industries with widely recognized brands through capital operations. Those enterprises with certain tangible assets but badly managed were considered as "shocked fish." Haier successfully took them over and with a brand new enterprise culture and managerial mechanism. The most successful case of "gulping down the shocked fish" was Haier's acquisition and revival of Red Star Electrical Appliances Company.

There were many voices of opposition towards Haier's pluralistic efforts. Which way is the better one: specialization or pluralism? Haier holds that specialization and pluralism all have risks; it is hard to say which one is more risky than the other. The secret is with the company itself: its brand, its management, and the maturity of the market. The fatal deficiency of many unsuccessful pluralistic attempts was attributed to the lack of competent human resources. Haier was facing the same problem: a shortage of qualified personnel to sustain company expansion. It was routine to carry out human resources training and adjustment after each expanding operation.

Some business leaders misunderstood the concept of pluralistic operation. They preferred to change quickly if they could not make money in one industry; if they lost money with one product, they chose to retreat. Haier believed in "persistence" theory: First, spare no efforts to become the most powerful one in the traditional industry before entering into

Table 3.4 Market performance and objectives of Haier products in 2003

Products	Sales revenue		Current market position		Planned position
	Domestic market in RMB 10,000	Exports (in US$10,000)	Domestic markets	Global markets	
Refrigerator	898,846	13,088	1	2	1 (global)
Air-conditioner	1,127,199	14,327	1	5	Top 3 (global)
Washing machine	537,760	3,615	1	3	1 (global)
Freezer	161,098	4,462	1	3	1 (global)
Water heater	103,326	n.a.	1	8	Top 3 (global)
Dish washer	n.a.	n.a.	1	6	Top 3 (global)
Microwave oven	40,402	591	4	17	Top 5 (global)
Gas kitchen range	n.a.	n.a.	6	16	Top 5 (global)
Color TV	n.a.	n.a.	6	–	Top 3 (domestic)
Cell phone	n.a.	n.a.	9	–	Top 3 (domestic)
Computer	n.a.	n.a.	After 10	–	Top 3 (domestic)

Sources: Haier Group; CHEAA Monthly Report.

other related industries; second, after entering into a new industry, strive to be one of the market leaders. From 1984 to 1991, Haier implemented that strategy step by step: first, refrigerators then air-conditioners, freezers, and washing machines. Table 3.4 shows Haier's market performance in 2003.

Phase three: globalization (1998–)

As the highest official of the Haier Group, Zhang Ruimin has been aiming at changing Haier into a world-class brand.[2] Having that in mind, Haier started its globalization after its brand and pluralistic developing phases. During this strategic phase, Haier insisted using the principles of "crack the hardest first" and "promote the brand through exporting" to construct a framework of international enterprise.

Global strategy: globalizing Haier

Early in 1997 Zhang claimed that "Haier always attaches great importance to *think globally and operate locally*. It must develop the whole world into its market." Haier's global expansion experienced three stages: OEM, export with its own brand and, finally to establish overseas manufacturing bases.

From OEM to exporting with its own brand

A basic requirement for competing in the global market is quality of products. A quality zealot, Zhang once took a sledgehammer and ordered workers to help him smash any refrigerator with the slightest flaw, bringing some employees to tears. Haier was among the first big companies to focus on customer care. Zhang said, "The quality of the goods represents not only a company, but the whole country. I figured I could not raise the entire worth of China, but I could raise the worth of this company."

As the product quality has been improved, Haier's export has expanded significantly. The export volume of Haier's refrigerators was 0.84 million in 2000, 1.34 million in 2001, and 1.80 million in 2003. The figure for the first nine months of 2004 reached 2.10 million. Exports of air-conditioners have seen the same momentum: 0.78 million in 2000, 1.33 million in 2003, and 1.17 million for the first nine months of 2004. The figures for exports of washing machines are 0.45, 0.77, and 0.95 for the same periods. The export share in total output for refrigerators and air-conditioners is 30 percent, and 26 percent for washing machines, as indicated in Table 3.5. The main export market of Haier's products were the US and Europe (mainly Germany), later expanded to Southeast Asia, Mid-East and Japan (as shown in Table 3.3).

Building the global brand of Haier

Haier is more "obsessed" with exporting products in its own brand than other Chinese manufacturers because of its belief in "brand strategy" and the immense benefit a successful brand implies. This belief was rooted in Haier's development from a weak refrigerator maker (ranked forty-first in China) to such a highly competitive market player.

Table 3.5 Total output and exports Haier (in 10,000 units)

Products	2000	2001	2002	2003	2004 (Jan.–Sept.)
Refrigerators					
Total output	305.0	368.0	459.0	502.0	543.0
Exports	84.0	134.0	180.0	161.0	210.0
Exports/total output	27.5	36.4	39.2	32.1	38.7
Air-conditioners					
Total output	210.0	281.0	289.0	438.0	560.0
Exports	52.0	78.0	89.0	133.0	117.0
Exports/total output	24.8	27.8	30.8	30.4	20.9
Washing-machines					
Total output	306.0	356.0	393.0	456.0	368.0
Exports	43.0	45.0	64.0	77.0	95.0
Exports/total output	14.1	12.6	16.3	16.9	25.8

Source: CHEAA Monthly Report.

Haier exported its OEM products to the US in the early 1990s and sales kept increasing over the next five years. Since 1996, Haier required its US partner to market the products in the Haier brand. Till the end of the 1990s, about 70 percent of Haier exports was not OEM products but in Haier's own name. Haier had a strong sense of crisis towards OEM production and low-price export sales even in the very early stage. Zhang said, "China exported a lot, but mostly we produced under the subcontracts of foreign companies. They preferred to sign contracts with us because of our low wages (low costs); if there were some Southeast Asian countries that could offer lower prices, they would definitely go there and abandon us. The only way out was to market and sell the products in our own brand."[3]

Developing global network through "crack the hardest first" strategy

Haier realized that it could not add more value to the assembled products and in the long run would have to have its own R&D capability and sales force. Therefore, Haier saw FDI as an important factor in globalization. 30 April, 1999 turned a new page for Haier. On that day, Haier laid the foundation for its US manufacturing base in South Carolina. The Haier (America) Industrial Park occupies an area of 445,000 square meters and it was projected to finish the construction in six phases. The first of the six phases began its operation in March 2000 and was ranked as sixth among US refrigerator makers with an annual capacity of 500,000 sets.

It was a common understanding that the biggest competitive advantage of Chinese products was the low price of labor, parts and components. So why was it necessary to give up this advantage and to produce in a rather higher-cost US? The reasons discussed below may explain Haier's motive of "crack the hardest first" strategy. First, direct investment in developed countries doesn't necessarily cause a dramatic increase in labor cost. In developing countries like China, the labor cost would be less than 10 percent of the total cost. Analyzing the costs of Haier's white goods, about 80 percent is the cost of purchasing from an outsider, so labor cost is less important. Even when producing in the US, major parts/components could be purchased through Haier's international network including China. The labor cost with the assembling process makes no substantial impact on the overall cost.

Second, the domestic demand in developed countries could be satisfied in a timely manner. The 18 design centers and other overseas information departments employed only locals. The purpose of doing that is to respond to the demands promptly and design better products to meet with local consumer habits and thus win the market.

Third, a production base in the US not only enables Haier to access advanced technology and market information, such as stricter environmental regulation and safety standards, but also effectively to evade the non-trade barriers in international trade. As Zhang Ruimin said, "The main motive for Haier establishing overseas factories was to enhance international competitiveness of its brand. Haier's global expansion is a long-term preparation for foul when it's still in fair weather. After entry to the WTO, Chinese products are facing the problem of the rather high technical standards in foreign countries. Another consideration is that by operating in the US, Haier would be qualified to bid for American govern-mental procurement."

Fourth, operating abroad assists Haier's domestic market exploitation with its international business expertise, technology, and brand influence. Like the US, China has one of the most dynamic groups of consumers of white goods. As Table 3.6 shows, before 2000, Chinese consumers' demand for refrigerators, washing machines, and TV accounted for about 20 percent of total world demand respectively, thus was recognized as a central demanding region for household electronical appliances. Japanese and European markets, on the contrary, remained stagnant. Haier locked market shares in both domestic and developing countries with experience, technology, and quality control consciousness learnt in the developed

Table 3.6 Capacity and shares of major manufacturing countries (in 1,000 units, percentage in brackets for market shares)

	Refrigerator					
	1993	*(%)*	*1999*	*(%)*	*2002*	*(%)*
US	6,900	(14.3)	10,600	(17.7)	14,163.8	(17.3)
China	6,000	(12.5)	11,050	(18.4)	8,111.8	(9.9)
Japan	4,490	(9.3)	4,770	(8.0)	4,646.5	(5.7)
Brazil	1,640	(3.4)	3,010	(5.0)	4,677.5	(5.7)
Germany	3,450	(7.2)	2,560	(4.3)	3,910.3	(4.8)
India	2,100	(4.4)	2,580	(4.3)	3,225.9	(3.9)
World	48,150	(100.0)	59,990	(100.0)	81,896.4	(100.0)
	Washing machine					
	1993	*(%)*	*1999*	*(%)*	*2002*	*(%)*
US	5,950	(15.4)	7,510	(12.8)	14,499.5	(19.1)
China	7,350	(19.0)	12,850	(21.8)	12.949.1	(17.1)
Japan	4,660	(12.1)	4,230	(7.3)	4,521	(6.0)
Germany	2,810	(7.3)	2,480	(4.2)	3,535.2	(4.7)
Brazil	–	–	3,130	(5.0)	1,302.5	(1.7)
India	–	–	2,940	(5.0)	1,326	(1.7)
World	38,630	(100.0)	58,870	(100.0)	75,842.7	(100.0)

Source: *Manual of Electronic Household Appliances Industry*, CHEAA.

market. That also explains why from 2000 to date, Haier's market shares have grown steadily despite the overall decrease in domestic demand.

Fifth, direct investment helps upgrade Haier's competitiveness with international brands. Zhang understood that the average salary of American workers is ten times that of Chinese workers. It's a great pressure, but Haier must undertake it. Although the safest way was to stay in China and never explore overseas markets sooner or later it would become more risky to keep that conservative attitude. Therefore a globalization strategy not only meant exploring foreign markets, but also getting Haier acquainted with a competitive atmosphere. The only question is whether we possess enough competitiveness.

Haier's competitive advantages

Haier has two major international competitive advantages: first, the low-cost advantage, second, Haier's unique enterprise advantage developed from years of globalization and exploration, such as organizational structure, R&D mechanism, and innovative enterprise culture. These advantages raised Haier's reactive speed and flexibility towards the market.

Cost advantage

The Chinese makers took advantage of the inexpensive offer from domestic components/parts providers ("the providers") to gain that cost advantage. Therefore, the household appliances manufactures had no incentive to produce the parts/components themselves but relied on the original parts providers. Haier produces refrigerators but no compressors. This competition between foreign and domestics providers served to reduce prices.

Haier's uniqueness: market scale advantage

As a large developing nation, China has an immense market scale and Haier profited immensely from this favorable demand market. As illustrated in Table 3.6, the shares of Chinese refrigerators in the global market increased rapidly in the 1990s. Haier grasped the opportunity and captured the market shares to become the largest company group in China's household electronical appliances industry. The crucial market position was to endow it with even great bargain powers.

Flow innovation: building a market chain theory for a flat structure

One of Haier's strengths is its ability and willingness to adjust and perfect itself to ever-changing strategic demands. Haier established its long-term goals and spared no effort in pursuing them. In relation to its globalization strategy, since 1999 Haier has begun its flow rebuilding and structural reorganization.

The household appliances industry is fiercely competitive and considered to be one of the most marginalized industries. Many companies found they could hardly survive in the long term. The company's organization would be restructured to implement order-based production. In the past, the organization of the company was like a pyramid, information came from the highest officials down to the lowest level but not directly from the market. This organizational structure caused employees to faithfully execute the wrong decisions. In a planned environment, a company had no responsibility as long as it could produce the right product at the right quantity and in a timely manner, but it would be a fatal mistake if the company were to produce something that could never be accepted by the market. Thus, it is unwise to rely on lowering prices to solve the problem, it's better to build a boundless structure with a suitable market chain.

The use of Market Chain theory and method is aimed at promoting Haier's company vigor by turning the outside market objectives to internal goals, and internal goals to personal targets, which are closely connected to personal income. In detail, Market Chain is based on Haier's enterprise culture and OEC management, centered on order information flows. The chain drives the flows of materials, goods, and funds, and guarantees the achievement of the "Three Zeros," (zero quality flaw, zero service distance, zero operating cost). With the speed of the simultaneous flow of the market chain and the strength of the SST mechanism (SST: salary claim, compensation claim, switch-off in Chinese), Haier stimulates employees to make customers' demands a top priority and to fulfill the order-sheet jobs in an innovative way.

The implementation of the internal market chain changed employees' attitude. They are no longer only responsible for their superiors but also for the market and customers (including internal customers); the key of the market chain is to switch from the "old" functional management to today's flow management. In fact, Haier's market chain transforms the outside market pressure to an internal one, thus preserving the capability of persistent innovation through its development. This new mechanism also provides employees with the freedom to accomplish assignments in an innovative way, thus satisfying the customized demands of the market.

R&D competence

When Haier develops a new product, it pays great importance to the exterior design and corresponding molding technologies (technologies related to informational household electronical appliances or general quality control, etc). Haier knew clearly that it owned no more advanced core producing technologies than its domestic competitors, so it attempted to differentiate itself in outlook design by acquiring from outside and enhancing its own design capability at the same time.

Haier owns first-class mold design and production technology in China. It cooperated with National Pie & Mold CAD Engineering Research Center to develop a new mold design system. Haier views it as a "short-cut" to import advanced producing equipments and computers to manu-facture molds, especially at the present stage. Haier has sufficient financial power but lacks sophisticated mold design information and experience. Digital technology offers an important tool for Chinese engineering enter-prises to reach world-class levels.

Haier shows a great interest in technologies in new areas or new prod-ucts, including those peripheral technologies. In 1998, Haier set up its Central Research Institute (CRI) and since then, has carried out joint R&D programs with more than 50 JVs, Chinese universities, and research bodies. Some of the major research areas are as follows: (a) digital/network technology, such as joint R&D on "blue tooth technology" with Ericisson, "National Public Data Transmission Technology" (Venus) program with Microsoft; (b) program design, such as the joint program on digital loop control technology with Tsinghua University; and (c) integra-tion technology of white goods' parts/components: convulsion control, noise control, Freon substitutions, etc. In addition Haier also has various R&D programs with domestic partners and institutions.

Innovative enterprise culture

Innovation is the soul and core value of Haier's enterprise culture. On its promotional logos or pamphlets, innovation is detailed in three principles: (i) The nature of innovation is to demolish and create – which means Haier is willing to overcome all obstructions to acquiring valuable order sheets; (ii) the objective of innovation; and (iii) the approach of innova-tion: to imitate creatively. In other words, Haier will immerse itself in open technology network, acquire knowledge and use it in the develop-ment of new products.

Speed and flexibility

In the world markets, household appliance manufacturers in developing countries are facing great challenges from multinational companies which have predominant advantages in brand, technology and financial resources. What Haier is doing is adopting different business strategies in an attempt to find a shortcut to plug the gaps with the multinationals.

For the time being, Haier's strategy is to combine available technical parts/components and resources into new products, and laid aside R&D on hardware-related product technology. Haier's proclamation to be "Dell in the Chinese household electronical appliances industry," and "Nike in the white goods industry" explains its long-term goals. Within a global open sourcing network, Dell, Nike and Haier all hope to fully employ available mature technology and standardized parts/components to develop more diversified products and sell to the customers as quickly as possible. Based on the competitive advantages acquired in the domestic market – low prices and rapid R&D capability – Haier has not only completed the restructuring of its managerial organization and gained the necessary technical reserves, but has also achieved certain competitive advantages that could hardly be imitated by its competitors. Haier's next step is to further strengthen its domestic dominance and become more aggressive in the international market. Haier is fully confident that it can implement its globalization strategy at first wave and take on any challenges from international multinationals in the household electronical appliances industry.

On the other hand, it will be disadvantageous for Chinese enterprises since they don't have core production technology and cannot run R&D on key technology independently. Haier's globalization seems to be a new attempt to shield itself against a frontal attack, to obtain advanced technology to improve its own technical performance, and to break through the developing (even developed) markets with available know-hows and reliable quality and services mechanisms.

Summary and conclusion

It will always be a challenge for Chinese enterprises to compete with multinational companies in the world markets. Without extensive brand influence, rich capital resources, first-class technological power and long-term international competitive experience, Haier is striving to find its own way out.

In a speech given at the end of 2000, Zhang proclaimed his strategy: "If Haier wants to be a multinational in such a global time, it has to become a wolf, otherwise it will be torn down and devoured by the wolves. The true meaning of competition is to satisfy the individual demands in the world market with speed. We want to build Haier into a world-class company, at the same time, accelerating our localization pace of all Haier overseas branches."

"We aim at high capital efficiency not low-level price wars. We'll follow Dell's production model based on order sheets. This model can increase the capital velocity instead of unexpected stocks. We also would like to learn Nike's successful example of making huge profits with its brand product developing capability, sales tactics and less than 1,000 employees. To us, capital is the boat, and the brand is the sail. We will set up more design, manufacturing and sales centers worldwide. We'll develop new products 24 hours all day long. We'll spare no resources to take full advantage of our global R&D network and human resources to achieve our goals. To promptly satisfy the diversified demands of the customers, to realize order-based production and zero stocks, all internal business operations will be carried out based on JIT. The organizational structure will be changed from 'pyramid type' to flat type. Furthermore, we must improve our logistic infrastructure and functions to get better results from JIT."

As Haier's experience shows, its global strategy assists it in heading off the traditional disadvantages and in fully make use of its international resources and domestic advantages of low cost, high speed and flexibility to build its own unique competitiveness.

Acknowledgment

The comments and suggestions on this chapter from Professor Kevin H. Zhang, the editor of this book, are very much appreciated.

Notes

1 *World managers*, 1st edn, 2004.
2 Zhang once said, "to establish a world brand is the top objective of Haier. It is such a great career I'd like to devote myself to my life time ... I would like to see one day, across the Pacific Ocean, our own brands will be known worldwide and the whole world will get to know the power of China through these brands. It is a dream we can and must realize sooner or later," The Haier Dream of Zhang Ruimin (TV special). The electronic edition was collected in Management and Entrepreneurs, Haier Experience (2000) produced by the Electronic Audio & Video Publishing House of China.
3 The business ideas of Zhang Ruimin, (Economic Department, CCTV (2000)).

References

CCTV (2000), "The Haier Dream of Zhang Ruimin" and "The Business Ideas of Zhang Ruimin," (TV specials, Economic Department).

CHEAA (various issues), *Monthly Reports of CHEAA*, Beijing: China Household Electronic Appliances Association.

CHEAA (1997, 2001, 2003), *Manual of Household Electronical Appliance Industry* (1997, 2001, 2003), Beijing: China Household Electronic Appliances Association.

Dunning, John (1993), *Multinational Enterprises and the Global Economy*, Harrow: Addison-Wesley.

Euromonitor (2002, 2004), "Top 100 World Most Influential Brands," *World Managers* (2002 and 2004).

General Office of Chinese Customs (2001), "Managerial philosophy of Zhang Ruimin," *Enterprise Management*, January, 2001: Custom Statistics 1993–2002.

Lall, Sanjaya (1998), "Export of manufactures by developing countries: emerging patterns of trade and location," *Oxford Review of Economic Policy*, 14 (2): 54–73.

Lall, Sanjaya (2000), "The technological structure and performance of developing countries manufactured exports," *Oxford Development Studies*, 28 (3): 337–369.

Newsweek (2005), "A Jack Welch of communists," 9 May 2005: 30–31.

United Nations (1993), *Transnational Corporations from Developing Countries*, New York: United Nations.

Zhang, Ruimin (2000), "Welcoming new challenge – Haier builds framework of an international enterprise," Haier Group: Haier's official website.

Zhang, Zhong (1999), *Retrospection of 20 Years of Reform and Opening to the World: Interviews with Zhang Ruimin, CEO of Haier Group*. China: Economics and Management Publishing House.

4   Cheap labor and China's export capacity

Yanling Wang[1]

Introduction

Since China opened its door to the world in 1978, it has not only been the world's fastest growing economy, but also an outstanding exporter and a recipient of substantial sums of foreign direct investment (FDI) – it has emerged as a world "workshop." Its imports and exports have grown at a hefty annual rate of 14.73 percent and 15.72 percent respectively from 1978 to 2003: imports increased from US$10.9 billion to US$412.8 billion, and exports from US$9.8 billion to US$438.4 billion. Its trade balance with the world turned into surplus in 1990 and peaked at US$43.5 billion in 1998. Trade accounts for a fairly large share in its economy and has become an important engine for China's continuous economic growth. Inflows of FDI have also increased at an impressive annual growth rate of 21 percent from 1983 to 2003, making China the largest FDI recipient among developing countries, with US$53.5 billion in 2003. Table 4.1a highlights China's trade and its shares in GDP for selected years since 1978 and Table 4.1b presents its FDI inflows and their shares in fixed capital formation and GDP for selected years since 1979.

This chapter examines China's competitiveness and its export capacity in the world market, along with the role of human capital in shifting the composition of trade. The basis of the analysis is China's huge labor endowment and its cheap labor cost.

Table 4.1a China's total merchandise trade (unit: US$ billion)

Year	1978	1980	1985	1990	1995	2000	2001	2002	2003
Imports (M)	10.9	19.6	42.2	53.3	132.1	225.1	243.6	295.2	412.8
Exports (X)	9.8	18.3	27.3	62.1	148.8	249.2	266.1	325.6	438.4
Trade balance	−1.1	−1.3	−14.9	8.8	16.7	24.1	22.5	30.4	25.6
(M + X)/GDP (%)	9.62	12.57	23.38	30.13	51.78	43.90	43.98	49.03	60.40

Sources: Imports and Exports are taken from the Ministry of Commerce at www.mofcom.gov.cn. GDP is from World Development Indicators from the World Bank. Percentages are calculated by the author. As shown, the share of trade in GDP increased steadily, and reached 60% in the year 2003.

Table 4.1b China's FDI inflows (unit: US$ billion)

Year	1979–1982	1983	1985	1990	1995	2000	2001	2002	2003
FDI inflows	1.77	0.92	1.96	3.49	37.52	40.72	46.88	52.74	53.50
FDI inflows as % of GDP	0.21*	0.28	0.54	0.98	5.12	3.55	3.76	3.89	3.79
FDI inflows as % of GCF	0.64*	0.83	1.44	2.83	12.54	9.78	9.78	9.64	9.01

Sources: FDI inflows are taken from the Ministry of Commerce at www.mofcom.gov.cn. Fixed capital formation and GDP are taken from the World Bank dataset (World Development Indicators), and the percentages are calculated by the author. *: the percentages are based on FDI flows of year 1982.

Note
GCF: Fixed Capital Formation.

Over the years the percentages of FDI of GDP and of fixed capital formation also showed an increasing trend. In 2003, FDI inflow accounted for almost 3.8 percentage points of GDP, and a little over 9 percentage points of total fixed capital formation. The large shares of trade and FDI of GDP makes China well integrated into the world economy.

The composition of China's trade shifted drastically from primary products to manufactures, which now accounts for about 90 percent of China's exports and 80 percent of its imports. The composition of manufactures also shifted from traditional unskilled to skilled labor-intensive products. In the early 1990s, light manufacturing accounted for more than 42 percent of China's exports and in the year 2003 the share declined to 28 percent, while machinery and transport (which includes electronics) increased from 17 percent in 1993 to 41 percent in 2003. However, the share of high-tech exports is relatively low, the majority of which are produced and exported by foreign-invested firms.

The growing importance of the Chinese economy has attracted numerous studies not only on its domestic economic reforms, but also on its role in the global economy. Mastel (1997) used the title in his book *The Rise of the Chinese Economy – The Middle Kingdom Emerges* argues why China should be brought into the world economy. Lardy (2002) also argues the importance of integrating China into the global economy. Recently, the International Monetary Fund published a book that focused specifically on China's economy. In that issue, Rumbaugh and Blancher (2004) analyzed China's impact on trade patterns both in the world market and in the Asian regional market. Martin and Manole (2004) examined the transformation of China's exports relative to those of India and other low-income exporters.

China has economic relationships with countries (regions) across the globe, but its top four trading partners account for big shares of its total trade. From January to June 2004, the European Union, Japan, the US, and Hong Kong represented over 54 percent in China's total merchandise trade with the world, with shares of 15.4 percent, 15.0 percent, 14.7 percent, and 9.3 percent respectively. The top four trading partners are also the top four FDI sources. As of year 2002, the share of cumulative FDI stocks from each source is: 45.73 percent from Hong Kong, 8.9 percent from the US, 8.11 percent from Japan, and over 6.38 percent from the European Union. Foreign-invested firms play an important role in China's high-tech trade. Given the significant importance of the top economic partners in China's economy, this chapter will analyze China's export capacity, and forecast its future structural change in light of the top economic partners.

Labor cost and its comparative advantage: an analytical framework

Resources and their costs play an important role in determining a country's comparative advantage in the world trading market. The classic Heckscher-Ohlin (H-O) trade theory offers a good analytical basis. In the H-O framework, there are only two countries (Home and Foreign), each producing two goods, cloth and machinery. There are only two factors of production, labor and capital – both mobile between sectors. Workers earn wages, and capital owners collect rents for capital. Suppose that for any given ratio of factor prices, cloth uses relatively more labor (labor-intensive good), and machinery uses relatively more capital (capital-intensive good). Finally let's suppose that Home is labor abundant, and Foreign is capital abundant (the ratio of labor to capital is higher in Home than that in Foreign). All other things are the same both in Home and in Foreign, such as technologies of production, and consumers' preferences, etc.

Since cloth is the labor-intensive good, Home's production possibility frontier relative to Foreign's is shifted out more in the direction of cloth than in the direction of machinery. Thus, other things equal, Home tends to produce a higher ratio of cloth to machinery. For any given ratio of the price of cloth to that of machinery, Home will produce a higher ratio of cloth to machinery than Foreign will: Home will have a larger relative supply of cloth. Thus, the relative price of cloth at Home is smaller than that in Foreign in a pre-trade world.

When Home and Foreign trade freely with each other, their relative prices converge (we assume away any trading costs). The relative price of cloth rises in Home and declines in Foreign, and a new world relative price of cloth is established at a point somewhere between the two pre-trade relative prices. In Home, the rise in the relative price of cloth leads to a rise in the production of cloth and a decline in the relative consumption, so Home becomes an exporter of cloth and an importer of machinery. Conversely, the decline in the relative price of cloth in Foreign leads it to become an importer of cloth and an exporter of machinery.

Thus, factor abundance is important in shaping a country's trade pattern and its export capacity. In fact, absolute large endowments of a factor often drives down its price, which may give a country even the absolute advantage in the products using that factor extensively. If a country has absolute advantage in labor cost, which is often the case for developing countries, its labor-intensive goods in general will be very competitive in the world market, which makes it an exporter of labor-intensive products. Besides that, and combined with other factors, that developing country might also be a favourite destination for FDI.

China's labor cost and its competitiveness in the global markets

Overview

China's labor and capital endowments and its labor cost could well explain its export capacity in the context of the H-O theory, and why it was a large FDI recipient. As shown in the introduction, both trade and FDI have become important players in China's continuously growing economy, and the following analysis will focus on what makes China competitive in the world market and what makes China so attractive for FDI. As the European Union, the US, Japan, and Hong Kong are the key players in both China's trade and FDI, the discussion will highlight how China's huge labor supply and thus cheap labor cost makes China relatively competitive in comparison with those of its key economic partners. Although some other factors, such as China's big market size and its human capital, are also important, this analysis will not touch these topics due to the length constraints. For attracting FDI, China's efforts and successes in steadily improving the investment climate (infrastructure, legal framework, etc.), and its relatively stable political environment are also key players.

In fact, comparing China's endowment of labor (agricultural, unskilled and skilled) and capital with those from its top trading partners does reveal that China is labor abundant, and its labor cost is the cheapest (comparison is made in the manufacturing sector).

China accounts for one-fourth of the world's total population and it has a massive supply of cheap labor. Table 4.2 shows that China has a huge

Table 4.2 Percentage share in world aggregate factor resources (1995)

	US	*EU*	*Japan*	*China*	*Rest of the world*
Agricultural labor	0.3	0.7	0.3	40.0	52.3
Unskilled labor	7.9	10.4	4.5	13.7	57.3
Skilled labor	14.5	15.6	3.6	17.5	45.8
Capital	19.3	30.7	22.7	2.0	23.3

Source: Abeysinghe and Lu (2003).

agricultural, unskilled and skilled labor force (40 percent, 13.7 percent and 17.5 percent respectively of the world labor force in each category). But it only has 2 percent of the world's capital (the number could be slightly bigger for year 2003 as China has been successfully attracting foreign direct investment over the last decade).

A simple comparison of China's labor cost in manufacturing with its top trading partners reveals that Chinese workers are much cheaper. For example, in 1998, a typical Chinese worker earned US$1,188 while a US worker earned US$35,639, and a Japanese worker earned US$47,238 (data are taken from LABORSTA, converted to US$ per year by the author).[2] In other words, it took 30 Chinese workers to make one US worker's salary, and 40 Chinese workers to one Japanese counterpart's. This low labor cost not only gives China the absolute advantage in attracting large amounts of FDI, but also the comparative advantage in labor-intensive goods in the world market.

According to the H-O theory, China will have a trade surplus in commodities which intensively use labor, and a trade deficit in commodities which intensively use capital. The H-O prediction is actually well evidenced by China's export capacity (labor-intensive and capital-intensive goods) with its top trading partners and with the world in general.

Trade in labor-intensive commodities

For labor-intensive goods, it is inevitable that we discuss China's exports of apparel and footwear which have been China's major components in exports accounting for big shares, and one of the main sources of trade surplus. In the early 1990s, light manufacturing accounted for more than 40 percent of China's exports, with products consisting of footwear, clothing, toys, and other miscellaneous manufactured articles. The share has been declining, but still was 28 percent in 2003.

In 2003, China had a big trade surplus on apparel and clothing accessories (SITC 84) and footwear (SITC 85) with each of its top trading partners (Table 4.3). In fact, China is so competitive in labor-intensive goods (not just compared with its top trading partners), that the statistics on world trade says it all. China had a huge trade surplus for miscellaneous manufactured articles (SITC 8) of US$50.24 billion, US$38.38 billion, and US$20.78 billion for year 2002, 2003 and January to July 2004 respectively. For example, in the US, imports from China account for 18.09 percent of its total imports of apparel and accessories from January to August 2004. No wonder when we go to a department store, a glance at the labels reveals that many items of apparel are "made in China." Moore (2002: 60) states that China was the largest exporter of both textiles and clothing in 1999, accounting for 9 percent and 16 percent of the international market, respectively, with an overall total market share of 13 percent.

Table 4.3 Imports and exports of apparel and footwear with its top trading partners (unit: US$ billion)

	Europe			Japan			US			Hong Kong		
	M	X	TB	M	X	TB	M	X	TB	M	X	TB
SITC 84	0.11	11.63	**11.52**	0.22	12.52	**12.31**	0.01	6.56	**6.55**	0.67	8.49	**7.82**
SITC 85	0.04	2.90	**2.87**	0.01	1.10	**1.09**	0.06	5.33	**5.27**	0.01	0.67	**0.66**
Subtotal	0.15	14.53	**14.38**	0.23	13.62	**13.39**	0.07	11.89	**11.82**	0.67	9.15	**8.48**

Source: Ministry of Commerce at www.mofcom.gov.cn. M = imports; X = exports; TB = trade balance.

China's export capacity in electronics is also enormous. Before Deng Xiaoping introduced economic reforms in 1978, home electronics manufacturing was trivial in China. Today, 20 percent of the world's refrigerators, 30 percent of air conditioners and TVs, and 50 percent of cameras are produced in China (Asian Development Bank, 2003) – this certainly makes China an important player in the world market for these goods. Huge exports in light manufacturing and electronics have led to the emergence of China as a world "workshop."

Trade in capital-intensive (high-tech) commodities

However, trade in high-tech (capital-intensive) commodities presents a very different picture (Table 4.4). Overall, China's technology base remains limited and the capital infrastructure needed to produce advanced, high-tech goods is largely absent. Chinese firms do not have any advantages in high-tech products, and most of their high-tech exports are mature commodities, such as DVD players and laser printers. The brains of these machines, namely their semiconductor chips, are almost all imported – reflected in China's high-tech trade deficit of around $9 billion in the year 2003. It is the same story with semiconductors. The country is a voracious consumer of chips and an increasingly important location for silicon-wafer plants, providing an estimated 19 percent of world capacity in 2003. Yet foreigners control most of the chip plants in China – its indigenous industry remains tiny and low-tech and in turn, concentrates on low-value assembly and testing rather than design and manufacture. Human capital, which is crucial for development of high-tech products, is relatively low. Overall, the percentage of high-tech exports is relatively small: 11 percent for 1998, 12.7 percent for 1999, 14.9 percent for 2000, 20.88 percent for 2001, and 22.44 percent for January 2003. Furthermore, the majority of the high-tech exports are from foreign-invested firms (Table 4.5). Table 4.4 shows the latest statistics on high-tech trade with the world and with Japan – one of its major trading partners.

Table 4.4 shows that in the year 2002, China had a trade deficit in high-tech products of US$ 5 billion with the world, while it had US$6.54 billion with Japan from January to October 2002. And in the year 2003, the trade deficit with the world was US$8.98 billion, and US$11.92 billion with Japan.

Even this small share of high-tech exports is "made in China," but not "made by China" – almost all of the value is captured by foreign-invested firms (see Table 4.5). In the year 2003, exports of high-tech products from foreign-invested firms accounted for over 94 percent, with a trade surplus of US$8.09 billion, while Chinese firms only accounted for less than 6 percent, and with a trade deficit of US$17.09 billion. It was a similar story from January to June 2004.

Table 4.4 China's high-tech merchandise trade (unit: US$ billion)

	Japan			The world		
	Imports	Exports	Trade balance	Imports	Exports	Trade balance
January to June 2004	13.74	7.46	**−6.28**	72.15	70.63	**−1.52**
2003	23.76	11.84	**−11.92**	119.30	110.32	**−8.98**
2002	12.60*	6.06*	**−6.54***	82.71	67.71	**−15.00**

Source: Ministry of Commerce.

Note
*: Statistics are for January to October 2002.

Table 4.5 China's imports and exports of high-tech products by company type (unit: US$ billion)

	January–June 2004					2003				
	M	% of total M	X	% of total X	TB	M	% of total M	X	X of total X	TB
State-owned	13.22	18.32	6.23	8.82	-6.99	26.77	22.44	11.48	10.41	-15.29
Foreign owned	**54.93**	**76.13**	**61.63**	**87.26**	**6.7**	**86.18**	**72.24**	**94.27**	**85.44**	**8.09**
Collective	1.06	1.47	1.11	1.57	0.05	1.73	1.45	2.04	1.85	0.31
Private	2.92	4.05	1.65	2.34	-1.27	4.51	3.78	2.53	2.29	-1.98
Other	0.02	0.03	0.01	0.01	-0.01	0.11	0.09	0.01	0.01	-0.1
Total	72.15	100	70.63	100	-1.52	119.3	100	110.3	100	-8.98

Source: Ministry of Commerce.

Note
M = imports; X = exports; TB = trade balance.

Climbing on the technology ladder?

China is a world "workshop" in labor-intensive goods such as clothing, footwear, and home electronics, like TVs and cameras. China's market share in major export markets increased steadily from 1970 to 2003 (Table 4.6), but it does not have any comparative (let alone absolute) advantage in high-tech products. Foreign-invested firms capture almost all of the values in high-tech exports but does China have any immediate incentives to climb the technology ladder?

A huge labor supply and cheap labor cost is China's greatest advantage. China's labor will remain cheap for decades. Statistics show that Chinese manufacturers are more productive and make more profits if they reduce the technology used in production and return to more people-heavy processes. In the mean time, labor-intensive industries can generate the millions of new jobs needed each year to maintain social stability sought by the leadership in Beijing. Robert Mundell, Nobel Laureate in economics, argues that "China can compete for the next 200 years on labor costs." (From his speech at the thirty-eighth annual meeting of the Canadian Economics Association, June 2004, Toronto.) He emphasizes China's competitiveness in low labor cost in a very exaggerated way, but Arther Kroeber, managing editor of *China Economic Quarterly*, has a similar argument. *The Economist* (20 December 2003, vol. 369, issue 8355, pp. 99–101) quotes him saying: "China has no real incentive to develop high-tech processes since … China can compete for the next 50 years on labor costs".

The above argument might be true in the short run, but in the long run, China will eventually climb the technology ladder and boost its indigent high-tech industries. The ability to compete in high-tech products is quite a common goal for most countries, and China is no exception. Actually, China does have superior technology in certain high-tech areas, for example, in the area of aerospace: it has successfully sent a Chinese (Yang Liwei) into space. With an enviable annual growth rate of about 9 percent of its GDP since 1978, and with its continuing economic reforms, the new Chinese government is actually paying more attention to building up its human capital, such as the legal and financial infrastructure which is

Table 4.6 Market share in major export markets (imports from China divided by total imports, in percent)

	1970	1980	1990	1995	2000	2002	2003
Japan	1.4	3.1	5.1	10.7	14.5	18.3	18.5
US	0	0.5	3.2	6.3	8.6	11.1	12.5
EU	0.6	0.7	2	3.8	6.2	7.5	8.9

Source: Rumbaugh and Blancher (2004).

needed for faster technological development. The Chinese government also has implemented a series of preferential policies to boost its high-tech trade. One of them is the "High-tech to Expand Trade" policy with a series of preferential treatments if a firm (city) develops high-tech products for exports (imports substituting). The government has already selected 20 cities that are currently using this preferential policy.

However, closing the gap with its top trading partners is a very long-term process. As shown in Table 4.2, China's physical capital endowment only accounts about 2 percent of that in the world, and there are reasons to argue that Chinese skilled labor is not as skilled as that in the US, though China and the US had about the same skilled shares in the world in 1995. Actually, in the case of human capital, China is far behind its top economic partners. For example, in year 1990, educational enrollment at third level per 1,000 population was 3.31 for China, 29.95 for France, and 53.95 for the US (taken from the United Nations common database). Averaged from 1980 to 1996, government spending on education as a percentage of GNP was 2.345 for China, 5.657 for France, and 5.188 for the US, and China actually experienced a negative growth rate of -0.4 percent, while it was 0.5 percent for France, and 0.7 percent for the US.[3]

On the other hand, its vast trade and huge inflows of FDI might also help domestic Chinese firms catch up with foreign counterparts. Some empirical studies have shown that trade promotes technology spillovers, and so does FDI, see Keller (2004) for a review on this. Empirical studies on China are quite limited due to the lack of access to the Chinese data. Nonetheless, Wei and Liu (2001) investigate the determinants and impact of foreign direct investment (FDI) in China while Cheung and Lin (2004) show that FDI has a positive impact on the number of domestic patent applications in China. If trade and FDI were to promote technology diffusion from foreign countries to Chinese firms, then the shift towards high-tech products would likely be a little faster though the magnitudes remain to be estimated.

Thus, any significant structural change of the composition of trade in high-tech exports is a long-term process. However, compared with other developing countries, China is, by all means, among the fastest growing economies. The composition of China's trade has already shifted from products relying heavily on unskilled labor to products relying on more skilled labor. The obvious example is the development of machinery and the transport (including electronics) industry. The proportion of China's exports represented by machinery and transport (which includes electronics) increased from 17 percent in year 1993 to 41 percent in year 2003, while the share of miscellaneous manufacturing declined from 42 percent to 28 percent. There are reasons to believe that this trade composition will continue to gradually shift towards high-tech products while maintaining its traditional advantages in labor-intensive products like apparel and electronics.

Conclusion

China has emerged as a major trading partner for several large countries (regions). It has a huge cheap labor supply to attract FDI, and makes it very competitive in labor-intensive goods, among others. Its large-scale exports of labor-intensive manufactures (providing a good size of trade surplus) has made China a world "workshop". The European Union, Japan, the US, and Hong Kong are not only its top trading partners, but also its major FDI sources. The comparison of endowments of labor and capital among China and its top trading partners reveals that China has a comparative advantage in labor-intensive products: a huge trade surplus with each one of them. However, China continues to have a trade deficit in high-tech products, and foreign firms capture almost all of the rents from high-tech exports. Although the new Chinese government has put more emphasis on the development of national high-tech products, its indigenous firms lack the technological capacity to compete. It is highly unlikely (and technologically impossible) for China to shift from its advantageous labor-intensive goods to the production of capital-intensive goods in the near future. However, in the long run, with its hugely successful economic development and continuing economic reforms, China might have the ability to gradually improve its human capital, foster the legal and financial infrastructure necessary for advanced technological development, while at the same time retaining its low labor cost advantage. This however, will be a lengthy and dynamic process.

Notes

1 I would like to thank Jean Daudelin, Kevin Honglin Zhang, Zhiqi Chen, Maurice Schiff, and an anonymous referee for their valuable comments.
2 Data were from LABORSTA, a database from the International Labor Organization, converted to US$ by the author.
3 Compiled and calculated by the author from the UN common database.

References

Cheung, Kui-yin and Ping Lin (2004): "Spillover effects of FDI on innovation in China: evidence from the provincial data", *China Economic Review*, 15, 1, 25–44.
Wei, Yingqi and Xiaming Liu (2001): *Foreign direct investment in China: Determinants and impact*, Cheltenham, UK and Northampton, MA: Edward Elgar.
Keller, Wolfgang (2004): "International technology diffusion", *Journal of Economic Literature*.
Asian Development Bank Annual Report, 2003.
Abeysinghe, Tilak and Luding Li (2000): "China as an economic powerhouse: implications for its neighbours", *China Economic Review*, 14, 164–185.
Lardy, Nicholas R. (2002): *Integrating China into the Global Economy*, Washington, DC: Brookings Institute Press.

Martin, Will and Vlad Manole (2004): "China's emergence as the workshop of the world", mimeo, The World Bank.

Mastel, Greg (1997): *The Rise of the Chinese Economy – the Middle Kingdom Emerges*, M.E. Sharpe, Inc.

Moore, Thomas G. (2002): "*China in the World Market: Chinese Industry and International Sources of Reform in the Post-Mao Era*", Cambridge: Cambridge University Press.

Rumbaugh, Thomas and Nicolas Blancher (2004): "International trade and the challenges of WTO accession", in Eswar Prasad (ed.) *China's Growth and Integration into the World Economy*, Washington DC: International Monetary Fund.

Part II
FDI, trade, and industrial development

5 Made by Taiwan but made in mainland China

The case of the IT industry

Chen-yuan Tung

Introduction

Over the past two decades, Taiwan's information technology (IT) industry[1] has grown very rapidly. In 1986, the value of its IT industry was only $2.1 billion; in 1992, it increased to $9.4 billion; in 2000, it reached as high as $47 billion. From 1986 to 2000, the average growth rate was 26 percent. This decreased slightly to $42.7 billion in 2001, due to the international economic downturn, but picked up to $48.4 billion in 2002 and $57.1 billion in 2003.

Consequently, the global market share of Taiwan's IT industry has been expanding dramatically. In 1986, the share in the world market was only 1.5 percent; by 2000, its market share among the world's ten largest producers increased significantly to 18.7 percent. These figures demonstrate clearly that the industry has been very competitive in the global market over the past two decades.

Furthermore, after 1990 Taiwan's IT industry began to invest abroad on a large scale. As a result, a huge share of Taiwan's IT products were manufactured abroad. In 1992, 90 percent were made in Taiwan, while 10 percent were made abroad. In comparison, in 2003 only 21 percent were made in Taiwan, while 79 percent were made abroad. In other words, nearly four-fifths of output was created by overseas production bases. Moreover, a significant portion of the overseas production bases were established in China. In 1995, only 14 percent of Taiwan's IT products were produced in China; by 2003, 63.3 percent were being produced in China.

Over the past ten years there were two obvious trends in the development of the industry. First, the competitiveness of products on the global market was persistently strengthened (the share of the world market constantly increased). Second, the share of products produced abroad increased rapidly, far exceeding Taiwan's local output; at the same time, the overseas production bases were located primarily in China. This trend characterized the fact that although Taiwan's IT products were mostly made by the Taiwanese, the majority of the products were increasingly being made in China.

The reason for Taiwan moving its production bases to China was definitely to increase its global competitiveness (the share of the global IT product market) through reducing its input cost and accessing the market, which were the top two reasons for outward investment. For instance, in 1993, the total cost savings from production in China rather than in Taiwan were as high as 8 percent of the final product value for monitors, 10 percent for motherboards, 16 percent for switch power supply, 21 percent for keyboards, and 22 percent for PC mice (Chung, 1997: 187–188). According to Taiwan's Institute for Information Industry, in 2003 the total production cost of IT products in China was only one-fourth to one-sixth of that in Taiwan (Jiang and Zhou, 2003: 3).

According to Taiwan's official surveys, between 1996 and 2002, "cheap and abundant labor" was the main reason that around 59–64 percent of Taiwanese business people conducted outward investment in the IT industry; and the "potential huge local market" was the second main reason (51–64 percent). Particularly, between 1996 and 2002, "cheap and abundant labor" was the reason given by 72–74 percent of Taiwanese business people for conducting outward investment in the IT industry in China and the "potential huge local market" was the second main reason (49–66 percent) (Ministry of Economic Affairs, 1997: 70–73, 2002: 312–315).

This chapter assesses the degree to which Taiwan's investment in the IT industry in China contributes to the competitiveness of their IT products in the global market. It measures the competitiveness in terms of the global market share of the domestic and overseas output value of Taiwan's IT products. If the global market share of their IT products is sustained, Taiwan maintains its original competitiveness, if, however, the global market share increases, then competitiveness is strengthened. If the market share declines competitiveness is reduced.

In addition, China's IT industry grew at an amazing pace in the 1990s. The global market share of Chinese high-tech products (including telecommunication equipment, automatic data processing machines, parts and accessories of computers) increased from 0.4 percent in 1985 to 6 percent in 2000. This result indicates that China is quite competitive in high-tech products in the global market (United Nations Conference on Trade and Development, 2002: 161–162). Since the Taiwanese have been transferring most of their production to China, this chapter also assesses the impact of Taiwan's direct investment on China's IT industry.

The structure of this chapter is as follows: First, it analyzes the impact of Taiwan's investment in the IT industry in China on the competitiveness of their IT industry as a whole. Second, to further clarify the impact, five case studies are conducted on: desktop computers, motherboards, keyboards, CD/DVD/CD RW drivers, and monitors. Third, it assesses the impact of Taiwan's direct investment on China's IT industry, and finally, it concludes the findings and discusses the pitfalls and limitations of this analysis.

Taiwan's direct investment in China was to utilize cheap Chinese production factors and access the Chinese market. These two factors would make a positive contribution to competitiveness in the global market. In addition, from 1996 to 2003, the average annual growth rate of Taiwan's IT products made in Taiwan was −0.7 percent while those made in China was 39.4 percent (elaborated below). Consequently, the expansion of the global market share of Taiwan's IT industry was driven mainly by the expansion of Taiwan's IT production in China.

To concretely measure the impact of Taiwan's investment in China on their competitiveness, this chapter establishes the index of competitiveness reinforcement (ICR). That is, for a fixed period of time, the ICR measures the change of the global market share of Taiwan's IT products, relative to the change of the share of its production of IT products in China to their overall production in both Taiwan and overseas production bases. The index formula is as follows:

The index of competitiveness reinforcement (ICR) = (The change of the global market share of Taiwanese businesspeople's IT products)/(The change of the share of Taiwanese businesspeople's production of IT products in China to their overall production in both Taiwan and overseas production bases).

For instance, in five years, if Taiwan increases the production of its IT products in China by 10 percent, and the global market share of Taiwan's IT products increases by 5 percent, the ICR is 0.5 (=5 percent/10 percent). That is, if the share of Taiwan's IT products made in China increases by 1 percent, the global market share will increase by half a percent. Therefore, the higher the ICR, the more competitive Taiwan becomes in the world industry.

The development of Taiwan's IT industry and its production bases in China

In 1986, the output value of Taiwan's IT industry was just $2.1 billion, increasing significantly to $47 billion in 2000. From 1986 to 2000, the output value (including the output value produced in Taiwan and abroad, hereinafter) increased by 22 times, with a 26 percent annual average growth rate. The vigorous performance of Taiwan's IT industry not only demonstrated the growth rate in the output value, but also the continuous expansion of the global market share of its IT products. The global market share of Taiwan's IT products was only 1.5 percent in 1986, reaching 4.9 percent in 1994 (see Table 5.1).

After 1994, because statistical data of the global market value of the IT products were not available, the "global market value" is replaced by the total output value of the ten largest producers of IT products in the world computed by the Institute for Information Industry in Taiwan. In 1994, according to the first indicator, the output value of Taiwan's IT products

Table 5.1 The global market share of Taiwan's IT hardware products (1986–1994) (unit: $ million; %)

Year	1986	1987	1988	1989	1990	1991	1992	1993	1994
Taiwan's output value	2,134	3,839	5,324	5,484	6,149	6,908	9,363	11,384	14,582
Global market value	145,000	160,000	170,000	180,000	200,000	224,000	244,160	269,300	295,150
Taiwan's global market share	1.5	2.4	3.1	3.1	3.1	3.1	3.8	4.2	4.9

Source: The Compilers of the *1997 IT Industry Yearbook 1997*: 58.

accounted for 4.9 percent of the world market, while the second indicator illustrated that they accounted for 7.9 percent of the total output value of the ten largest producers of the IT products in the world. Therefore, the disparity between these two indicators might be around 3 percent. Based on the second indicator, in 1995, Taiwan's IT products accounted for 9.9 percent of the total output value of the ten largest producers of IT products in the world, rising to 18.7 percent in 2000 (see Table 5.2).

Since the 1990s, Taiwan's IT industry began to invest abroad on a large scale and many production bases were rapidly transferred overseas, particularly to China. In 1992, 90 percent of Taiwan's IT products were produced domestically in Taiwan, while only 10 percent were produced abroad. After 1992, the trend of Taiwan's outward investment prevailed further. The proportion of Taiwan's overseas production to its total production increased nearly 10 percent every two years: from 10.4 percent in 1992, to 20.6 percent in 1994, 32.1 percent in 1996, 42.7 percent in 1998, 50.9 percent in 2000, 64.3 percent in 2002, and 79.1 percent in 2003.

In particular, after the mid-1990s the overseas production bases of IT products for the Taiwanese were mostly transferred to China. From 1995 to 2003, the proportion of overseas production increased by 51.1 percent. During the same period, the proportion of production of IT products in China for the Taiwanese increased by 49.3 percent. Since the mid-1990s, almost all the outward investment of Taiwan's IT industry has been invested in China (see Table 5.2).

Taiwanese investment in the IT industry in China can be divided into three stages: the first half of the 1990s, the second half of the 1990s, and the period after 2000. In the first stage, Taiwan's investment in China consisted mainly of labor-intensive small- and medium-sized enterprises. The major products made in China included electrical home appliances, consumer electronic products, scanners, mice, keyboards, and computer cases.

The second stage was prompted by the Taiwanese government allowing medium- and large-sized enterprises to indirectly invest in China. At this stage, Taiwan's investors in China focused primarily on periphery production and system assembling, such as production of CD/DVD/CD RW drivers and motherboards, and assembling of PCs.

In the third stage, along with mature development of PC products and fierce global market competition, after Taiwan relaxed its policy, the high-technology-intensive industry in Taiwan (such as notebook computers and LCD monitors) formed the third wave of upsurge of investment.

After the Taiwanese invested rapidly in China, their global market share increased dramatically. In 1994, the share of the output value of Taiwan's IT industry to the output value of the ten largest producers in the world was 7.9 percent. By 2000, Taiwan's global market share increased to 18.7 percent – more than double that of six years earlier.

As a matter of fact, the expansion of the global market share of Taiwan's IT industry is predominantly driven by the expansion of

Table 5.2 Production bases of Taiwan's IT hardware products and its global market share (1992–2003) (unit: %)

Year	1992	1993	1994	1995	1996	1997	1998	1999	2000	2001	2002	2003
Proportion of production in Taiwan	89.6	85.2	79.4	72.0	67.9	62.6	57.3	53.0	49.1	47.1	35.7	20.9
Proportion of overseas production	10.4	14.8	20.6	28.0	32.1	37.4	42.7	47.0	50.9	52.9	64.3	79.1
Proportion of production in China	–	–	–	14.0	16.8	22.8	28.9	33.0	31.3	36.9	47.5	63.3
Taiwan's global market share	–	–	7.9	9.9	11.4	10.7	11.3	17.3	18.7	–	–	–

Sources: The Compiler Committee of the *1996 IT Industry Yearbook* 1996: 19; The Compiler Committee of the *1997 IT Industry Yearbook* 1997: 7 and 658; The Compiler Team of the *1998 IT Industry Yearbook* 1999: 1, 2 and 7; The Compiler Committee of the *2000 IT Industry Yearbook* 2001: III–2; The Compiler Team of the *2002 IT Industry Yearbook* 2002: III–3 and III–4; Qin 2003: 8.

Notes
1 Taiwan's output value includes the output value produced at home and abroad.
2 The global market value refers to the output value of the ten largest producers of IT hardware products in the world.

Table 5.3 Comparison of growth rates for Taiwan's IT products made in Taiwan and China (1996–2003) (unit: %)

Year	1996	1997	1998	1999	2000	2001	2002	2003	Average
The growth rate of Taiwan's IT products made in Taiwan and overseas bases	28.1	20.5	11.9	18.1	17.9	−9.2	13.5	17.2	11.0
The growth rate of Taiwan's IT products made in Taiwan	20.8	11.1	2.5	9.2	9.2	−12.9	−14.1	−31.4	−0.7
The growth rate of Taiwan's IT products made in China	53.7	63.6	41.9	34.8	11.8	7.0	46.1	56.2	39.4

Source: Calculated by the author.

Taiwan's IT production in China. From 1996 to 2003, the average growth rate of Taiwan's IT products made in both domestic and overseas bases was 11 percent. In that period, the growth rate of Taiwan's IT products manufactured in Taiwan was mostly under 20 percent and became negative after 2000 – −0.7 percent of the average annual growth rate. In comparison, in the same period, the growth rate of Taiwan's IT products made in China were mostly above 40 percent – with 39.4 percent of the average annual growth rate (see Table 5.3).

Obviously, Taiwan's production in China was extraordinarily helpful to its overall competitiveness in the global market. From 1995 to 2000, the share of production in China increased by 17.3 percent. During the same period, the global market share increased by 8.8 percent. Therefore, the ICR was 0.51 (=8.8 percent/17.3 percent). That is, as long as Taiwan increased its share of production in China by 1 percent, the global market share increased by more than half a percent. The following section will further analyze the impact of Taiwan's investment in the IT industry in China by looking at the competitiveness of their individual IT products in the global market.

The development of Taiwan's individual IT products and its production bases in China

By 1999, Taiwan had transferred more than 80 percent of production of desktop computers, CDT monitors, CD/DVD/CD RW drivers to overseas production bases. Taiwan's Institute for Information Industry predicted that by 2002, this proportion would reach around 95 percent. Among them, 52 percent of desktop PCs, 71 percent of CDT monitors, and 92 percent of CD/DVD/CD RW drivers would be produced in China (see Table 5.4).

Table 5.4 Share of Taiwan's IT hardware products made in overseas bases (1999–2002) (unit: %)

Year	Notebook computer	Desktop computer	Motherboard	Server	LCD monitor	CDT monitor	CD/DVD/CD RW driver	Digital camera
1999	3.3	84.0	40.5	–	0.5	80.0	80.0	–
2000	6.7 (0)	84.0 (45.0)	48.0 (45.0)	45.0 (9.0)	3.0 (1.0)	92.0 (58.0)	86.0 (78.0)	58.0 (44.0)
2001	11.5 (5.2)	86.0 (48.0)	55.1 (52.8)	49.0 (16.0)	32.8 (28.4)	97.9 (66.3)	93.9 (91.2)	60.0 (54.0)
2002 (f)	40.0 (37.0)	94.0 (52.0)	57.3 (54.8)	54.0 (24.0)	72.0 (69.4)	98.0 (70.9)	94.6 (91.8)	67.0 (63.0)

Source: The Compiler Team of the *2002 IT Industry Yearbook* 2002: III–3.

Note
The figures in parentheses are the shares of Taiwan's IT hardware products made in China.

In addition, by 2000, Taiwan had transferred about half of the production of motherboards, servers, and digital cameras to overseas production bases. The pace of transfers has been accelerating in 2001–2002. According to the estimate of the Institute for Information Industry, in 2002 the share of the above products produced overseas would increase by 10 percent. Moreover, the destination of Taiwan's transfers was mostly to China. In 2000, 45 percent of motherboards, 44 percent of digital cameras, and 9 percent of servers were produced in China; by 2002, these figures would increase to 55 percent, 63 percent, and 24 percent. respectively (see Table 5.4).

The last wave of IT products to be transferred to production bases abroad includes notebook computers and LCD monitors. In 1999, Taiwan transferred only 3.3 percent of notebook computer production and 0.5 percent of LCD monitor production abroad. According to the estimate of the Institute for Information Industry, by 2002 the above figures would increase to 40 percent and 72 percent.

Even more surprisingly, the majority of production bases were transferred to China. In 2000, Taiwan did not make any investment in China to produce notebook computers, and they transferred only 1 percent of LCD monitor production to China. By 2002, 37 percent of Taiwan's notebooks and 69 percent of its LCD monitors would be produced in China. In other words almost all of the transfers were shifted to China (see Table 5.4).

Regarding the changes of its global market shares as a result of massively shifting the production to overseas production bases, Taiwan's individual IT products can be divided into three categories: First, the global market shares of Taiwan's individual IT products decline, remain stable, or slightly increase (under 10 percent). Second, the global market shares of Taiwan's individual IT products increase moderately (10–20 percent). Third, the global market shares of Taiwan's individual IT products increase by a large margin (above 20 percent).

The first category of products includes: motherboards, monitors, graphics cards, terminals, networking cards, and mice. During the seven years between 1994 and 2001, Taiwan's motherboards maintained around 80 percent of the global market share, while monitors retained 55 percent, graphics cards 32 percent (between 1994 and 1999), terminals 25 percent (between 1994 and 1996), and networking cards 35 percent (between 1994 and 1999). The global market share of Taiwan's mice declined from 80 percent in 1994 to 58 percent in 1999. Nevertheless, Taiwan's motherboards, monitors, and mice all maintain very high global market shares of more than 50 percent. Therefore, Taiwan's investment in China, to some degree, should make a positive contribution to their competitiveness. At least, it is helpful for Taiwan to maintain such high global market shares (see Table 5.5).

The second category of products includes: desktop computers and keyboards. From 1994 to 2000, the global market share of desktop computers

Table 5.5 Global market share of Taiwan's major IT products (1994–2002) (unit: %)

Year	1994	1995	1996	1998	1999	2000	2001	2002
Notebook computer	28.0	27.0	32.0	40.0	49.0	52.5	54.8	60.6
Motherboard	80.0	65.0	74.2	78.3	79.2	84.7	86.3	87.8
Desktop computer	8.0	10.0	10.2	17.0	19.0	24.5	24.0	–
Monitor	56.0	57.0	53.7	58.0	58.0	53.7	51.2	–
Keyboard	52.0	65.0	61.0	65.0	68.0	–	–	–
CD/DVD/CD RW driver	1.0	11.0	15.0	34.0	34.0	38.9	31.9	–
Desktop scanner	61.0	64.0	52.0	84.0	91.0	92.5	–	–
SPS	31.0	35.0	55.3	66.0	70.0	74.0	–	–
Sound card	11.0	22.0	50.0	–	–	–	–	–
Mouse	80.0	72.0	65.0	60.0	58.0	–	–	–
Graphics card	32.0	32.0	38.3	31.0	31.0	–	–	–
Terminal	22.0	27.0	24.6	–	–	–	–	–
Networking card	34.0	38.0	–	36.0	40.0	–	–	–
Video card	24.0	35.0	55.0	–	–	–	–	–

Sources: The Compilers of the *1995 IT Industry Yearbook* 1995: 24; The Compiler Committee of the *1996 IT Industry Yearbook* 1996: 184; The Compiler Committee of the *1997 IT Industry Yearbook* 1997: 655; The Compiler Team of the *1999 IT Industry Yearbook* 2000: III–7; The Compiler Committee of the *2000 IT Industry Yearbook* 2001: III–3, III–6, VIII–5; The Compiler Team of the *2002 IT Industry Yearbook* 2002: VIII–13 and XVII–1; Institute for Information Industry (2003b); Institute for Information Industry (2003c).

increased from 8 percent to 24.5 percent – an increase of 16.5 percent. The global market share of keyboards increased from 52 percent in 1994 to 68 percent in 1999 – an increase of 13 percent (see Table 5.5).

The third category of products includes: notebook computers, CD/DVD/CD RW drivers, desktop scanners, and switching power supplies (SPS), sound cards, and video cards. From 1994 to 2000, the global market share of notebook computers increased by 24.5 percent, CD/DVD/CD RW drivers by 37.9 percent, desktop scanners by 31.5 percent, SPS by 43 percent, sound cards by 39 percent (from 1994 to 1999), and video cards by 31 percent (from 1994 to 1996). During this short period of six years, the products mentioned above increased by around one-third of the global market share – demonstrating the remarkable competitiveness (see Table 5.5).

In the following sections, this chapter further analyzes desktop computers, motherboards, keyboards, CD/DVD/CD RW drivers, and monitors as case studies. This will concretely illustrate the impact of Taiwan's investment in China on the competitiveness of their IT products in the global market.

Desktop computers

In 1995, 91.2 percent of Taiwan's desktop computers were produced in Taiwan, while 8.8 percent were produced overseas. At that time, the global market share of Taiwan's desktop computers was just 10 percent. In the four years prior to 1996, the global market share was maintained between 8 percent and 10 percent.

From 1997 to 1999, Taiwan conducted massive outward investment in the desktop computer industry. In 1999, only 16 percent of Taiwan's desktop computers were produced in Taiwan, while 84 percent were produced overseas and 30 percent were produced in China. In that year, the global market share of Taiwan's desktop computers was 19.6 percent. During the three years, the global market share of desktop computers doubled.

From 1999 to 2001, Taiwan transferred its production bases of desktop computers primarily to China. Consequently, the share of their production in China increased from 30 percent in 1999 to 48 percent in 2001. During the same period, the global market share of desktop computers increased from 19.6 percent to 24 percent. Therefore, the ICR was 0.24 (=4.4 percent/18 percent) (see Table 5.6).

Motherboards

In 1997, 60 percent of motherboards were produced in Taiwan, while 40 percent were produced in China. At that time, the global market share was 68 percent. After 1998, Taiwan continued expanding its investment in

Table 5.6 Production bases and the global market share of Taiwan's desktop computers (1993–2001) (unit: %)

Year	1993	1994	1995	1996	1998	1999	2000	2001
Proportion of production in Taiwan	–	–	91.2	85.6	–	16.0	15.0	12.0
Proportion of production in China	–	–	–	–	–	30.0	45.0	48.0
Taiwan's global market share	8.0	8.0	10.0	10.2	17.4	19.6	24.5	24.0

Sources: The Compiler Committee of the *1997 IT Industry Yearbook* 1997: 658; The Compiler Team of the *1998 IT Industry Yearbook* 1999: 1 and 7; The Compiler Team of the *2002 IT Industry Yearbook* 2002: VIII–23, VIII–24, and VIII–27.

China. In 2002, only 37.6 percent of motherboards were manufactured in Taiwan, while 63 percent were made in China. At that year, the global market share of motherboards increased to 87.8 percent.

Between 1997 and 2002, the share of production in China increased by 23 percent, with their global market share increasing by 19.8 percent. Therefore, the ICR was 0.86 (=19.8 percent/23 percent). That is, as Taiwan shifted their production of motherboards in China by 1 percent, the global market share of motherboards increased by 0.86 percent (see Table 5.7).

Keyboards

Taiwanese business people shifted its production of keyboards abroad earlier than other IT products. In 1993, only 32 percent of keyboards were still produced in Taiwan. Nevertheless, most of their keyboard production was shifted towards Southeast Asian countries, with only 11 percent in China. At that time, the global market share of Taiwan's keyboards was 49 percent.

After the mid-1990s, not only did the production of Taiwan's keyboards massively move to China, but also the production of Taiwanese goods in Southeast Asian countries was shifted to China. Consequently, in 1997, only 9.8 percent of keyboards were made in Taiwan, while 61.9 percent of their keyboard production was transferred to China. In that year, the global market share increased to 62.2 percent.

In the five-year period between 1993 and 1998, the share of production in China increased by 52 percent, and the global market share of keyboards increased by 15.9 percent. As a result, the ICR was 0.31 (=15.9 percent/52 percent). The process of shifting their production to China is continuing, with that, the global market share is increasing as well – reaching 68 percent in 1999 (see Table 5.8).

CD/DVD/CD RW drivers

Before 1994, the production of CD/DVD/CD RW drivers was in the preliminary stages. In that year, Taiwan only accounted for 1.1 percent of the global market share. In 1996, 67.2 percent of CD/DVD/CD RW drivers were produced in Taiwan and only 4 percent in China. At that time, the global market share of Taiwan increased to 12 percent.

After 1996, Taiwanese began to conduct massive outward investment, particularly in China. At the same time it enormously redirected its overseas production to China. By 2001, only 7.1 percent of CD/DVD/CD RW drivers were made in Taiwan, while 91.2 percent were made in China. In 2000, the global market share increased to 38.9 percent.

During the period of four years between 1996 and 2000, the share of production of CD/DVD/CD RW drivers in China increased by 68.4

Table 5.7 Production bases and the global market share of Taiwan's motherboards (1997–2002) (unit: %)

Year	1997	1998	1999	2000	2001	2002
Proportion of production in Taiwan	60.0	61.0	56.0	52.0	45.0	37.6
Proportion of production in China	40.0	39.0	43.0	46.0	53.0	63.0
Taiwan's global market share	68.0	78.3	79.2	84.7	86.3	87.8

Sources: The Compiler Team of the *2000 IT Industry Yearbook* 2001: X–15 and X–18; The Compiler Team of the *2002 IT Industry Yearbook* 2002: VIII–23, VIII–24, and VIII–27; Institute for Information Industry (2003b).

Note
The figures of proportion of production in China for 1997 and 1998 are not available. Because the difference between the proportion of overseas production and the proportion of production in China was only 1–2 percent from 1999–2001, the figures of the proportion of production in China in 1997 and 1998 use those of the proportion of overseas production in the same years.

Table 5.8 Production bases and the global market share of Taiwan's keyboards (1993–2000) (unit: %)

Year	1993	1994	1996	1997	1998	1999	2000
Proportion of production in Taiwan	32.0	31.0	7.0	9.8	9.3	8.2	5.0
Proportion of production in China	11.0	18.0	52.0	61.9	63.0	–	86.0
Taiwan's global market share	49.0	52.0	61.0	62.2	64.9	68.0	–

Sources: The Compiler Team of the *1995 IT Industry Yearbook* 1995: 164–165; The Compiler Team of the *1998 IT Industry Yearbook* 1999: 135; Institute for Information Industry (2000).

percent, and the global market share increased by 26.9 percent. Therefore, the ICR was 0.39 (=26.9 percent/68.4 percent) (see Table 5.9).

Monitors

In 1993, 68.6 percent of monitors were still made in Taiwan, and only 31.4 percent were made abroad. In that year, the global market share was 51 percent. Thereafter, Taiwan continued to invest outwardly, transferring its production abroad. In particular, after the mid-1990s, its investment was heavily focused in China. In 1997, 44.9 percent of monitors were produced in Taiwan, and 21.5 percent in China. In that year, the global market share was 54.6 percent. By 2001, only 2.1 percent of monitors were still produced in Taiwan, while 66.3 percent were produced in China. In that year, the global market share was 51.2 percent.

During the four-year period between 1997 and 2001, the share of production in China increased by 44.8 percent, and the global market share of declined by 3.4 percent. Therefore, the ICR was −0.08 (=−3.4 percent/44.8 percent). That is, investment in monitors in China might not reinforce their competitiveness. However, the global market share increased once to 58 percent in 1999, higher than 54.6 percent in 1997 (see Table 5.10).

The impact on China's IT industry

Between 1996 and 2003, the average annual growth rate of Taiwan's IT products that were made in China was 39.4 percent. In 2003, 63.6 percent of Taiwan's IT products were already produced in China. As a result, during this period, Taiwan's direct investment in China should have significantly contributed to the development of China's IT industry.

China's official statistics of IT hardware products are scattered and incomplete. Nevertheless, most of China's high-tech products have currently consisted of IT products. For instance, the share of computer and telecommunication products in China's total high-tech products was 49.1 percent in 1997, increasing rapidly to 80.4 percent in 2002. As a result, this chapter primarily uses the statistics of China's high-tech industry,[2] supplemented by some statistics from China's electronics and information industry and IT hardware industry.

Since the mid-1990s, China's high-tech industry has grown very rapidly. The value-added to China's high-tech industry increased almost three times in six years – from RMB108.1 billion in 1995 to RMB309.5 billion in 2001. Between 1995 and 2001, the average annual growth rate of the value-added reached 19.3 percent. In addition, the share of value-added to the high-tech industry in China's total industries increased from 8.8 percent in 1995 to 13.9 percent in 2001. More astonishing, the share of high-tech exports in China's total exports increased from 7.9 percent in 1995 to 19.4

Table 5.9 Production bases and the global market share of Taiwan's CD/DVD/CD RW drivers (1994–2001) (unit: %)

Year	1994	1995	1996	1997	1998	1999	2000	2001
Proportion of production in Taiwan	–	79.1	67.2	52.0	29.6	19.5	13.9	7.1
Proportion of production in China	–	–	4.0	28.0	–	–	72.4	91.2
Taiwan's global market share	1.1	10.0	12.0	22.7	34.4	34.0	38.9	–

Sources: The Compiler Team of the *1998 IT Industry Yearbook* 1999: 117–119; The Compiler Team of the *2000 IT Industry Yearbook* 2001: X–35; The Compiler Team of the *2002 IT Industry Yearbook* 2002: VIII–94.

Table 5.10 Production bases and the global market share of Taiwan's monitors (1992–2001) (unit: %)

Year	1992	1993	1994	1995	1996	1997	1998	1999	2000	2001
Proportion of production in Taiwan	84.7	68.6	59.9	51.3	45.3	44.9	28.6	19.2	8.0	2.1
Proportion of overseas production	15.3	31.4	40.1	48.7	54.7	55.1	71.4	81.8	92.0	97.9
Proportion of production in China	–	–	–	–	–	21.5	34.6	43.4	58.0	66.3
Taiwan's global market share	–	51.0	56.0	–	53.7	54.6	57.8	58.0	53.7	51.2

Sources: The Compiler Team of the *1994 IT Industry Yearbook* 1994: 150; The Compiler Team of the *1995 IT Industry Yearbook* 1995: 23, 147; The Compiler Team of the *1998 IT Industry Yearbook* 1998: 109–112; The Compiler Team of the *2002 IT Industry Yearbook* 2002: III–3, VIII–66, VIII–68.

percent in 2001, while the share of high-tech imports in China's total imports increased from 20.3 percent in 1995 to 32.4 percent in 2001 (see Table 5.11).

The value of China's high-tech exports was just $4 billion in 1992, increasing enormously to $67.9 billion in 2002. As a matter of fact, the majority of China's high-tech trade was "processing trade." In 1993, the share of processing exports in China's total high-tech exports was already 70.2 percent. This ratio increased to 86.2 percent in 1998 and further to 89.6 percent in 2002. In addition, in 2002, 61.6 percent of high-tech imports belonged to the processing trade (see Table 5.12).

Moreover, the majority of China's high-tech exports were produced by foreign-invested enterprises (FIEs, including Taiwan-, Hong Kong-, and Macao-invested enterprises). The share of the FIEs in China's total high-tech exports was 71.5 percent in 1996, increasing to 76 percent in 1999 and further to 82.2 percent in 2002. It is very obvious that the rapid expansion of China's exports of high-tech products was predominantly driven by the FIEs through processing trade. These figures suggest that most FIEs in China have been utilizing China's cheap labor, along with imported materials, to increase their competitiveness in the global market (see Table 5.12).

In 2001, of China's high-tech industrial enterprises' revenues and capital, the share of the FIEs was 47.7 percent and 49 percent, respectively. According to China's National Bureau of Statistics, between 1996 and 2001, 62 percent of China's high-tech industrial growth was contributed by FIEs (National Bureau of Statistics, 2003). These figures exemplify the significant contribution of FIEs to the development of China's high-tech industry in the late 1990s and early 2000s.

Statistics from China's electronics and information industry, which is broader than Taiwan's classification, also indicate the rapid expansion of China's IT industry. The output of the electronics and information industry increased from RMB69.8 billion in 1990 to RMB1.78 trillion in 2002, expanding by almost 30 times within 12 years. The share of value-added to the industry to GDP increased from 1 percent in 1998 to 2 percent in 2002. The share of exports of the industry to China's total exports increased from 11 percent in 1995 to 28 percent in 2002 (Lou, 2003: 148–161).

FIEs have played a very important role in the development of China's electronics and information industry. In 2002, the output, sale, value-added, and exports of the industry were RMB1.78 trillion, RMB1.4 trillion, RMB298 billion, and $92 billion, respectively. At that year, the shares of FIEs in the output, sale, and value-added of the industry were 67.8 percent, 67.6 percent, and 49.1 percent, respectively (Ministry of Information Industry, 2003). In 2001, 90 percent of China's exports of the electronics and information industry were processing exports, while FIEs contributed to 78.6 percent of China's exports. In the first half of 2003, FIEs contributed to 82.7 percent of China's exports.

Table 5.11 Statistics on China's high-tech industry (1995–2001)

	1995	1996	1997	1998	1999	2000	2001
Number of enterprises	18,834	18,909	17,411	9,348	9,493	9,758	10,479
Value-added (RMB billion)	108.1	127.2	154.0	178.5	210.7	275.9	309.5
Growth rate of value-added (%)	n.a.	17.7	21.1	15.9	18.0	30.9	12.2
Share of value-added in all industries (%)	8.8	9.4	9.8	11.7	12.5	14.0	13.9
Share of high-tech exports in total exports (%)	7.9	9.8	10.3	12.4	14.1	16.6	19.4
Share of high-tech imports in total imports (%)	20.3	19.8	21.0	24.9	27.1	29.4	32.4

Source: China Science and Technology Statistics 2003.

Table 5.12 Exports of China's high-tech products (1992–2002) (unit: $ billion, %)

	1992	1993	1994	1995	1996	1997	1998	1999	2000	2001	2002
Value of high-tech exports	4.0	4.7	6.3	10.1	12.7	16.3	20.3	24.7	37.0	46.5	67.9
Growth rate of high-tech exports	38.9	14.9	34.0	60.3	25.7	25.7	24.2	22.0	49.8	25.4	46.1
Share of high-tech exports in total exports	4.7	5.1	5.2	6.8	8.4	8.9	11.0	12.7	14.9	17.5	20.8
Share of processing exports in total high-tech exports	n.a.	70.2	n.a.	n.a.	n.a.	n.a.	86.2	87.3	n.a.	n.a.	89.6
Share of foreign-invested enterprises in total high-tech exports	n.a.	n.a.	n.a.	n.a.	71.5	n.a.	73.7	76.0	n.a.	81.5	82.2

Source: China Science and Technology Statistics 2003.

Table 5.13 The value of China's IT hardware products and Taiwanese business
people's contribution (1999–2001)

Year	1999	2000	2001
Value ($ billion)	18.5	25.5	28.2
Taiwanese business people's contribution (%)	71.3	57.6 (72.0)	55.9

Sources: Institute for Information Industry 2003a; "70% of Mainland's Computer Equipments Come From Taiwanese Businesspeople"(2001).

Note
The figure of 72 in parenthesis is from China's Ministry of Foreign Trade and Economic Cooperation. Other figures are compiled by Taiwan's Institute for Information Industry.

Based on the compilation of Taiwan's Institute for Information Industry, the sale of China's IT hardware products increased from RMB13.4 billion in 1992 to RMB62.6 billion in 1995, to RMB115.5 billion in 1998, and further to RMB181.5 billion in 2001. Between 1992 and 2001, the average annual growth rate of the sale of China's IT hardware products was 36.1 percent (Institute for Information Industry, 2003a). These figures exemplify the rapid expansion of China's IT industry after 1992.

According to Taiwan's Institute for Information Industry, the value of IT hardware products manufactured by both local enterprises and FIEs in China was $18.5 billion in 1999, $25.5 billion in 2000, and $28.2 billion in 2001, respectively. Among the FIEs, the Taiwan-invested enterprises (TIEs) in China played a principal role in expanding China's IT hardware production. The share of these products manufactured by TIEs was 71.3 percent in 1999, 57.6 percent in 2000, and 55.9 percent in 2001, respectively. Nevertheless, according to China's Ministry of Foreign Trade and Economic Cooperation (now renamed to the Ministry of Commerce), 72 percent of China's total IT hardware products were manufactured by TIEs in 2000. For instance, TIEs produced 73.5 percent of China's monitors and Chinese enterprises manufactured only 9.5 percent in 2001 (Lou, 2003: 195). Generally speaking, in 1999–2001, TIEs contributed to around 60–70 percent of China's IT hardware products (see Table 5.13).

Conclusion

Does Taiwanese investment in the IT industry in China improve the competitiveness of its IT products in the global market? The answer is quite obvious: there is a very positive effect through reducing input cost and accessing the Chinese market. For instance, in 2003 the total production cost of IT products in China was only one-fourth to one-sixth of that in Taiwan. From 1996 to 2003, the average annual growth rate of Taiwan's IT products made in Taiwan was −0.7 percent while that in China was

39.4 percent. Consequently, the expansion of the global market share of Taiwan's IT industry was driven mainly by the expansion of its IT production in China.

For Taiwan's IT industry as a whole, in the second half of the 1990s, the ICR was 0.51. That is, from 1995 to 2000, as the proportion of its production of IT products in China increased by 1 percent, the global market share increased by 0.51 percent.

For Taiwan's individual IT products, in the second half of the 1990s, the effects were as follows: desktops ICR was 0.24, motherboards 0.86, keyboards 0.31, CD/DVD/CD RW driver's 0.39, and monitors −0.08. Except for monitors, Taiwan's investment in China had a very positive impact on the competitiveness of their IT products in the global market. Even though the impact was not positive, monitors still maintained more than 50 percent of the global market share by 2001. Despite the pressure of global competition, investing in China might be the reason why Taiwan sustained such a high global market share.

In addition, Taiwan's direct investment in China has clearly played a vital role in the rapid expansion of China's IT industry. During the period of 1999–2001, 62 percent of China's high-tech industrial growth and approximately 80 percent of China's high-tech exports (around 75 percent of which was IT hardware products) were contributed by FIEs. In terms of China's electronics and information industry, the share of FIEs in output was 67.8 percent in 2002, and the share of FIEs in exports was 82.7 percent in the first half of 2003. Among the FIEs, between 1999 and 2001, the TIEs contributed to around 60–70 percent of China's IT hardware products. Based on the proportion of FIEs' contribution to China's exports, it is very plausible that the TIEs might contribute to at least 60–70 percent of China's IT hardware exports in this period.

To conclude, "made by Taiwan but made in China" would be a new expression to describe the global division of labor across the Taiwan Strait driven by Taiwan's direct investment in China. Over the past decade, both sides of the Strait benefitted tremendously from this economic division of labor in the IT industry. Based on the market force it is likely that this economic division of labor in the IT and other industries would be broadened and deepened in the future.

Finally, though the ICR concisely tells us the impact of Taiwan's investment in the IT industry in China on the competitiveness of their IT products in the global market, there are some pitfalls and limitations to this analysis. First, because the period of sampling is very short (six years), the result of the ICR does not completely reflect the facts.

Second, because Taiwan's global market share fluctuates the timing might well have influenced the results. For instance, the global market share of Taiwan's monitors was 54.6 percent in 1997, it increased to 58 percent in 1999, and then declined to 51.2 percent in 2001.

Third, if there is enough statistical data, we should run a regression analysis on the two levels of the whole IT industry and individual IT products. This will help further clarify the degree of the impact of Taiwan's investment in China has had on its competitiveness in the global market.

Finally, this chapter adopts a very strict definition of competitiveness reinforcement; that is, the global market share of Taiwan must increase. Although the global market share might not increase, if Taiwan can maintain a considerably high global market share (for example, more than 50 percent), its investment in China should, to some degree, have a positive impact on its competitiveness in the global market.

Notes

1 According to Taiwan's Institute for Information Industry, IT products include PCs, CD/DVD/CD RW drivers, scanners, monitors, digital cameras, game machines, multimedia, servers, notebook computers, printers, motherboards, graphics cards, sound cards, video cards, PCMCIA cards, CPUs, memories, palm computers, radios, printed circuit board, projectors, and hard disks.
2 According to China's official definition, the high-tech industry includes eight categories of technologies: biological technology, life science technology, opto-electronic technology, computer and telecommunication, electronic technology, computer integrated manufacturing technology, materials technology, and aerospace technology.

References

"70% of mainland's computer equipment comes from Taiwanese businesspeople," *Gongshang Shibao, Commerce Times*, 14 April 2001.

China Science and Technology Statistics 2003. Available from: http://www.sts. org.cn (accessed 25 August 2003).

Chung, C. (1997) "Division of labor across the Taiwan Strait: macro overview and analysis of the electronics industry," in B. Naughton (ed.) *The China Circle: Economic and Technology in the PRC, Taiwan, and Hong Kong*, Washington, DC: Brookings Institution Press, 164–209.

The Compiler Team of the 1994 IT Industry Yearbook (compiled) (1994) *The 1994 IT Industry Yearbook*, (in Chinese), Taipei: Institute for Information Industry.

The Compiler Team of the 1995 IT Industry Yearbook (compiled) (1995) *The 1995 IT Industry Yearbook*, (in Chinese), Taipei: Institute for Information Industry.

The Compiler Committee of the 1996 IT Industry Yearbook (compiled) (1996) *The 1996 IT Industry Yearbook* (in Chinese), Taipei: Institute for Information Industry, 1996.

The Compiler Committee of the 1997 IT Industry Yearbook (compiled) (1997) *The 1997 IT Industry Yearbook* (in Chinese), Taipei: Institute for Information Industry.

The Compiler Team of the 1998 IT Industry Yearbook (compiled) (1999) *The 1998 IT Industry Yearbook* (in Chinese), Taipei: Institute for Information Industry.

The Compiler Team of the 1999 IT Industry Yearbook (compiled) (2000) *The 1999 IT Industry Yearbook* (in Chinese), Taipei: Institute for Information Industry.

The Compiler Committee of the 2000 IT Industry Yearbook (compiled) (2001)

The 2000 IT Industry Yearbook (in Chinese), Taipei: Institute for Information Industry.

The Compiler Team of the 2002 IT Industry Yearbook (compiled) (2002) *The 2002 IT Industry Yearbook* (in Chinese), Taipei: Institute for Information Industry.

Institute for Information Industry (2000) "The Outward Transfer of the IT Industry and Response Strategies: Part I," (in Chinese).

Institute for Information Industry (2003a). Available from: http://mic.iii.org.tw/itdb/ResourceDisplay.asp?sno=MSERLOMO (accessed 25 August 2003).

Institute for Information Industry (2003b) "The Current Situation and Prospect of the Development of Taiwan's Motherboard Industry in 2002," (in Chinese).

Institute for Information Industry (2003c) "The Current Situation and Prospect of the Development of Taiwan's Notebook Computer Industry in 2002," (in Chinese).

Jiang, F.Y. and Zhou, S.X. (2003) "The analysis on the operation management style of Taiwan's PC industry across the Taiwan Strait," (in Chinese), Taipei: Institute for Information Industry.

Lou, Q.J. (ed.) (2003) *Zhongguo Dianzixinxi Chanye Fazhan Moshi Yanjiu* [The Study on the Development Model of China's Electronics and Information Industry], Beijing: Zhongguo Jingji Chubanshe.

Ministry of Economic Affairs (Taiwan) (1997) *Zhizaoye Duiwai Touzi Shikuang Diaocha Baogao* [The investigation Report on Outward Investment of the Manufacturing Industry], Taipei: Ministry of Economic Affairs.

Ministry of Economic Affairs (Taiwan) (2002) *Zhizaoye Duiwai Touzi Shikuang Diaocha Baogao* [The Investigation Report on Outward Investment of the Manufacturing Industry], Taipei: Ministry of Economic Affairs.

Ministry of Information Industry (China) (2003) "Summary of the data of the Electronics and Information Industry Yearbook 2002," (in Chinese). Available from: www.mii.gov.cn/mii/hyzw/tongji/2003071902.htm (accessed 29 October 2003).

National Bureau of Statistics (China) (2003) "Census Analysis XII: The Problems and Policies of Hi-Tech Industrial Development in China," (in Chinese). Available from: www.stats.gov.cn/tjfx/ztfx/decjbdwpc/1200305230104.htm (accessed 21 August 2003).

Qin, S.X. (2003) "The New Position of Taiwan's IT Hardware Industry in the Global Division of Labor," (in Chinese), Taipei: Institute for Information Industry.

United Nations Conference on Trade and Development (2002) *World Investment Report 2002: Transnational Corporations and Export Competitiveness*, New York: United Nations.

6 Japanese FDI in China

Trend, structure, and exchange rates

Yuqing Xing

Introduction

Today "Made in China" is available almost at every corner of the global market, and is occupying increasing market share. What are the reasons for the sudden popularity of "Made in China"? Observers may point to relatively low labor cost as a secret of the success. However, labor in China was even cheaper ten years ago compared with that of today. Why was "Made in China" not popular then? Decomposing China's exports according to their producers may provide an answer for the rising popularity of "Made in China". In 2001, exports of foreign-invested firms in China amounted to $133.23 billion, more than 50 percent of China's total exports (CSB, 2002). It is the first time that the exports of foreign-invested firms exceeded that of domestic firms. From 1994 to 2001, the exports of foreign-invested firms grew on average about 21 percent annually. In contrast, the exports of China's domestic firms grew merely 6.4 percent, even lower than the growth of China's GDP (Xing and Zhao, 2003). Unambiguously, foreign-invested firms are a major force driving the robust export growth and promoting the popularity of "Made in China". Without the contribution of foreign-invested firms, the so-called export-driven growth in China could not be possible.

Actually, it is very difficult for firms from a developing country to penetrate markets of industrialized countries, even if their products are of equal quality. First of all, products from developing countries lack brand name recognition, which is important for sophisticated consumers in industrialized countries. Second, compared with firms in industrialized countries, those from developing countries do not have internationally established distribution and marketing networks, making market access even harder.

However, with the entry of multinational enterprises (MNE), either in the form of joint ventures, or wholly foreign-owned firms, "Made in China" has been produced with advanced technology (e.g. fashionable electronics), distributed in global market, and sold under globally recognized brand names. Chinese firms have established alliances with foreign

MNEs, becoming fragments of global production chains. Further, Chinese workers have been integrated into the international division of labor. Therefore, export-oriented FDI not only enhances the competitiveness of "Made in China", but also functions as a mechanism facilitating the utilization of China's comparative advantages such as a relatively rich labor endowment.

Among all foreign investors, Japanese MNEs have played a leading role in fostering China's manufacturing exports. In 2001, they invested more than 2.9 billion US dollars in China (CSB, 2002), making Japan the third largest single source by origin. Excluding the reinvestment by existing Japanese affiliated manufacturers in China, Japanese direct investment in China's manufacturing accumulated to 1.88 trillion yen from 1981 to 2002.[1] Unlike American MNEs focusing basically on China's domestic market, Japanese MNEs are mainly export-oriented and consequently promoting China's exports greatly. In 2002 Japanese affiliated manufacturers in China exported 2,245 billion yen, about 65 percent of their products to overseas market (METI, 2003). Using China as a production base for Japan and the global market is the strategy being utilized by Japanese MNEs to strengthen their global competitiveness and to avoid the negative impact of the yen's appreciation.

In 2003, Sino-Japan trade reached a record $132 billion. Examining the fast expansion of Sino-Japan bilateral trade suggests that direct investment from Japan performed a critical role in strengthening the economic integration between the two economies. Japanese affiliated manufacturers in China contributed to the surging bilateral trade in dual ways: exporting their products as final products and intermediate inputs to Japan, and importing intermediate goods from Japan as their production inputs. In 2002, Japanese affiliated manufacturers exported 1,057 billion yen products to Japanese market (METI, 2003). The effect of Japanese affiliated manufacturers' operation on China's exports and its national economy is tremendous.

The influx of Japanese FDI benefits China not only at a macro level, but also at a micro level. Despite more than a decade long economic stagnation, Japanese firms are still the global leaders in the manufacturing industries such as electronics, machinery, and transportation equipment. Japanese firms own most of the globally recognized brands in these sectors (Porter and Sakakibara, 2004). As Japanese MNEs continue to relocate their production facilities into China and expand their investment scale, China's domestic industry will continue to benefit substantially from the positive externality of the investments. Direct investment from Japan creates a prime opportunity for Chinese firms to access the information on product innovation, advanced production technology, and sophisticated global marketing channels. Further, it functions as a critical mechanism for technological progress and productivity growth, consequently transforming China's industry fundamentally.

Growth of FDI

Japanese firms started to invest in China as early as 1981. Figure 6.1 shows trends of FDI in both manufacturing and non-manufacturing sectors. The scale of FDI from Japan was relatively moderate before 1990 and the investment mainly concentrated on the non-manufacturing sector. According to the data complied by the Japanese Ministry of Finance,[2] in 1990 Japanese firms invested 50.7 billion yen in China, of which 27 billion yen was invested in non-manufacturing while 23.7 billion yen was invested in manufacturing sector. An unprecedented investment boom began in 1991 as inflows increased sharply to 73.1 billion yen, 44 percent higher than that in the preceding year. The rising trend continued and peaked in 1995 with a total 421.8 billion yen of annual inflows, of which 336.8 billion yen flowing into the manufacturing sector and only 85 billion yen into non-manufacturing. The rising trend, however, reversed abruptly in 1996 as FDI plunged to 278.1 billion yen, 34 percent lower than the peak level. The contraction of Japanese direct investment in China continued and reached its bottom 81 billion yen in 1999. It is important to notice that the declination of Japanese FDI was much earlier than the Asian financial crisis, contrary to conventional wisdom claiming that the declination was due to the Asian financial crisis. In fact the yen's sharp depreciation triggered the contraction of FDI inflows. The weaken yen eroded the relative wealth of Japanese MNEs and raised relative production cost in China (Xing, 2006), thus mitigating the influx of FDI. In 2000 direct investment from Japan revived to grow again and surged to 200 billion yen subsequently in 2002, but still much lower than its peak level in the 1990s.

Coinciding with the robust growth, sectoral composition of direct investment from Japan also experienced significant changes. The focus of Japanese MNEs switched to manufacturing after 1990. Table 6.1 summa-

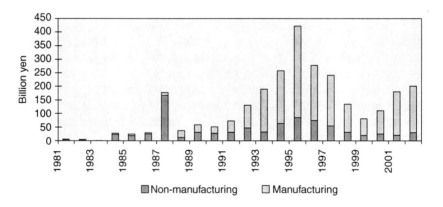

Figure 6.1 Japanese FDI in China (1981–2002) (source: *Monthly Statistics*, various issues, Japanese Ministry of Finance).

Table 6.1 Japan's FDI in China's manufacturing sectors (billion yen)

Sectors	1989		1995		2001		Cumulative FDI: 1989–2001	
	Value	Share (%)	Value	Share (%)	Value	Share (%)	Value	Share (%)
Food	1.82	6.60	13.69	4.07	1.29	0.81	94.13	5.66
Textile	1.45	5.26	45.53	13.52	4.23	2.66	200.36	12.06
Lumber and Pulp	0.19	0.69	6.75	2.00	2.67	1.68	26.22	1.58
Chemical	1.50	5.44	13.78	4.09	18.55	11.67	118.91	7.16
Metal	0.82	2.97	34.71	10.31	16.26	10.23	141.81	8.53
Machinery	5.73	20.78	46.31	13.75	16.25	10.22	206.65	12.44
Electrical	10.68	38.74	90.44	26.86	63.93	40.21	455.43	27.41
Transport	0.16	0.58	37.01	10.99	25.79	16.22	179.84	10.82
Others	5.22	18.93	48.54	14.41	10.03	6.31	238.26	14.34
Total	27.57	100	336.76	100.00	159.00	100.00	1,661.61	100.00

Source: Monthly Statistics by the Japanese Ministry of Finance, shares are authors' calculations.

rizes shares and values of FDI from 1989 to 2001 in nine manufacturing sectors: food, lumber and pulp, chemical, metal, textile, electrical, machinery, transportation equipment, and others. Over the period, FDI inflows in manufacturing accumulated 1,661.6 billion yen, more than tripled cumulative investment in non-manufacturing, indicating that Japanese manufacturers have established mass production capacity in China for serving both the global market as well as China's domestic market. The Japanese electrical industry, which has been the leader in engaging FDI in Asia, also took the lead in China. It invested 455.4 billion yen during the period which accounted for more than 27 percent of the total investment. The machinery industry ranked second with 206.7 billion yen cumulative investment. It is well known that Japanese electrical and machinery industries are very competitive globally and export most of their products to the world market. The huge investment should strengthen the competitiveness of Chinese electrical and machinery industries, and enhance their exports. Textiles was the third largest sector in terms of cumulative FDI. It received a total 200.4 billion yen direct investment from Japan from 1989 to 2001. The investment in the textile industry basically reflects the international division of labor between the two countries, as textiles is labor intensive and China has a comparative advantage in producing textile products due to its rich labor endowment. Transportation equipment represents another sector observing drastic growth of FDI inflows. In 1989, the investment in the sector was merely 0.16 billion yen, less than 1 percent of annual FDI. It emerged as the second largest sector in terms of FDI in 2001, with 25.8 billion yen, more than 16 percent of Japanese FDI in China's manufacturing. Cumulative investment in transportation equipment from 1989 to 2001 amounted to 179.8 billion yen, making it the fourth largest sector receiving direct investment from Japan. In the mass media, domestic market-oriented projects by major Japanese auto-makers such as Toyota, Honda, Nissan, etc. are often widely reported. However, it is noteworthy that Japanese MNEs' investment in transportation equipment is not only for occupying China's domestic automobile market, but also a strategic move to integrate China into their global production chains, making China a supplier of intermediate inputs such as auto parts. According to the *Quarterly Survey of Business Activities* (METI, 2003), the sales in the local market in 2002 accounted for only one-third of the annual sales of Japanese affiliated manufacturers in transportation equipment.

Export-oriented FDI

Japanese direct investment in developing countries is traditionally export oriented. By relocating production capacities of mature industries into developing countries, Japanese MNEs combine their advanced technology, brand name recognition, and well-established global distribution system, with relatively low production cost of host countries, consequently strengthening their global competitiveness. Extending oligopoly power into local markets, the strategy often adopted by US MNEs, is not the prime objective of Japanese MNEs. Kojima (1978) identified this kind of FDI as the "Japanese model" of foreign direct investment. According to the survey conducted by the Japan External Trade Organization (JETRO, 2003), 61.6 percent of Japanese firms operating in China stated that they exported at least 70 percent of their products. In Asia, only 55.9 percent of Japanese affiliated manufacturers exported at least 70 percent of their products. Thus, the export intensity of the Japanese affiliated manufacturers in China was much higher than the average.

The export-oriented nature of Japanese MNEs in China can also be illustrated with the structure of their sales destinations. Figure 6.2 depicts export intensities of Japanese affiliated manufacturers in China in electrical machinery, industrial machinery, transport equipment, textile, and all manufacturing together for the period of 1997 to 2002. The export intensity is defined as the ratio of exports to total sales. First, exports of Japanese affiliates far exceeded the sales in the local market. The manufacturers as a whole exported more than 60 percent of their products to overseas market on average. Although China's GDP expanded about 8 percent annually during the period and China's domestic market grew significantly, the export intensity did not decrease. The exports of Japanese affiliated manufactures still accounted for 65 percent of their total sales in 2002, only 2 percentage points lower compared with that in 1997. Moreover, export intensities tended to be higher in the sectors with more FDI. In industrial machinery, exports accounted for more than 80 percent of total sales on average, the highest among all sectors. In electrical machinery, except for 1999, export intensity ranged from 65 percent to 73 percent. In transportation equipment where China is now considered as the largest unexplored market, the importance of the overseas market still dominated that of the local market. In both 2001 and 2002, Japanese affiliated manufacturers in the sector made about 65 percent of sales from the Japanese market and other overseas markets. The sales structure illustrated in Figure 6.2 is actually consistent with the phenomenon, that most of the "Made in China" products available in the Japanese domestic market carry Japanese brands, and many products under Japanese MNEs' brands available in the global market are made in China. For example, Pioneer Co. produced more than 90 percent of Pioneer's DVD recording devices in its plant located in Guangdong Province, most of them earmarked for personal computer and mainly for exports. These facts unequivocally indicate that, Japanese domestic investment in China's manufacturing was export-oriented, and using China as a production base serving the Japanese domestic market as well as global market was the primary objective of Japanese MNEs.

In terms of value and growth, the performance of Japanese affiliated manufacturers is also very impressive. Figure 6.3 shows the annual exports of these firms and corresponding growth rates from 1997 to 2002. In 1997, the exports of all Japanese affiliated manufacturers was 1,205 billion yen. It surged to 2,245 billion yen in 2002, representing a 13.5 percent annual growth, much higher than the growth of China's overall exports. Exports intensity, value, and the growth of Japanese affiliated manufacturers in

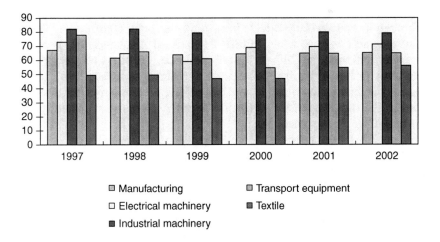

Figure 6.2 Export intensities of Japanese affiliated manufacturers in China (source: Author's calculation based on *Quarterly Survey of Business Activities*, METI).

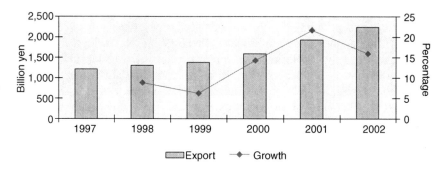

Figure 6.3 Exports of Japanese affiliated manufacturers in China (source: Author's calculation based on *Quarterly Survey of Business Activities*, METI).

China together demonstrates unequivocally that Japanese MNEs performed a crucial role in fostering China's exports, in particular the exports of manufactured goods.

Reverse imports and FDI

Another significant characteristic of Japanese MNEs in China is that they actively engaged in reverse imports, which refers to the products made at overseas Japanese plants and exported to the Japanese market. Coping with the rising yen and a shrinking domestic demand, many Japanese firms have relocated their domestic production capacity into China, or simply outsourced their production to Chinese firms. Fast Retailing Co., which markets the UNIQLO casual wear brand in Japan is a typical example. It designs, distributes, and markets UNIQLO brand products in Japan, but exclusively produces the products in its affiliated manufacturers in China, or subcontracts to local firms. Hitachi Household Appliance Co. producing air conditioners in China's Anhui province, exported 60 percent of them back to Japan. Unlike the exports of Chinese domestic firms, there exist no barriers in distribution and brand name recognition for reverse imports. The rapid expansion of reverse imports enhanced significantly the growth of China's exports to Japan.

Figure 6.4 shows ratios of reverse imports to total sales in selected industries. The overall ratio of reverse imports is relatively high compared with the ratio of local sales. On average Japanese affiliated manufacturers sold about one-third of their products back to Japan. In industrial machinery, more than half of the products were exported to the Japanese domestic market either as final goods or intermediates inputs. In textile and transportation equipment sectors the ratios of reverse imports actually increased from 1997 to 2002. In 1997, only 31 percent of textile products were produced for the Japanese market while the share rose to 47 percent in 2002. In transportation equipment, Japanese affiliated manufacturers

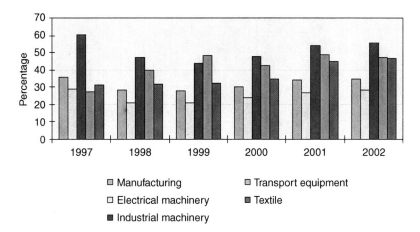

Figure 6.4 Reverse imports as the percentage of total sales of Japanese affiliated manufacturers in China (source: Author's calculation based on *Quarterly Survey of Business Activities*, METI).

also exported 47 percent of their products to Japan in 2002, much higher than 27 percent reverse import ratio in 1997. Rising reverse imports activities demonstrate that China has become an important production base for final products consumed in the Japanese market and the intermediate inputs of Japanese firms.

Unequivocally reverse imports directly contributed to the growth of China's exports to Japan. In 1997, Japanese affiliated manufacturers sold 565 billion yen of their products in the Japanese domestic market. Reverse imports of manufactured goods surged to 1,057 billion yen in 2002. Due to the Asian financial crisis which weakening Japanese domestic demand, reverse imports decreased 5 percent in 1998 and showed zero growth in 1999. However, reverse imports turned to growth drastically and increased 23 percent in 2000, and continued to grow 36 percent and 16 percent respectively in 2001 and 2002. Rapid expansion of reverse imports indicates a high level of vertical integration between Japanese and Chinese industries, and creates a close linkage between firms in the two economies, not only in production chains, but also in marketing networks, deepening interdependence of the two countries. Further, it leads to a win–win scenario for industries in both countries. Japanese companies benefit from low production costs and Chinese firms take advantages of the extensive marketing networks and advanced production technology of their Japanese partners.

Shifting to China

China has emerged as one of the most popular destinations for Japanese direct investment since the middle of 1990s. According to the survey of

JETRO (2001), among the Japanese firms with overseas production facilities, 54.4 percent of them have production facilities in China, the highest
among all foreign countries hosting Japanese FDI. The Asian NICs (Singapore, Korea, Hong Kong, and Taiwan) and ASEAN-4 (Indonesia,
Malaysia, Philippines, and Thailand) had been the primary destinations
for Japanese FDI in manufacturing. After 1990, China gradually became
one of the main destinations of Japanese FDI. The share of Japanese FDI
in China's manufacturing increased rapidly, compared with that of other
regions. In 1990, Japanese FDI in China accounted for merely 5 percent of
the Japanese total direct investment in Asian's manufacturing while the
NICs received about 42 percent and ASEAN-4 about 47 percent. By 1995,
China became the largest recipient of Japanese FDI. Its share jumped to
43 percent while the share of the NICs shrank to 14 percent and that of
ASEAN-4 decreased to 35 percent (Figure 6.6).

The shift to China is usually interpreted with the flying-geese theory,
with Japan at the highest level of economic development, followed by the
NICs, ASEAN-4, and China. Economic development at a high level
results in the migration of mature industries, especially those in which
labor costs are critical for competitiveness, to less developed economies.
Japanese MNEs searching for low production cost location have relocated
their production facilities in the same fashion across Asia (Kwan, 2001;
Edgington and Hayter, 2000). The flying-geese theory, however, may not
explain the whole story on Japanese FDI in China, especially when we
consider that many Japanese firms started to produce high-tech products
at the initial stage of their investment, not just labor-intensive products.
For instance, Fuji Zerox Co. develops and produces digital copy machines
tailored to industrialized countries in Shanghai for exporting to Japan, the
US, and Europe. Leading notebook computer maker Toshiba produced

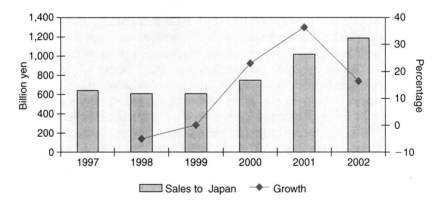

Figure 6.5 Reverse imports by Japanese affiliated manufacturers in China (source:
Author's calculation based on *Quarterly Survey of Business Activities*,
METI).

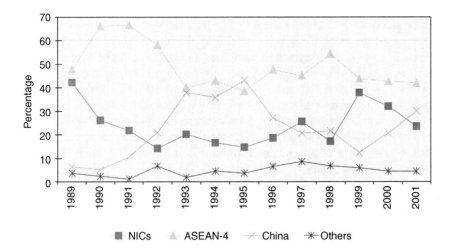

Figure 6.6 The distribution of Japanese FDI in Asia's manufacturing (source: Author's calculation based on *Quarterly Survey of Business Activities*, METI).

about 70,000 notebook computers per month in China. Further, after two decades' rapid economic growth, China's economic development has exceeded that of Indonesia and the coastal region, where most of the FDI was made and at least enjoys comparable economic development as Malaysia and Thailand. The classification in the flying-geese theory on the relative economic development between ASEAN-4 and China fails to outline the reality appropriately. In addition, before the Asian financial crisis, ASEAN-4 maintained relative stable political environment and sound economic fundamentals. In other words, there existed almost no other apparent structure problems that forced Japanese MNEs to switch to China from ASEAN-4, where they have established production bases for more than two decades. A new theory examining other dimensions of decision making on FDI is needed.

Factors determining FDI

The factors determining Japanese direct investment in China consist of push (Japan side) and pull factors (China side). The cumulative appreciation of the yen has raised the production cost in Japan substantially. The rising yen widened production cost gaps between Japan and other countries and eroded competitiveness of Japanese MNEs in global market. The moderate productivity growth at Japanese MNEs could not offset the negative impact of the yen's appreciation. As a consequence, relocating domestic production capacity to a country with low production costs evolved as a means of reducing production costs and maintaining competitiveness. The sharp appreciation of the yen as the result of the Plaza Accord of 1985 has been recognized as one of the major factors pushing Japan to be the largest capital exporting country, through either green field FDI or acquisition activities (Wong and Yamamura, 1996). Moreover, since the bubble burst, the long lasting economic stagnation has seriously weakened Japanese domestic demand. Facing a deteriorating economy, Japanese consumers have changed their consumption behavior fundamentally. They are willing to substitute expensive "Made in Japan" for cheap "Made in China", and demand more for their money. To cope with the changing economic environment, Japanese MNEs have extended their exodus into China.

For the pull factors on the China side, there are numerous studies on why China is so attractive to FDI. Branstetter and Feenstra (2002) showed that FDI inflows reflected political openness and the reform on the state ownership; Cheng and Kwan (2000) found that large regional market, good infrastructure, and preferential policy are important determinants of FDI in China; Lardy (1995), Henly et al. (1999), and Zhang (2001) identified potential market size, low labor cost, preferential policies (e.g. tax credits), openness, geographic proximity, and political stability as primary factors attracting FDI into China.

On the other hand, the role of exchange rates in determining FDI in China is largely ignored in the literature, despite the fact that the Chinese yuan devaluated sharply after 1989 as the result of the transition from the dual exchange rate system to a unified single exchange rate one. Few studies investigate to what extent the drastic devaluation contributed to the surge of foreign direct investment.

The mechanism through which exchange rates affect FDI flows has been modeled in a few theoretical studies (e.g. Kohlhagen, 1977; Cushman, 1985; Froot and Stein, 1991). Most of these studies reached a conclusion that a devaluation in the value of FDI hosting country's currency stimulates inflows of FDI and conversely an appreciation leads to a reduction in FDI inflows. Fundamentally, there are two channels through which exchange rates impact FDI: wealth effect channel and relative production cost channel. A devaluation in the currency of FDI receiving country induces a reduction in local production costs in terms of foreign currency, raising profit of export-oriented foreign investors accordingly. A higher return naturally attracts more FDI inflows. The wealth effect – the relative wealth of foreign investors to domestic investors, is also raised after the devaluation. From the point of view of foreign investors having capital measured in foreign currency, all production inputs such as labor, land, machines, and assets in an FDI hosting country becomes cheaper after the devaluation, encouraging them to acquire more domestic assets. As most Japanese MNEs in China are involved in reverse imports, Xing and Zhao (2003) argue that the yuan's devaluation further intensified the reverse import activity, thus leading more Japanese FDI into China.

The believers of the efficient capital market hypothesis usually ignore the role of exchange rates in the context. They argue that possible higher return induced by the currency devaluation will disappear as soon as domestic firms chase the higher return through borrowing foreign currency denominated loans. The efficient market assumption, nonetheless, does not hold in China, where international capital flow is under strict control and its capital account has not been liberalized yet. Therefore, the potential capital return differential between domestic and foreign capitals due to the currency devaluation could only be erased by continuous inflows of foreign direct investment.

Exchange rates and Japanese FDI in China

In examining Japanese FDI inflows closely along with the bilateral exchange rate between the yen and the yuan, there is a noticeable correlation between the two variables. Figure 6.7 plots trends of annual Japanese direct investment in China and the real bilateral exchange rate during 1981 to 2001. The real exchange rate is defined as the price of the Japanese basket in terms of the Chinese basket. Higher real exchange rates implies an appreciation of the yen. The figure shows that the real appreciation of the yen was always followed by an increase in FDI while the devaluation of yen was associated with a decrease. It is imperative to notice that FDI did not increase monotonically. It decreased sharply after 1995. However, in both high and low cycles, FDI closely followed the path of the real exchange rate.

From 1989 to 1995, nominal exchange rate between the yen and the yuan dropped to 9.9 yen/yuan from 38.58 yen/yuan, due to the yuan's official devaluations and pegging the yuan to the dollar policy. Excluding inflation, Japanese yen appreciated against Chinese yuan more than 46 percent cumulatively for the period. Real exchange rate measures the relative price level between the two countries. The change of real exchange rates reflects the variation of the purchasing power of one country's currency in term of goods and services of the other. Therefore, the wealth effect due to the cumulative devaluation of the yuan was tremendous and too large to be ignored by Japanese MNEs. It must have boosted the inflows of Japanese FDI. Actually, 1989 to 1995 is the period that direct investment from Japan jumped from 59 billion yen to 422 billion yen, the highest annual inflows so far. It is also the period that China replaced the ASEAN-4 as the number one destination of Japanese FDI in Asia. All these facts suggest that there must exist a non-coincidental relationship between the bilateral exchange rate and Japanese direct investment. The exchange rate might be one of the major factors determining FDI inflows. Further, it is highly likely that Japanese MNEs strategically took advantage of the exchange rate fluctuation, making more direct investment as the yen appreciated and lowering the pace of their investment as the yen depreciated. Xing (2006) analyzed empirically the effect of exchange rates on Japanese FDI in China's nine manufacturing sectors from 1981 to 2002, and reached the conclusion that the real exchange rate is one of significant factors determining direct investment from Japan.

Additionally, the wealth and production cost effects due to the yuan's devaluations effectively strengthened China's position in competing for FDI with other developing countries, consequently resulting in the shift of Japanese FDI to China from ASEAN-4. Before the Asian financial crisis, Indonesia, Malaysia, Thailand, and Philippines all pegged their currencies to the dollar. The yuan's sharp devaluation naturally gave rise to the appreciation of these countries' currencies to the yuan and reduced the relative costs of Chinese labor and other production inputs such as land, enhancing China's competitiveness for export-oriented FDI. China's cumulative economic growth in the last two and half decades should raise the real wage of Chinese workers proportionally. On the other hand, measured in foreign currency such as the yen or the dollar, the increase in the real wage was moderate. The yuan's cumulative devaluations offset the growth of the real wage in terms of foreign currency, thus preventing China from losing its competitiveness in the labor-intensive industry to other developing countries such as ASEAN-4, at least in the short run. Xing and Wan (2006) studied the competition for FDI in the context of China and ASEAN-4 and its relation with the exchange rate regimes.

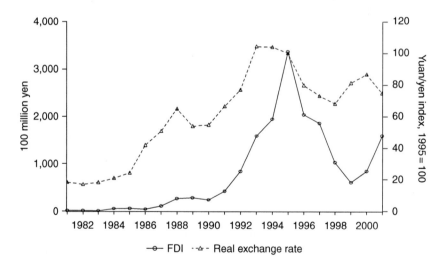

Figure 6.7 The correlation between Japanese FDI in China and the real exchange rate (sources: compiled by the author based on *Monthly Statistics* (Japanese Ministry of Finance), and *International Financial Statistics* (IMF).

They found that China's exchange rate policy contributed significantly to the shift of Japanese FDI from ASEAN-4 to China.

Conclusion

Examining Japanese FDI inflows into China in the last two decades demonstrates a few unique characteristics. First of all, Japanese direct investment was mainly export oriented. Using China as a production base serving the global market still dominated the agenda of Japanese MNEs. The investment strategy of Japanese MNEs was consistent with China's outward looking development strategy and created less competition pressure for domestic firms compared with domestic market-oriented FDI. More importantly, the export-oriented FDI effectively integrated Chinese firms into fragments of global production chains, and expanded the channel for utilizing China's comparative advantages.

Second, reverse imports, which contributed directly to Sino-Japan bilateral trade, accounted for more than one-third of the sales of Japanese affiliated manufacturers. The extraordinarily high ratios of reverse imports among Japanese affiliated manufacturers indicate a comprehensive economic integration between the two economies, far beyond the scope simply defined by FDI. Through reverse imports, the vertical integration between industries in the two countries has been developed in production processes, and extended into distribution and marking networks, greatly enriching the dimensions of technology spillovers associated with FDI.

Finally, the bilateral exchange rate between the yen and the yuan affected Japanese FDI significantly. The yuan's devaluation and pegging the yuan to the dollar policy enhanced China's competitiveness for FDI and triggered the shift of Japanese FDI from ASEAN-4 to China. Whether the Chinese yuan should appreciate or not has been debated among scholars and policy makers recently. Considering the critical role of the yuan's exchange rate in determining Japanese FDI and the importance of the latter for Chinese economy, the appreciation of the yuan will undermine China's competitiveness in attracting export-oriented FDI, thus weakening China's export growth, which has been one of the growth engines for the Chinese economy.

Export-oriented Japanese FDI created a win–win scenario for both economies. In fact, many Japanese MNEs such as Matsushita, Olympus, and Omron stated that relocating production facilities into China was a factor contributing to their profit increase in the fiscal year of 2003. At present, China's relative low production cost definitely served as a quick solution for Japanese firms' restructure. By moving production facilities into China, Japanese MNEs combined their comparative advantages in production technology and global marking networks with China's low production cost, reinforcing their competitiveness in the global market. Looking into the future, as the Chinese economy continues to grow, it will provide an enormous market for existing Japanese affiliated manufacturers, thus giving an option for these firms to switch the focus to the domestic market. The option could be an insurance for the long-term profitability of Japanese affiliated manufacturers operating in China.

Notes

1 Author's calculation, based on *Monthly Statistics*, Japanese Ministry of Finance.
2 FDI data compiled by the Ministry of Japanese Finance does not include the reinvestment by existing Japanese affiliates.

References

Branstetter, L.G. and Feenstra, R.C. (2002) "Trade and foreign direct investment in China: a political economy approach", *Journal of International Economics*, 58(2): 335–358.
Cheng, L.K. and Kwan, Y.K. (2000) "What are the determinants of the location of foreign direct investment? The Chinese experience", *Journal of International Economics*, 51(2): 379–400.
China Statistics Bureau (CSB) (2002) *China Statistics Yearbook 2002*, Beijing: China Statistics Press.
Cushman, D.O. (1985) "Real exchange rate risk, expectation, and the level of direct investment", *Review of Economics and Statistics*, 67(2): 297–308.
Edgington, D.W. and Hayter, R. (2000) "Foreign direct investment and the flying geese model: Japanese electronic firms in Asia-Pacific", *Environment and Planning*, 32(2): 281–304.
Froot, K.A. and Stein, J.C. (1991) "Exchange rates and foreign direct investment: an imperfect capital market approach", *Quarterly Journal of Economics*, 106(4): 1191–1217.
Japan External Trade Organization (JETRO) (2003) *Japanese-affiliated Manufacturers in Asia: Survey 2002*, Tokyo: JETRO.
Japan External Trade Organization (JETRO) (2001) *Current and Future Prospects of Foreign Direct Investment by Japanese Companies in 21st Century*, Tokyo: JETRO.
Kohlhagen, S. W. (1977) "Exchange rate changes, profitability, and direct foreign investment", *Southern Economic Journal*, 44(1): 43–52.
Kojima, K. (1978) *Direct Foreign Investment: A Japanese Model of Multinational Business Operations*, London: Croom Helm.
Kwan, C.H. (2001) *Yen Bloc*, Washington D.C.: Brookings Institution Press.
Henley, J., Kirkpatrick, C., and Wilde, G. (1999) "Foreign direct investment in China: recent trend and current policy issues", *World Economy*, 22(2): 23–43.
Lardy, N. (1995) "The role of foreign trade and investment in China's economic transformation", *China Quarterly*, 144: 1065–1082.
Ministry of Economy, Trade and Industry (METI) (2003), *Quarterly Survey of Business Activities*, Tokyo: METI.
Porter, M.E. and Sakakibara, M. (2004) "Competition in Japan", *Journal of Economic Perspectives*, 18(1): 27–50.
Wong, K. and Yamamura, K. (1996) "Japan's direct investment in the United

States: cause, patterns, and issues", in L. Hollerman and R. H. Myers (ed.) *The Effect of Japanese Investment on the World Economy*, Stanford, CA: Hoover Institute Press.

Xing, Y. (2006) "Why is China so attractive for FDI? The role of exchange rates", *China Economic Review*, forthcoming.

Xing, Y. and Wan, G. (2006) "Exchange rates and competition for FDI in Asia", *The World Economy*, forthcoming.

Xing, Y. and Zhao, L. (2003) "Reverse imports, foreign direct investment, and exchange rates", working paper 2003–2004 in International Development Series, the Research Institute of International University of Japan.

Zhang, K.H. (2001) "What attracts foreign multinational corporations to China?", *Contemporary Economic Policy*, 19(3): 336–346.

7 Foreign competition and productivity of Chinese firms

Bin Xu

1 Introduction

The last two decades of the twentieth century saw China emerge as an important force in the world economy. China's exports increased more than ten times, from $18 billion in 1980 to $249 billion in 2000.[1] China's share in world exports increased from 0.9 percent (ranked 26) in 1980 to 3.9 percent (ranked 7) in 2000.[2] The share of exports in GDP increased from 6 percent in 1980 to 23 percent in 2000 (Figure 7.1).[3] The fast growth of foreign trade was accompanied by even faster growth of foreign direct investment (FDI) inflows. China's utilization of FDI increased from $916 million in 1983 to $41 billion in 2000, making it the world's second largest host country of FDI next only to the US.[4]

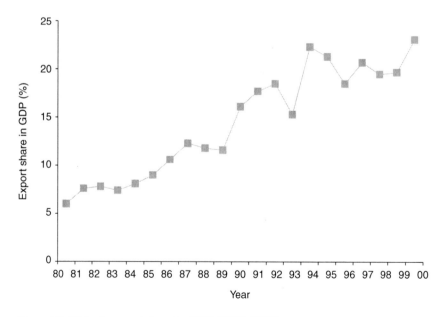

Figure 7.1 China's export share in GDP (1980–2000).

Trade and investment openness has been widely cited as one of the most important reasons for China's extraordinary GDP growth at around 10 percent over the past two decades. As is well known, GDP growth can come from factor accumulation and productivity increase. China had a GDP growth of over 5 percent before 1978, the year that economic reform started. GDP growth during that period, however, was driven mainly by factor accumulation (Chow 1985). In contrast, many studies of China's productivity growth in the period after 1978 find a positive and significant contribution of productivity growth to GDP growth. For example, Li (1997) uses a sample of 272 state-owned firms and estimates that TFP growth was 4.68 percent per year between 1980 and 1989 and accounted for over 73 percent of output growth.

The existing literature has established a link between China's TFP growth and economic reform.[5] Li (1997) shows evidence that over 87 percent of the TFP growth in his sample of state-owned firms was attributable to improved incentives, intensified market competition, and improved factor allocation resulted from China's economic reform. While acknowledging the contribution of trade and investment openness as an important part of China's economic reform, there has been little research linking the TFP growth explicitly to trade and investment openness. Because of data availability, previous studies are based mainly on samples of state-owned firms. As China's economic reform progresses, however, the non-state part of the Chinese economy, including foreign-funded firms, joint ventures, and private firms, has grown significantly and accounted for half of the gross output value of industrial enterprises in China in 2000.[6] Moreover, the share of exports by foreign-funded firms in China increased from near zero in 1980 to 50 percent in 2000 (Figure 7.2).[7] These new developments call for a study of the impact of trade and FDI (and their interactions) on the TFP growth of Chinese firms.

This chapter is an attempt to meet this demand. Based on a recent World Bank survey, we study a sample of 822 non-state-owned Chinese firms. In section 2 we describe the sample. In section 3 we run growth regressions to estimate TFP growth of firms. In section 4 we investigate the link between TFP growth and export participation. In section 5 we examine the link between TFP growth and foreign ownership. In section 6 we divide samples by industry and by city to show further evidence of effects of trade and FDI on TFP growth. In section 7 we conclude.

2 The sample

Our data comes from a World Bank survey of 1,500 Chinese firms.[8] The World Bank conducted the survey in 2001, which drew 300 firms each from five large cities: Beijing, Chengdu, Guangdong, Shanghai, and Tianjin. Firms in the sample belong to five manufacturing sectors and five service sectors. The five manufacturing sectors are apparel and leather

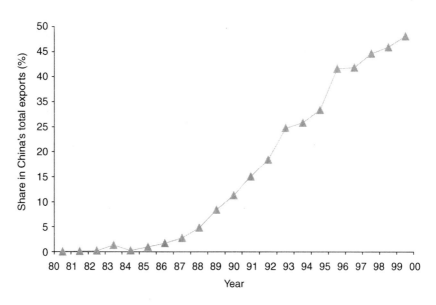

Figure 7.2 Exports of foreign-funded enterprises in China (1980–2000).

goods, consumer goods, electronic components, electronic equipment, and vehicles and vehicle parts. These sectors reflect China's current or potential comparative advantage in manufacturing. The five service sectors are accounting and related services, advertising and marketing, business logistics, communication services, and information technology services.[9] The data covers the period 1998 to 2000. After 20 years of economic reform, the non-state-owned part of the Chinese economy was very much market-oriented. The state-owned part, however, was still running in a non-market way to a great degree. The sharp difference between state-owned and non-state-owned firms makes it inappropriate to pool them together in a cross-section study. Thus, we choose to focus on a sample of non-state-owned firms.

Table 7.1 provides summary information about our sample. In the 1,500 firms surveyed by the World Bank, 323 are state-owned firms. Our study requires information on sales, unskilled labor, skilled labor, fixed assets, and R&D expenditure, however, 355 non-state-owned firms in the survey do not have the necessary information. This leaves us a sample of 822 non-state-owned firms. Among them, 283 firms are majority foreign owned with foreign ownership exceeding 50 percent and account for 34.3 percent of the sample; 81 firms are minority foreign owned with foreign ownership above zero but below (including) 50 percent and account for 9.9 percent of the sample. The remaining 459 firms are non-foreign, non-state-owned firms and account for 55.8 percent of the sample.

Table 7.1 also reports the export status of firms in the sample. During

Table 7.1 Sample distribution

	Number	Percentage
Sample	822	100.0
Ownership status:		
Foreign majority owned	282	34.3
Foreign minority owned	81	9.9
Non-foreign, non-state-owned	459	55.8
Exporting Status:		
Exporting in 1998	283	34.4
Exporting in 2000	309	37.6
Exporting in 1998 or 2000	320	38.9
Exporting in 2000 but not in 1998	37	4.5

the sample period, 320 firms (38.9 percent of the sample) had positive export sales; 283 firms (34.4 percent of the sample) exported in 1998, and 309 firms (37.6 percent of the sample) exported in 2000. There are 37 firms (4.5 percent of the sample) that had zero export sales in 1998 but became exporters during 1999 or 2000.

Table 7.2 provides summary statistics of key variables for our study. The sample mean of sales is RMB163,400 in 1998 and RMB265,200 in 2000. The sample mean of sales growth over the two years is 26.8 percent. The average firm employed 431 unskilled workers in 1998 and the number dropped to 400 in 2000. The average firm employed 123 skilled workers in 1998 and the number rose to 129 in 2000. Although the sample mean of unskilled labor falls over the two years, the sample mean of its growth rate is positive and equal to 7.5 percent. The sample mean of growth rate of skilled labor is 9.1 percent. The average firm had RMB149,400 fixed assets in 1998 and RMB169,500 fixed assets in 2000.[10] Fixed assets grew by 25.2 percent in the sample mean. The sample mean of R&D intensity or export intensity does not change much from 1998 to 2000, but the sample mean of their growth rates is 13.1 percent and 3.6 percent, respectively. Notice that there are large variations across firms in all these variables, as indicated by the large standard deviations.

3 Growth regressions

We ran a log linear growth regression to estimate the output elasticities of major inputs, assume a Cobb-Douglas production function with three production factors, unskilled labor, skilled labor, and physical capital. Without data on output, we used sales as a proxy. We measured capital by fixed assets. All values are in 1998 prices.

Table 7.3 reports regression results. The estimation method is OLS with heteroskedasticity adjustment. The dependent variable is growth rate of sales from 1998 to 2000. Regression (1) indicates that the estimated output

Table 7.2 Summary statistics

Variable	Definition	1998	2000	1998–2000, growth (%)
Y	Sales (in thousands)	163.4 (1,157.8)	265.2 (1,665.4)	26.8 (99.3)
L	Unskilled labor	431 (1,722)	400 (940)	7.5 (51.0)
H	Skilled labor	123 (498)	129 (459)	9.1 (40.6)
K	Fixed assets (in thousands)	149.4 (1,462.2)	169.5 (1,401.0)	25.2 (53.0)
R/Y	R&D expenditure/sales	0.090 (1.361)	0.091 (1.481)	13.1 (128.3)
X/Y	Exports/sales	0.202 (0.365)	0.208 (0.364)	3.6 (102.9)

Notes
All value in 1998 price. Mean reported and standard deviation in parenthesis.

Table 7.3 Regression results, OLS, N = 822

	(1)	*(2)*	*(3)*
Δlog L	0.41 (0.15)***	0.40 (0.15)***	0.38 (0.15)***
Δlog H	0.45 (0.17)***	0.43 (0.16)***	0.44 (0.16)***
Δlog K	0.41 (0.10)***	0.40 (0.10)***	0.39 (0.10)***
R&D intensity in 1998		15.4 (3.4)***	14.9 (3.55)***
Exporting in 1998		14.0 (6.8)**	15.8 (8.0)**
Majority foreign ownership		15.3 (7.0)**	12.6 (7.3)*
Industry dummies	No	No	Yes
City dummies	No	No	Yes
R²	0.23	0.29	0.30

Notes
The dependent variable is $\Delta \log Y \equiv \log Y(2000) - \log Y(1998)$. R&D intensity is defined as R/Y. Numbers in parentheses are heteroskedasticity-adjusted standard errors. *** indicates statistical significance at the 1% level, ** 5% level, and * 10% level.

elasticities of unskilled labor (L), skilled labor (H), and physical capital (K) are all around 0.4. This implies increasing returns to scale for the sample. In regression (2), we introduce three more independent variables: R&D intensity (R/Y), exporting dummy, and dummy for majority foreign ownership. These variables are included in the regression to explain the growth in output not accounted for by growth in factor inputs, i.e. the growth in total factor productivity (TFP). The 1998 value of these variables is used to alleviate the endogeneity problem.

Regression (2) shows that TFP growth depends positively on R&D intensity, export participation, and majority foreign ownership. The level of R&D intensity measures a firm's capability of technology innovation and absorption. Since TFP growth is driven mainly by technological progress, we expect firms' R&D intensity to be significant to TFP growth. Export participation is a measure of exposure to international competition and technology diffusion. International competition drives firms to adopt new technology, which is a source of TFP growth. Exporting also exposes firms to international technology diffusion, which is another source of TFP growth. We find that majority foreign ownership enters the regression significantly, while minority foreign ownership and non-foreign, non-state ownership do not. One interpretation is that majority foreign ownership facilitates transfer of foreign technology.

Regression (2) shows that the estimated output elasticities remain at around 0.4 for all three production factors. This is still true when we include industry dummies and city dummies in regression (3). The three variables important to TFP growth, namely R&D intensity, export participation, and foreign majority ownership, remain statistically significant. Most industry dummies and city dummies are statistically indifferent from zero, and the R-squared does not increase much after controlling for these dummies.

The growth regressions in Table 7.3 allow us to estimate TFP growth rates for firms in the sample. Under the assumption that firms share the same Cobb-Douglas production function,[11] we can compute TFP growth as equal to $\Delta \log Y - a_L \Delta \log L - a_H \Delta \log H - a_K \Delta \log K$, where a_L, a_H, and a_K are estimated output elasticities of unskilled labor, skilled labor, and capital, respectively. In the following analysis, we will use TFP growth rates computed from regression (3).

4 Export competition

China has had phenomenal growth in international trade since the early 1980s. Casual observation suggests that China has benefitted greatly from trade openness not only in consumption but also in production technology. There has not been much firm-level research on how China's trade openness affects its total factor productivity. We make an attempt here with our data.

In Table 7.4 we show TFP growth and its contribution to output growth. For the full sample of 822 firms, TFP grew by 10.1 percent over the period of 1998 to 2000. During the same period sales (a proxy for output) grew by 26.8 percent. Thus the contribution of TFP growth to output growth is about 38 percent. Looking at the sample of 320 exporting firms, we find that on average they grew significantly faster than firms in the full sample in both TFP and sales. Moreover, the contribution of TFP growth to output growth is 55 percent for exporting firms. In contrast, the 502 non-exporting firms in the sample, while achieving 15 percent growth in sales, grew only by 0.6 percent in TFP. The contribution of TFP growth to output growth is merely 4 percent for non-exporting firms.

The higher TFP growth and TFP contribution of exporting firms was due partly to their higher R&D intensity. As Table 7.4 shows, the average R&D intensity of exporting firms is 0.14 compared with 0.06 of non-exporting firms. The fact that 61 percent of the exporting firms are majority foreign owned may have also contributed to its extraordinary TFP performance. In comparison, only 17 percent of the non-exporting firms are majority foreign owned. As argued before, majority foreign ownership better positions a firm in receiving transfer of foreign technology than minority foreign-owned firms and non-foreign-owned firms.

For our study of the relationship between exporting and productivity growth, it is important to discuss the issue of causality.[12] Is exporting making firms more productive, or more productive firms become exporters? In the first two rows of Table 7.4 we show the TFP levels of firms in 1998 and 2000. Notice that exporting firms had on average *lower* TFP levels than non-exporting firms in both 1998 and 2000. In the last column of Table 7.4, we have a sample of 37 firms that switched from non-exporting in 1998 to exporting in 2000. These firms had an average TFP level of 0.56 in 1998, and their average TFP level increased to 0.70 in 2000.

Table 7.4 TFP growth and export status

	All firms	Exporting firms	Non-exporting firms	New exporting firms
TFP 1998	0.56 (1.36)	0.50 (1.02)	0.60 (1.54)	0.56 (1.18)
TFP 2000	0.66 (2.10)	0.62 (1.22)	0.68 (2.51)	0.70 (1.39)
TFP growth (%)	10.1 (87.3)	25.0 (91.5)	0.6 (83.2)	26.7 (76.8)
Sales growth (%)	26.8 (99.3)	45.2 (107.2)	15.0 (92.0)	61.0 (91.1)
TFP contribution	38%	55%	4%	44%
R&D intensity	0.09 (1.36)	0.14 (2.02)	0.06 (0.67)	0.07 (0.18)
Foreign majority	34%	61%	17%	41%
Number of firms	822	320	502	37

Notes
Mean reported and standard deviation in parenthesis. TFP is computed based on regression (3) of Table 7.3. R&D intensity is measured as the ratio of R&D expenditure to sales in 1998. TFP contribution is computed as the ratio of mean of TFP growth to mean of sales growth. Exporting firms are firms that exported in 2000 but not in 1998. New exporting firms are firms that exported in 1998 or 2000. New exporting firms are firms that exported in 1998 or 2000 but not in 1998.

These firms experienced an average 26.7 percent growth in TFP and 61 percent growth in sales; TFP contributed 44 percent to total growth. Notice that the average R&D intensity of these firms is 0.07, similar to that of non-exporting firms. While 41 percent of these firms are majority foreign owned, which is higher than the 17 percent of the non-exporting group, the number is significantly lower than the 61 percent of the exporting group. Based on these observations we may conclude that the high TFP growth of these 37 firms is mainly a result of their becoming exporters. The entry into the international market brings a higher standard and more competition, pushing firms to use resources more efficiently and become more productive.

5 Foreign production

China's opening to the outside world has been impressive in both international trade and foreign direct investment. In our sample period of 1998 to 2000, China became the second largest destination of FDI next only to the US. To understand the TFP growth of Chinese firms, one cannot neglect the role of FDI.

In Table 7.5 we display the results for three groups: majority foreign-owned firms, minority foreign-owned firms, and non-foreign, non-state-owned firms. It is clear that the group of majority foreign-owned firms experienced the fastest growth in both TFP (25.3 percent) and sales (49.5 percent). The contribution of TFP growth to total growth is 51 percent for this group. By contrast, the group of minority foreign-owned firms had only 6.1 percent growth in TFP and 16 percent growth in sales, and a TFP contribution of 38 percent. The performance of non-foreign, non-state-owned firms was even poorer. Their TFP grew by merely 1.4 percent although their sales grew by 14.7 percent. TFP growth contributed to total growth by only 10 percent. The poor TFP performance of the non-foreign firms may be traced to their low R&D intensity (0.03) and low exporting participation ratio (19 percent).

Table 7.5 provides evidence that majority foreign ownership matters for TFP growth. Notice that the average R&D intensity of minority foreign-owned firms (0.21) is higher than that of majority foreign-owned firms (0.15). Despite this higher R&D intensity, the TFP growth of minority foreign-owned firms (6.1 percent) is significantly lower than that of majority foreign-owned firms (25.3 percent). One reason is that export participation ratio is significantly higher in the group of majority foreign-owned firms (70 percent) than in the minority foreign owned firms (48 percent). Exporting is not the entire reason for majority foreign-owned firms to be more productive. Recall the regression results reported in Table 7.3, which show that when export participation is controlled for, the effect of majority foreign ownership is still positive and statistically significant.

Table 7.5 TFP growth and foreign ownership

	Majority foreign-owned	Minority foreign-owned	Non-foreign, non-state-owned
TFP 1998	0.82 (1.81)	0.41 (0.82)	0.42 (1.06)
TFP 2000	1.11 (3.25)	0.37 (0.50)	0.43 (1.10)
TFP growth	25.3 (101.1)	6.1 (78.7)	1.4 (77.9)
Sales growth	49.5 (118.1)	16.0 (79.1)	14.7 (86.8)
TFP contribution	51%	38%	10%
R&D intensity	0.15 (2.15)	0.21 (1.64)	0.03 (0.14)
Exporting	70%	48%	19%
Number of firms	282	81	459

6 Industries and cities

The 822 firms in our sample belong to ten industries and five cities. In Table 7.6 we report TFP growth of firms by industry and by city. In the five manufacturing industries, the industry of vehicles and vehicle parts had the highest TFP growth (24.5 percent) and TFP contribution (65 percent). This can be explained mainly by its high R&D intensity (0.39). The electronic equipment industry and the electronic components industry had low R&D intensities (0.03) but TFP growth around 14 percent. This may be explained by the high exporting participation and majority foreign ownership ratios, both above 40 percent. Despite 59 percent of the firms were exporting and 37 percent of them were majority foreign-owned, the industry of apparel and leather products had a TFP growth rate of only 7.9 percent, probably due to its very low R&D intensity (0.004). The relatively low export participation ratio (36 percent) and majority foreign ownership ratio (33 percent) may explain the relatively low TFP growth rate (4 percent) of the consumer product industry.

Not surprisingly, the five service industries had little exporting. Because of government regulation, the service sectors did not have many majority foreign-owned firms, especially in the communication service industry. The information technology (IT) industry had the highest TFP growth (18.8 percent) among the five service industries because of its high R&D intensity (0.16). The communication service industry shows a negative growth in both TFP and sales. It should be pointed out that our model may not fit well with industries that are heavily regulated by the government so caution should be taken in interpreting the results for such industries.

Table 7.6 also reports results by city. Among the five cities in the survey, Shanghai saw the highest average TFP growth (25.3 percent) and TFP contribution (58 percent) in its firms. This is not surprising considering the average R&D intensity (0.28) of the sample firms from Shanghai, which is significantly higher than that of the firms from other four cities.

Table 7.6 TFP growth by industry and by city

	Apparel and leather	Electronic components	Electronic equipment	Consumer products	Vehicles and parts
TFP growth	7.9	13.9	13.6	4.0	24.5
Sales growth	13.4	45.0	36.2	13.8	37.8
TFP contribution	59%	31%	38%	29%	65%
R&D intensity	0.004	0.03	0.03	0.03	0.39
Exporting	59%	45%	63%	36%	44%
Foreign majority	37%	40%	44%	33%	36%
Number of firms	139	107	131	110	140

	IT services	Communication services	Financial services	Marketing services	Logistics services
TFP growth	18.8	−40.0	14.6	7.1	−0.2
Sales growth	51.9	−36.5	38.5	32.5	8.5
TFP contribution	36%	NA	38%	22%	NA
R&D intensity	0.16	0.01	0.03	0.01	0.00
Exporting	7%	0	0	0	5%
Foreign majority	24%	8%	26%	25%	28%
Number of firms	42	38	35	40	40

	Beijing	Chengdu	Guangzhou	Shanghai	Tianjin
TFP growth	6.0	4.2	7.1	25.3	11.1
Sales growth	18.8	22.8	31.6	43.7	19.7
TFP contribution	32%	18%	22%	58%	56%
R&D intensity	0.10	0.03	0.04	0.28	0.02
Exporting	24%	19%	62%	62%	33%
Foreign majority	27%	6%	43%	69%	36%
Number of firms	179	181	170	141	151

Shanghai also had the highest export participation ratio (62 percent) and foreign majority ownership ratio (69 percent), which contributed to TFP growth according to our model. Among the five cities Chengdu had the lowest TFP growth rate (4.2 percent) and TFP contribution (18 percent). This can be explained by the fact that Chengdu had the lowest export participation ratio (19 percent) and foreign majority ownership ratio (6 percent) among the five cities. It is interesting to observe that although Guangzhou had higher R&D intensity, higher export participation ratio, and higher foreign majority ownership ratio than Tianjin, its TFP growth was lower than that of Tianjin and its TFP contribution is even lower. This suggests that there are unobserved city effects that contributed to variation in TFP growth across firms. Recall that we controlled for the city effects in regression (3) of Table 7.3 and our analysis has been based on that regression.

7 Conclusion

In this chapter we investigate the effects of international trade and foreign direct investment on total factor productivity growth of Chinese firms. Our investigation uses a sample of 822 non-state-owned Chinese firms from five large cities, covering five manufacturing industries in which China has a current or potential comparative advantage, and five service industries. Using estimates from a growth regression, we obtain estimates of TFP growth rates for these firms. We then examine if TFP growth is associated with export status and foreign ownership of firms.

Our study yields two main findings. First, exporting enhances TFP growth. In our sample, exporting firms had significantly higher TFP growth rates than non-exporting firms. The contribution of TFP growth to output growth was also significantly higher for exporting firms than for non-exporting firms. We find evidence that the causality runs from exporting to productivity. In the sample 37 firms were non-exporting firms in 1998 and became exporting firms in the following two years. Their 1998 TFP level was similar to other non-exporting firms but their 2000 TFP level was significantly higher than the firms that remained non-exporting. The effect of exporting on TFP growth remains positive and statistically significant when we control for R&D intensity, foreign ownership, and unobserved industry and city effects.

Second, we find that majority foreign ownership enhances TFP growth. Majority foreign-owned firms had significantly higher TFP growth rates than minority foreign-owned firms and non-foreign firms. One reason for this link is that many majority foreign-owned firms are also exporting firms. Our results show, however, that majority foreign ownership has a positive effect on TFP growth even after controlling for the effects of exporting. This finding supports the view that majority foreign ownership facilitates transfer of foreign technology and hence enhances TFP growth.

Notes

1 *Almanac of China's Foreign Economic Relations and Trade* (2001: 579).
2 *Almanac of China's Foreign Economic Relations and Trade* (2001: 581).
3 *World Merchandise Trade by Region and Selected Economy* (2001), World Trade Organization.
4 *Almanac of China's Foreign Economic Relations and Trade* (2001: 764).
5 See a recent literature survey by Zhang *et al.* (2003).
6 *China Statistical Yearbook* (2001: 403).
7 *World Merchandise Trade by Region and Selected Economy* (2001), World Trade Organization.
8 We thank the World Bank and the Davidson Data Center & Network (DDCN) for providing the data.
9 For more descriptions of the data, see Hallward-Driemeier *et al.* (2003).
10 All values are converted to 1998 value using the GDP deflator computed from the *China Statistical Yearbook* (2001). The GDP deflator is 0.978 for 1999 and 0.986 for 2000, with 1998 as the base year. Notice that China experienced deflation in 1999 and 2000 with respect to 1998. We use the book value of a firm's fixed assets as a proxy for its capital stock. The fixed assets cover buildings, production machinery and equipment, office equipment, vehicles, etc.
11 This is a strong assumption and may cause biased estimates. An alternative approach, developed by Gordon and Li (1995), allows the production function to differ arbitrarily across firms. Preliminary estimation using the Gordon–Li approach yields similar qualitative results. For this chapter we report only the results from the conventional approach, which is widely used in productivity study despite its limitation.
12 See Bernard and Jenson (1999) for a discussion of the causality between exporting and productivity.

References

Bernard, A. and Jensen, B. (1999) 'Exceptional exporter performance: cause, effect, or both', *Journal of International Economics* 47: 1–25.
Chow, G. (1985) 'A model of Chinese national income determination', *Journal of Political Economy* 93: 782–792.
Gordon, R.H. and Li, W. (1995) 'The change in productivity of Chinese state enterprises, 1983–1987', *Journal of Productivity Analysis* 6: 5–26.
Hallward-Driemeier, M., Wallsten, S., and Xu, L.C. (2003) 'The investment climate and the firm: firm-level evidence from China', Working Paper, World Bank.
Li, W. (1997) 'The impact of economic reform on the performance of Chinese state enterprises, 1980–1989', *Journal of Political Economy* 105: 1080–1106.
Zhang, J., Shi, S., and Chen, S. (2003) 'The industry reform and efficiency change in China: methodology, data, literatures and conclusions', *China Economic Quarterly*, 3: 1–38.

8 The role of FDI in China's export performance

Kevin Honglin Zhang

China's export boom has been accompanied by huge inflows of foreign direct investment (FDI) since its opening-up in the late 1970s. As China became the third largest exporting nation ($594 billion) in the world in 2004 from the thirty-second ($18 billion) in 1978, its FDI inflows rose from zero to $61 billion in the same period, with the accumulated FDI being as much as $560 billion by the end of 2004 (Figure 8.1 and Table 8.1). The exports generated by foreign-invested enterprises (FIEs) in 2004 were $339 billion, comprising 57 percent of China's total exports. What role does FDI play in China's export expansion? How does FDI affect China's export performance? This chapter attempts to address the questions.

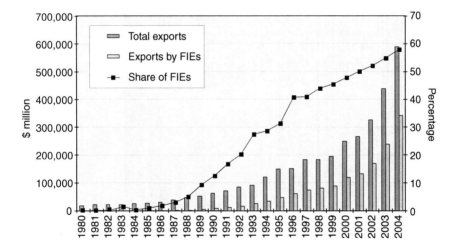

Figure 8.1 Share of foreign-invested enterprise (FIEs) in China's total export (1980–2004) (sources: *China Statistical Yearbook 2003* (SSB, 2004) and *China Foreign Economic Statistical Yearbook 1979–2003* (SSB, 1979–2003). The data for 2004 are taken from the official website of China's Ministry of Commerce (http://www.mofcom.gov.cn).

Table 8.1 FDI flows, total exports, and exports by foreign-invested enterprises (FIEs) (1980–2004)

Year	FDI inflows ($ billion)	Cumulative FDI ($ billion)	Total exports ($ billion)	Exports by FIEs ($ billion)	Share of FIEs (%)
1980	0.036	0.570	18.119	0.082	0.05
1985	1.661	4.587	27.350	0.297	1.08
1990	3.487	18.848	62.091	7.814	12.58
1995	37.521	133.024	148.797	46.876	31.51
2000	40.715	346.634	249.211	119.441	47.93
2001	46.878	393.512	266.150	133.218	50.05
2002	52.743	446.255	325.570	169.985	52.21
2003	53.505	499.760	438.370	240.340	54.83
2004	60.630	560.390	593.370	338.610	57.07

Sources: *China Statistical Yearbook 2004* (SSB, 2004) and *China Foreign Economic Statistical Yearbook 1979–2003* (SSB, 1979–2003). The data for 2004 are taken from the official website of China's Ministry of Commerce (www.mofcom.gov.cn).

FDI and exports in China 1980–2004

Figures 8.1 and 8.2 along with Table 8.1 show the growth of FDI, total exports, exports generated by FIEs, and the share of exports by FIEs in total exports in 1980–2004. The small amount of FDI in the early 1980s initially made a negligible contribution to China's total exports. As late as 1985, six years after the passage of China's foreign investment law and five years after the establishment of special economic zones, the exports by FIEs were only $297 million, barely over 1 percent of China's total exports. From that modest base they expanded dramatically, reaching about 47 billion by 1995 (32 percent of total exports), and even almost $339 billion in 2004, 57 percent of China's total exports.

The dramatic rise of exports by FIEs is a result of the establishment of an export-processing program, under which inputs and components needed for the production of goods for exports were imported duty free, with a minimum of administrative interference. This can be seen from the fact that exports created by FIEs are predominantly products assembled from imported parts and components. In addition, many Chinese firms also produce processed exports using parts and components supplied by or purchased from foreign firms. In fact, the total processed exports in 2003 were more than $242 billion, 55 percent of China's exports (Table 8.2).

The fundamental factor behind the rise of exports by FIEs has been related to China's export-promotion regime in which FIEs operate under

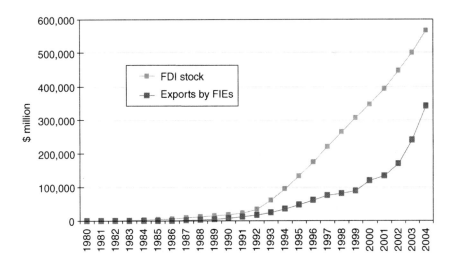

Figure 8.2 FDI and exports by foreign-invested enterprises (FIEs) (1980–2004) (sources: *China Statistical Yearbook 2003* (SSB, 2004) and *China Foreign Economic Statistical Yearbook 1979–2003* (SSB, 1979–2003). The data for 2004 are taken from the official website of China's Ministry of Commerce (http://www.mofcom.gov.cn).

Table 8.2 Nation's processing exports and processing exports by foreign-invested enterprises (FIEs) (1995–2002)

Year	Nation's processing exports		Processing exports by FIEs		
	Value ($ billion)	Share in total exports (%)	Value ($ billion)	Share in FIE exports (%)	Share in total processing exports (%)
1995	73.70	49.5	42.07	89.7	57.1
1996	84.34	55.8	53.09	86.3	62.9
1997	99.66	54.5	63.85	80.4	64.1
1998	104.47	56.9	69.18	85.5	66.2
1999	110.88	56.9	74.56	84.1	68.1
2000	137.66	55.2	97.23	81.4	70.6
2001	147.44	55.4	106.60	80.1	72.3
2002	179.95	55.3	136.16	80.1	75.7
2003	241.85	55.2	190.27	80.1	78.7

Sources: *China Foreign Economic Statistical Yearbook* (SSB, 1996–2003); Jiang (2002).

an entirely different set of institutions and regulations from those applying to most domestic enterprises. The most important of these institutions is the duty-free processing of imported materials and components into exports. Two types of the duty-free processing trade in China may be identified: processing materials and processing imports. The processing materials may take place under a contract in which a foreign business ships materials to Chinese firms for processing or assembly and subsequent re-export. In the second type of the duty-free trade (processing imports), factories in China import materials and organize production and then export. FIEs (mainly joint ventures) account for the bulk of export value under this arrangement (about 74 percent in 1995).

As shown in Table 8.2, export processing has grown rapidly along with the growth of FIEs. In 1995 export processing accounted for half of all exports and 90 percent of FIE exports. At the end of 2003, the national processing exports rose more than three times of 1995 (from $74 billion to $242 billion), constituting 55 percent of total exports. While the processing-export share in FIE exports declined from 90 percent to 80 percent in 1995–2003, the value increased more than four times from $42 billion to $190 billion, and the share in total processing exports rose from 57 percent to 79 percent. Many export-processing arrangements are made between Hong Kong firms and factories in China. Chinese factories import raw materials and semi-manufactures, then export finished product after processing and assembling (Naughton, 1996).

Conceptual framework of the FDI–export link

Theoretical positions on the FDI–export nexus can be very divergent. Standard proposition of the neoclassical types suggest that FDI promotes exports of host countries by: (a) augmenting domestic capital for exports; (b) helping transfer of technology and new products for exports; (c) facilitating access to new and large foreign markets; and (d) providing training for the local workforce and upgrading technical and management skills (UNCTAD, 2002a).[1]

In a discussion of export-promoting effects of FDI, it is convenient to divide export activities of foreign affiliates into three categories according to production characteristics as follows: (a) Local raw materials processing: foreign affiliates in host countries may have better export potential than indigenous firms, because of their business contacts abroad, marketing skills, superior technology, both in product and processes, and greater general know-how; (b) New labor-intensive final product exports: firms in developing countries seeking to export usually lack such skills in the design, packaging, distribution and servicing of the products as well as production technology. FDI in which these skills are embodied thus may help developing country exporters to enter the world markets through special arrangements of links to final buyers; and (c) Labor-intensive processes and component specialization within vertically integrated international industries: Exports of labor-intensive goods within vertically integrated production obviously depend on the participation of multinational corporations (MNCs). Generally, these exports are thought of as intra-firm trade, but a great part of them are arm's-length transactions between MNCs and indigenous host country firms (Zhang and Markusen, 1999).

Foreign affiliates can also promote host-country manufacturing exports in several indirect ways. These include demonstration effects on local firms (Haddad and Harrison, 1993), spillovers of new technologies and improvement in competitiveness, and forward and backward linkages with foreign affiliates (Din, 1994; UNCTAD, 2001).

Contributions of FDI to China's export expansion

China has great potential to become a significant exporter of labor-intensive products, such as textiles and other consumer goods. However, the Chinese firms faced immense difficulties at the initial stage in setting up a distribution network, keeping in close touch with rapid changes in consumer tastes, mastering the technicalities of industrial norms and safety standards, and building up a new product image. In many cases, the design, packaging, distribution, and servicing of the products are as important as the ability to produce them at, or below, ruling prices in world markets. The lack of such skills constituted a key barrier for China to enter the world markets.

The simulative effects of FDI on China's exports mainly derive from the additional capital, technology, and managerial know-how MNCs bring with them, along with access to global, regional, and especially home-country, markets. These resources and market access brought with FDI have complemented China's resources and capabilities and provided some of the missing elements for greater competitiveness. China therefore has built upon these to enter new export activities and improved its performance in existing ones.

FDI helps exports by investing capital in the exploitation of China's low-cost labor, especially in the 1980s, when domestic investment was limited by financial constraints. Such FDI bridged the resource gap and took the risk of developing new exports. The provision of additional capital has been critical for China to build up its initial base of labor-intensive manufacturing exports.

FDI provides China with competitive assets for export-oriented production in technology-intensive and dynamic products in the world trade (Zhang and Song, 2000). Such assets are often firm-specific, costly and difficult for the Chinese firms to acquire independently. The transfer of such assets by foreign affiliates or non-equity partners in China through training, skills development, and knowledge diffusion opens up prospects for further dissemination to other enterprises and the economy at large. Thus more firms (including domestic enterprises) can develop their exports and the factors underlying competitiveness get rooted in the Chinese economy.

FDI promotes exports by facilitating China access to new and larger markets. This involves foreign affiliates' privileged access to not only MNCs' international production systems, but also MNCs' intra-firm markets and access at arm's length to MNCs' customers in global, regional and home-country markets. Moreover, these links to world markets extend to suppliers and other domestic firms. In addition, as happened in the US, China also benefitted from the lobbying activities of MNCs in their home countries for favorable treatment of exports from their affiliates abroad.

Export-oriented foreign affiliates provide training for the local workforce and upgrade technical and managerial skills that benefit the Chinese exports. This is especially true for export-oriented investments in advanced technological capabilities. China has already attracted significant MNC export activities at labor-intensive and low-technology levels. The strategic challenge facing China is that its future competitiveness depends on the host government's ability to boost the human capital and technological infrastructure. In turn, MNCs feed benefits back into local skill and technology systems, providing information, assistance, and contracts.

The positive role of FDI in China's exports may be summarized in terms of direct and indirect effects. The direct effects refer to exports by foreign affiliates themselves. The spillovers of FDI on export activities of local firms make up the indirect effects (Blomström *et al.*, 2000; UNCTAD, 2002a). The direct effects include the following four aspects:

1   Exports through processing and assembling: by processing components and assembling in which domestic firms import unfinished and intermediate goods, China became a dominant exporter of labor-intensive products (toys, shoes, clothes, and sporting goods) and some technology-intensive products (machinery and equipments, including electronic circuits, automatic data-processing machines, and mobile phones) (UNCTAD, 2002a). Generally, these exports are organized by MNCs within vertically integrated international production network (Markusen *et al.*, 1996; Zhang, 2000). Most of the exports created by FDI (80 percent in 2003 as indicated in Table 8.2) take place in this form, which constitutes three-quarters of China's total processing-assembling exports (SSB, 2004). Table 8.3 shows the FIE shares in selected exporting products in 1996 and 2000. Exports of these goods by FIEs rose substantially in 1996–2000, and so did their shares except toys and travel bags. FIEs played dominant role in exporting such goods as electronic circuits, data processing, office machines and related products, and mobile phones.

2   Exports through converting import-substituting industries: many developing countries including China restrict imports of manufactur-

Table 8.3 Shares of foreign-invested enterprises (FIEs) in selected exporting goods in 1996 and 2000 ($ million)

Products	Total exports		Exports by FIEs			
	1996	2000	1996		2000	
	Value	Value	Value	%	Value	%
Yarns and fabrics	4,547	5,900	1,107	24	1,677	28
Toys	5,473	8,293	2,494	46	3,699	45
Travel bags	2,653	3,767	1,192	45	1,406	37
Electronic circuits	996	4,105	781	78	3,817	93
Data processing, office machines and related products	5,391	16,547	4,451	83	13,996	85
Mobile phone (transmitter-receiver apparatus)	487	2,931	450	92	2,823	96

Source: Adapted from the *World Investment Report 2002* (UNCTAD, 2002a).

ing products but may allow FDI in these sectors. With well-designed policies, China started and increased exports of the import-substituting products by combining its cheap labor with advanced technology embodied in FDI (Zhang, 2005). This has been happening in home appliances (TV sets, VCD, DVD players, cameras, refrigerators, and washers) and the automobile industry.

3   Exports of new labor-intensive final products: the success of some Chinese brand names of light consumer goods in entering world markets is partly due to FDI providing links to final buyers, especially in the US markets (Zhang, 2002, 2005).

4   Exports of local raw materials processing: in the processing of locally produced raw materials, foreign affiliates may have better export potential than indigenous firms, because of their business contacts abroad, marketing skills, and superior technology, both in product and processes, and greater general know-how. This is especially true in the 1980s, when the Chinese firms lacked these assets and FDI was the only means, at least for the time being, of increasing exports.

FDI enhances as well China's manufacturing exports through spillover effects on local firms' exporting activities. For instance, local firms increase their exports by observing the export activities of foreign affiliates ("learning by watching") and by making use of the infrastructure of transport, communications, and financial services that develops to support those activities. The second spillover effect involves the influence of FDI on the competitiveness of domestic firms' exports and the diffusion of new technologies. By bringing their advanced product-process technology, management, and marketing competence, MNCs may increase competition in the

Chinese markets and force local firms to adopt more efficient methods. The third spillovers are related to the linkage between foreign and local firms. If export-oriented foreign subsidiaries increase their purchase of inputs from local firms as the subsidiary matures, China's exports increase (UNCTAD, 2001, 2002a).

Other contributions

In addition to contributing export volume, FDI helped in improving China's export-commodity structure through expanding exports in manufactures and high- and new-technological products (HNTP). Table 8.4 presents manufacturing shares in total exports and exports by FIEs over 1992–2000. In most years of the period, FIEs' manufacturing shares are over 92 percent of their total exports, while the national share in 1992 was only 80 percent. In other words, almost all exporting goods by FIEs are manufacturing, which speeds up the process of China's transformation as an exporter of industrial products. Among the manufacturing exports by FIEs are machinery and electronics, which make up two-thirds of total FIE export in 2003 (Table 8.5). From 1992 to 2003, China's exports in machinery-electronics rose by $207 billion (from $20 billion to $227 billion), 73 percent of the increase ($151 billion) comes from FIEs. In fact, More than two-thirds (69 percent) of China's machinery-electronics exports in 2003 are created by FIEs, compared with the share of 31 percent in 1992.

The role of FDI in China's HNTP exports is astonishing as well. As indicated in Table 8.6, China's exports of HNTP in 1996 were $12.7 billion (8 percent of total exports), of which nearly 60 percent came from FIEs. After seven years, the exports increased almost ten times, reaching $119.2

Table 8.4 Manufacturing shares in total exports and exports by foreign-invested enterprises (FIEs) (1992–2000)

Year	Total exports		Exports by FIEs	
	Export value ($ billion)	Manufacturing share (%)	Export value ($ billion)	Manufacturing share (%)
1992	84.94	80.0	17.36	93.9
1993	91.76	81.8	25.24	92.7
1994	121.04	83.7	34.71	92.4
1995	148.77	85.6	46.88	93.6
1996	151.07	85.5	61.51	80.8
1997	182.79	86.9	74.90	81.0
1998	183.76	88.8	80.96	94.2
1999	194.93	89.8	88.63	94.1
2000	249.21	89.8	119.44	83.0

Source: *China Foreign Economic Statistical Yearbook* (SSB, 1993–2001).

Table 8.5 Growing exports of machinery-electronics and contributions by foreign-invested enterprises (FIEs) (1992–2003)

Year	Nation's exports		Exports by foreign-invested enterprises		
	Value ($ billion)	Share in total exports (%)	Value ($ billion)	Share in FIE exports (%)	Share in machinery-electronics exports (%)
1992	19.65	23.0	6.10	35.1	31.2
1993	22.71	24.7	8.39	33.2	37.0
1994	32.00	26.4	13.28	38.3	41.5
1995	43.86	29.5	20.62	44.0	47.0
1996	48.21	31.9	26.91	43.8	55.8
1997	59.32	32.5	34.33	45.8	57.9
1998	66.54	36.2	40.12	49.6	60.3
1999	76.97	39.5	46.42	52.4	60.3
2000	105.31	42.3	66.73	55.9	63.4
2001	118.79	44.6	76.66	57.5	64.5
2002	157.08	48.2	101.60	59.8	64.7
2003	227.46	51.9	156.77	65.2	68.9

Sources: *China FDI Report 2004* (Ministry of Commerce, 2004); Jiang (2002).

Table 8.6 Exports of high- and new-technological products (HNTP) and contributions by foreign-invested enterprises (FIEs) (1996–2003)

Year	Nation's HNTP exports		HNTP exports by FIEs		
	Value ($ billion)	Share in total exports (%)	Value ($ billion)	Share in exports by FIEs (%)	Share in total HNTP exports (%)
1996	12.663	8.4	7.421	12.1	58.6
1997	16.310	8.9	10.915	14.6	66.9
1998	20.251	11.0	14.939	18.5	73.8
1999	24.704	12.7	18.775	21.2	76.0
2000	37.043	14.9	29.967	25.1	80.9
2001	46.457	17.5	37.881	28.4	81.5
2002	67.707	20.8	55.658	32.7	82.2
2003	119.179	27.2	91.738	38.2	77.0

Sources: *China FDI Report 2004* (Ministry of Commerce, 2004); *China Statistical Yearbook* (SSB, 2004); *China Foreign Economic Statistical Yearbook* (SSB, 1997–2003); *FDI in China* (Jiang, 2002).

billion (27 percent of total exports). Most of the increase (79 percent or $84 billion) is generated by FIEs, and the FIE share is 77 percent. One may conclude that China's HNTP exports are mainly driven by FDI.

Foreign-invested enterprises tend to export more and grow faster than domestic enterprises. Table 8.7 shows the export propensity of industrial products by FIEs and domestic firms. In 1996, export propensity (defined as the export share in total output) of domestic firms was 8.5 percent, one-fifth of that for FIEs (42 percent). Although the domestic firms expanded their exports over time, the propensity (14 percent in 2002) was much lower than that for FIEs (43 percent). In fact, FIEs' export propensity was three times that of domestic firms in 2002. Moreover, FIE exports grow much faster than exports by domestic firms (Figure 8.3). Over the period of 1993–2004, the increase in exports for FIEs is larger than that for domestic firms for most years, and the gap has even become bigger since 2001, when China entered World Trade Organization.

Some negative effects of FDI

Some negative effects are associated with FDI as well on China's export performance. In particular, depending on multinational corporations in promoting exports brings its own risks for China. Four problems have emerged: (i) unusually low local value-added in foreign affiliate exports; (ii) FDI's hindering China from industrial upgrading and moving up in dynamic comparative advantage; (iii) possible relocation of export-oriented FDI away from China; and (iv) relatively high costs of attracting and keeping export-oriented foreign affiliates.

Table 8.7 Export propensity of industrial output by domestic and foreign-invested enterprises (FIEs) (1996–2002)

Year	Domestic enterprises		Foreign-invested enterprises	
	Total output (RMB billion)	Export share (%)	Total output (RMB billion)	Export share (%)
1996	8,747.8	8.50	1,211.7	42.13
1997	9,933.4	9.01	1,439.9	43.17
1998	10,129.8	8.43	1,775.0	37.86
1999	10,603.3	8.32	2,007.8	36.64
2000	6,220.9	13.87	2,346.4	42.25
2001	6,822.8	13.70	2,722.1	40.41
2002	7,831.7	13.96	3,245.9	43.31

Sources: *China Statistical Yearbook* (SSB, 2004); *China Foreign Economic Statistical Yearbook* (SSB, 1997–2003).

Note
The total output by domestic enterprises for years after 1999 is recorded in a different measurement from that in previous years.

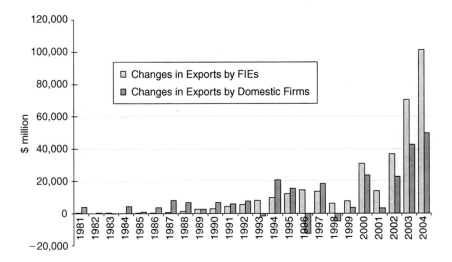

Figure 8.3 Annual changes in exports by foreign-invested enterprises (FIEs) and
by domestic firms (1981–2004) (sources: *China Statistical Yearbook 2003*
(SSB, 2004) and *China Foreign Economic Statistical Yearbook
1979–2003* (SSB, 1979–2003). The data for 2004 are taken from the
official website of China's Ministry of Commerce (http://www.
mofcom.gov.cn).

Figure 8.4 shows a trade deficit of foreign-invested enterprises until
1997 and modest surplus after that year. This suggests that the trade-
related benefits of FDI for China are quite limited because of the high
import content. In other words, multinational corporations seem just to
take advantage of China's cheap labor for simple processing and assembling work, leaving a small part of value-added in China.[2] Profits earned
by FIEs exceed their exports surplus by a wide margin (UNCTAD,
2002b). China's export surplus (at least until 997) is generated by nation
firms, rather than high import-content FIEs. An informative example is
given in Table 8.8. A globe with some educational functions made in
China is sold in the US for $88, but the value added within China is only
$20, and the factory that makes the globe receives only $15 for each globe
(17 percent of the total value).

Multinational corporations are more interested in focusing solely on the
static comparative advantages of China. While this might resolve some of
the short-term efficiency-related problems of MNCs, a number of the
benefits that can be associated with export-oriented foreign affiliates may
fail to materialize in China. In particular, dynamic comparative advantages
may not be developed, local value-added may not be increased, and affiliates may not embed themselves in the local economy by building linkages
to the domestic entrepreneurial community, by further developing labor
skills, or by introducing more complex technologies.

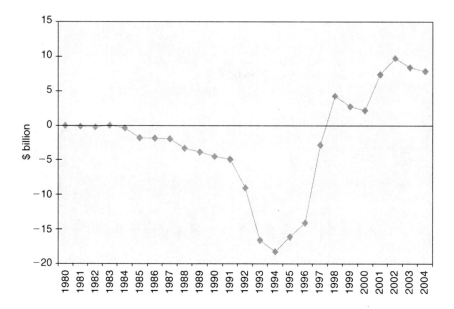

Figure 8.4 Trade balance of foreign-invested enterprises (FIEs) (1980–2004) (sources: *China Statistical Yearbook 2003* (SSB, 2004) and *China Foreign Economic Statistical Yearbook 1979–2003* (SSB, 1979–2003). The data for 2004 are taken from the official website of China's Ministry of Commerce (http://www.mofcom.gov.cn).

Table 8.8 Distribution of value-added in the production chain: the case of the globe

	Value-added ($)	Share
A US company designing the globe	28.00	31.82
A US retail store selling the globe	20.00	22.73
A Hong Kong company taking the order from the US	20.00	22.73
A Chinese trading company taking the order from Hong Kong	5.00	5.68
A Chinese factory producing the globe	15.00	17.04
Price of the globe sold in US	88.00	100.00

Source: *What We Should Know About America?* (Zhang, 2002).

Foreign affiliates can leave China when conditions change and profit prospects are affected. Usually export-oriented FDI activities are particularly sensitive to changes in the cost of production, market access, regulatory conditions, or perceptions of risks. If relocation of foreign affiliates occurs with little warning, China can face serious problems. Over time, there is also a risk of relocation of labor-intensive production to lower-cost sites (for example, Indian, Pakistan, Bangladesh, and some countries in Africa), as the wage level increases with income growth. Although the ability of multinational corporations to switch locations diminishes with the technology intensity of exports for the poorer host economies, it represents a serious problem requiring policy attention.

China also has a risk in attracting export-oriented FDI (for which international competition is particularly strong) through incentives and by lowering labor standards, environmental standards, or other economic or social standards. This can lead to a race to the top as far as incentives are concerned and a race to the bottom in terms of social benefits for workers and the economy as a whole. In addition, if all developing countries aim at exporting the same products at the same time, most of them including China may well be worse off.

Conclusion

Export promotion through FDI has been one of the key reasons for the government's desire to attract FDI. FDI can help to channel capital into industries that have the potential to compete internationally, and the global linkages of MNCs can facilitate their access to foreign markets. In addition to exports that are generated directly by foreign affiliates, FDI can also promote exports through the teaching of proper marketing strategies, methods, procedures, and channels of distribution. Given that the absolute volume of China's total exports has also been increasing substantially, China's effort on attracting FDI has proved a remarkable achievement.

China's success in promoting exports through FDI reported here might be somewhat special due to its unique advantage over other developing countries in bargaining with multinational corporations. While FDI has potential in helping host countries' exports, the benefits do not accrue automatically or evenly across countries. National policies and host government bargaining power relative to multinational corporations matter for attracting export-oriented FDI and for reaping its full benefits for exports. China's unique advantages in sheer size, strong centralized government, large number of rich overseas Chinese who set up most of the export-oriented affiliates, and well-designed FDI strategy, have provided it with negotiating power to minimize the adverse effects and realize positive effects of FDI.

In the post-WTO-entry period, China needs to pay special attention not only to attracting export-oriented FDI activities, which are the basis for benefitting from them. It also needs to pursue active policies to increase the benefits from export-oriented FDI activities once it has attracted them. The trade balance is relevant here, but particular attention needs to be given to upgrading of the export-oriented production.

Notes

1 On the other hand, however, the radical, neo-Marxist or left-leaning positions suggest that FDI may (a) lower or replace domestic savings and investment; (b) transfer technologies that are low level or inappropriate for the host country's factor proportions; (c) target primarily the host country's domestic market and thus not increase exports; (d) inhibit the expansion of indigenous firms that might become exporters; and (e) not help developing the host country's dynamic comparative advantages by focusing solely on local cheap labor and raw materials. Caves (1996) and Helleiner (1989) provide detailed discussion and a survey on the topic.

2 The reality is, however, more complex. A closer examination of the composition of FIE imports reveals that a significant proportion consists of capital goods, such as machinery and related equipment, to create or expand and upgrade production capacity in affiliates. The share of such imports was high (23–39 percent) during the period 1992–1997 (SSB, 2003). Moreover, since 1994, the deficits have decreased and turned to surplus in 1998. This may be a sign of rising value-added within China.

References

Blomström, Magnus, Ari Kokko, and Mario Zejan (2000), *Foreign Direct Investment: Firm and Host Country Strategies*, London: Macmillan Press.

Caves, Richard (1996), *Multinational Enterprises and Economic Analysis*, 2nd edition, Cambridge, MA: Cambridge University Press.

Din, Musleh-ud (1994), "Export processing zones and backward linkages," *Journal of Development Economics*, 43: 369–385.

Haddad, Mona and Ann Harrison (1993), "Are there positive spillovers from direct foreign investment?" *Journal of Development Economics*, 42: 51–74.

Helleiner, G. (1989), "Transnational corporations and direct foreign investment," in Chenery and Srinivasan (ed.) *Handbook of Development Economics*, Elsevier Science Publishers B.V.: 1441–1480.

Jiang, Xiaojuan (2002), *FDI Economies in China*, China People's University Press.

Markusen, James, A. Venables, D. Konan, and K. H. Zhang (1996), "A unified treatment of horizontal direct investment, vertical direct investment, and the pattern of trade in goods and services," NBER Working Paper No. 5696.

Ministry of Commerce (2004), *China FDI Report 2004*, Beijing: Ministry of Commerce.

Naughton, Barry (1996), "China's Emergence and Prospects as A Trading Nation," *Brookings Papers on Economic Activity*, 2: 273–344.

State Statistical Bureau (SSB) (2004), *China Statistical Yearbook 2004*, Beijing: China Statistical Press.

State Statistical Bureau (SSB) (1979–2003), *China Foreign Economic Statistical Yearbook* (1979–2003), Beijing: China Statistical Press.

United Nations Conference on Trade and Development (UNCTAD) (2001 and 2002a), *World Investment Report* (2001 and 2002), New York: United Nations.

United Nations Conference on Trade and Development (UNCTAD) (2002b), *Trade and Development Report, 2002*, New York: United Nations.

Zhang, Haiyang (2002), *What We Should Know about America?* Beijing: Central Edition & Translation Press.

Zhang, Kevin H. (2000), "Human capital, country size, and north-south manufac-turing multinational enterprises," *Economia Internazionale/International Economics*, 53 (2): 237–260.

Zhang, Kevin H. (2002), "China as a new power in world trade," in Fung, Pei, and Johnson (eds) *China's Access to WTO and Global Economy*, Beijing: Yuhang Publishing House, 32–49.

Zhang, Kevin, H. (2005), "FDI and host countries' exports: the case of China," Working Paper, Illinois State University.

Zhang, Kevin H. and James R. Markusen (1999), "Vertical multinationals and host-country characteristics," *Journal of Development Economics*, 59: 233–252.

Zhang, Kevin H. and Shunfeng Song (2000), "Promoting exports: the role of inward FDI in China," *China Economic Review*, 11(4): 385–396.

Part III

WTO, exchange rates, and labor markets

9 China's increasing openness

Threat or opportunity?

Ramesh B. Adhikari and Yongzheng Yang

Introduction

China's increasing openness has caused considerable concerns in the rest of the world. These concerns have been exacerbated by China's recent accession to the World Trade Organization (WTO) and its recently signed free trade agreement with the Association of South-East Asian Nations (ASEAN). Many developing countries, especially those in Asia, fear that competitive manufactures from China will not only flood their domestic markets, but also replace their exports in third country markets, especially in industrial countries. As China becomes increasingly attractive to foreign direct investment (FDI) with its WTO accession, these developing countries also fear that FDI may be further diverted away from them, in addition to luring their domestic investors away from home.

This chapter examines these two questions based on a growing body of research on China's integration with the global economy. We argue that given China's sheer size, its growing openness is bound to cause some dislocation in some developing countries in the short to medium terms, but it also provides tremendous opportunities for exports and investment from other developing countries, especially in the long run. Further inflows of FDI to China will likely grow at a moderate pace and are unlikely to cause large diversions away from other developing countries. Overall, China's increasing openness should benefit the rest of the world in the long run despite the adjustment pressure it will generate in the short to medium term.

China's increasing openness

Pre-WTO reforms

China's pre-WTO policy reforms included dismantling central planning, establishing border protection, decentralizing and liberalizing trade, relaxing foreign exchange controls, reducing exchange rate distortions, and removing anti-export biases in the trade regime (Adhikari and Yang, 2002;

Table 9.1 Simple average tariff rates in China, selected years (1982–2002) (in percent)

Year	Tariff
1982	55.6
1985	43.3
1988	43.7
1991	44.1
1992	42.9
1993	39.9
1994	36.3
1996	23.6
1997	17.6
1998	17.5
2000	16.4
2001	14.0
2002	12.7

Sources: Yang (2003), which in turn is based on Ianchovichina and Martin (2001), Lardy (2002), and IMF staff estimates.

Suppachai and Clifford, 2002). The simple average tariff has been falling consistently from 42.9 percent in 1992 to a low of 12.7 percent in 2002 (Table 9.1). These policy reforms led to a rapid expansion of external trade. The value of trade has exceeded 40 percent of GDP since the late 1990s, as opposed to 10 percent in 1978, when reforms began. China has also attracted large FDI inflows since it introduced its first law on joint ventures in 1979. Annual FDI inflows now account for about 10 percent of total gross investment.

Further reforms – the WTO commitments

China has made strong commitments to opening its markets and to complying with WTO rules, providing unprecedented opportunities for exports from its trading partners (Table 9.2).[1] China is also expected to further expand its exports of labor-intensive goods, increasing the competitive pressure on its trading partners with similar export structures. China's opening up of its domestic markets is expected to attract more FDI from Asia as well as from other parts of the world.

China-ASEAN FTA

China and ASEAN have signed an agreement to establish a free trade area (FTA) between them within a decade. This agreement has the potential to create an FTA of more than $2 trillion GDP, with 30 percent of the world's population (1.7 billion). Although initially focusing on

Table 9.2 Summary of China's WTO commitments

Industries	Key commitments
Agriculture	Farm subsidy – 8.5% of value of domestic production. Eliminate export subsidies. Average bound tariff down to 15% (1–3% in-quota rate and up to 65% above-quota rate on cereals), further reductions mostly by 2004.
Industrial goods	Average bound tariff down to 8.9% (highest 47% on photo films).
Automobiles	Import tariffs on automobiles to 25% by mid-2006 from current 80–100%. Restrictions on category, type and model of vehicles produced to be lifted in two years.
Banking	Foreign bank local currency business: with local corporate identities within two years after accession, with local residents five years. Geographic restrictions on foreign banking business to be lifted over five years.
Insurance	Foreign ownership: 50% of life-insurance and 100% of non-life insurance (property/casualty); geographic/business restrictions will be gradually phased out.
Securities	Minority foreign-owned joint ventures in fund management industry. Foreign ownership up to 49% in five years.
Distribution	Foreign companies are allowed to set up joint ventures within two years after accession with majority ownership and without geographic restrictions, with exceptions for a few products.
Accounting firms	Foreign accountants who pass China's registered accountant tests can enjoy national treatment in setting up accounting firms (joint ventures).
Telecommunications	Foreign company stakes: 25% in mobile phone, up to 35% in one year and 49% after three years; area restriction will be lifted after five years.
State trading and trading rights	State trading will continue in cereals, tobacco, fuels, and minerals. All enterprises will be free to import or export after three years.
Rules on Chinese exports	Transitional safeguard mechanism against import surges for 12 years. Antidumping procedures based non-market economy rules for 15 years. Textile and clothing quotas to be removed at the beginning of 2005, but a special safeguard remains valid until the end of 2008.

Source: Authors' compilation from WTO documents.

merchandise trade, the FTA may eventually cover other key areas such as information technology, human resources, direct investments, and the development of the Mekong River basin. It is designed to tap complementarities among the participants and promote intra-regional trade and economic cooperation (OAPP, 2001).

Implications of China's increasing openness

Overall impact

Recent studies consistently show that China's WTO accession will benefit the global economy; China and industrial countries will benefit the most, and some developing countries that directly compete with China may lose (Ianchovichina and Martin, 2001; Wang, 2001; Lardy, 2002; Li, 2003; Roland-Holst *et al.*, 2003).[2] However, there is considerable uncertainty about the timing, magnitude, and the duration of these effects. These studies tend to focus on short- to medium-term effects of tariff reductions; they generally do not take into account the potential effects of further reforms of domestic policies for WTO compliance, the opening up of the services sector, or possible long-term, dynamic effects (such as productivity improvements). Figures 9.1–9.3 (adopted from Asian Development

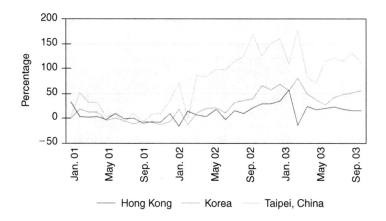

Figure 9.1 Growth of East Asian exports to China.

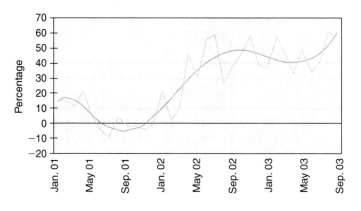

Figure 9.2 Growth rate of ASEAN-5 exports to the PRC.

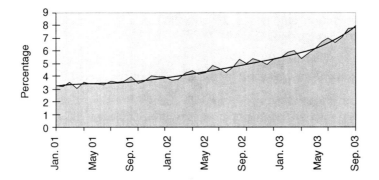

Figure 9.3 Share of ASEAN-5 exports to the PRC.

Bank (2003)) show that the growth of exports from East Asian and ASEAN countries has accelerated after China's WTO accession in December 2001, confirming the positive impact of Chinese liberalization.

Impact on ASEAN countries

There has been a general perception that ASEAN goods have a 20–30 percent cost disadvantage against Chinese goods (Ramli, 2002). It is feared that the China–ASEAN FTA would adversely affect local industries and employment in ASEAN countries. However, the ASEAN–China FTA would also mean opening up of China's huge domestic market for ASEAN goods. Thus, the ensuing trade policy and strategic concern should be how to export more to China under the FTA, rather than trying to protect inefficient domestic industries. At the same time, ASEAN and China should continue to pursue unilateral and multilateral trade liberalization to minimize the trade diversion effect of the ASEAN–China FTA.

It is important to emphasize that China cannot be competitive in everything. There is considerable complementarity between China and ASEAN countries. Some ASEAN countries are well positioned to provide China with competitive manufactured goods (e.g. intermediate inputs), and others can become large suppliers to China of commodities. In general, ASEAN countries, particularly those having comparative advantage in agriculture, natural resources, and high-tech goods are likely to benefit the most from the FTA with China, as long as they keep their most-favored-nation tariffs low.

The China-ASEAN FTA has the potential to influence trade and economic groupings in the region, including East, Central, and South Asia. As trade between ASEAN and China expands, other regional economies and groupings in Asia are likely to seek an FTA with ASEAN and strengthen their economic relationships with China to avoid being disadvantaged.

This may help improve regional security as well as lead to greater economic cooperation among the key regional players, particularly Japan, China, India, Korea, and ASEAN.

Will China remain a price-maker for labor-intensive goods?

China has an abundant supply of unskilled labor. Further reforms of state-owned enterprises and agriculture will result in additional effective supply of labor. The large pool of surplus labor in the vast undeveloped west China will also help keep wages low in China. Thus, China will remain competitive in labor-intensive exports in a foreseeable future. In fact, in some industries, China's competitiveness will increase after its WTO accession. In the past, some of China's most competitive exports, particularly textiles and clothing, were subjected to various restrictions in overseas markets. Many of these restrictions will be phased out as a result of China's WTO accession. Developing countries that also specialize in these products will be under increasing pressure from Chinese exporters. However, as most restrictions on Chinese exports will be phased out only gradually, developing countries should take this opportunity to restructure their industries and enhance their export competitiveness (Adhikari, 2001).

China is, however, likely to have a stronger hold in more skill- and capital-intensive goods over time, e.g., semi-conductors. So far, the FDI-driven assembling-type industries have specialized in low value added products. As China's human and technological base develops, it is likely that China will move up along the value added chain. This should leave more room for low-income developing countries, such as South Asian countries and poorer ASEAN countries, to expand their labor-intensive exports.

In this context, it is important to note that so far Asian developing countries have generally adjusted well to China's emergence. They have begun to differentiate their exports from Chinese products. For example, while China's exports to the US market are largely wearing apparel, footwear and household goods, followed by semiconductors and related goods, NIEs' exports are primarily semi-conductors, followed by apparel, footwear, and household goods. ASEAN-4 exports are broadly similar to China, but they seem to be moving away from apparel, footwear, and household goods to semiconductors and/or related goods (Fernald *et al.*, 1999; Loungani, 2000). Poorer ASEAN (such as Vietnam and Cambodia) and South Asian countries are gaining competitiveness in very labor-intensive products, such as textiles and clothing.

Thus, China does not always compete with other countries in the region even when the latter have similar factor endowments. For example, China and India are broadly similar in terms of underlying sources of comparative advantage. They compete on some export markets, but they also compliment bilaterally. According to the IMF Direction of Trade Statistics, China's trade with India more than quadrupled between 1995 and 2002, with India's exports to China increasing more than fivefold during the period. Potential for further trade growth with South Asia is large with China's increased openness and ongoing trade reforms in South Asia.

China has established itself as a formidable competitor in export markets largely based on productivity improvement (OAAP, 2002a). From 1997 to 2000, Chinese exports to the US increased from 20 percent of Asia's total to 24 percent, while ASEAN's share declined slightly. In particular, ASEAN's market share in unskilled labor-intensive goods like clothing and household goods is decreasing (Kwan, 2002). The key issue for ASEAN countries is not so much China's increasing competition, rather, it is their domestic policy that is critical to facilitate structural changes and increase their competitiveness in exports that are not in direct competition with Chinese products.

Will there be FDI diversion at the expense of other developing countries?

China has the world's third largest stock of FDI, after the US and the UK (OAAP 2002b). After attracting a total $47 billion in 2001, China's annual FDI inflows exceeded $50 billion in 2002 and 2003, taking an increasing share of FDI inflows to Asia.[3] WTO membership will continue to boost investor confidence in the country's economic prospects and business environment. Foreign firms are attracted by China's high GDP growth; growing demand for consumer goods; an increasingly skilled and educated workforce; improved infrastructure; and a more predictable business environment. Since the early 1980s China has drawn significant investment from regional conglomerates as well (OAAP, 2002a). ASEAN policy-makers would prefer to keep such investment at home. Moreover, FDI flows into ASEAN countries are increasingly in the form of mergers and acquisitions, compared with "greenfield" (new) investment in China.

While China's increasing openness may raise the cost for other develop-ing countries to attract FDI, it also represents a window of opportunity for foreign investors, including those from other developing countries (Prasad and Rumbaugh, 2003; Rumbaugh and Blancher, 2004). For example, the services sector will provide many opportunities in the future, particularly in banking, insurance, distribution, telecommunications, and professional services. Restructuring of manufacturing (e.g. machine tools, electrical equipment, information technology, pharmaceuticals, and biotech) will need foreign capital, technology, and managerial skills. India, for example, has begun to invest in China's information technology industry and increased its exports of computer software to China. Technology exporters are likely to gain in manufacturing as well as farming (Japan, the EU, and the US). So are energy suppliers (e.g. Indonesia and some Pacific Island countries, in addition to OPEC countries) and cereals exporters (e.g. Thailand, Vietnam, Australia, and the US). In this context, it is worth noting that China's increasing import demand for commodities, such as petroleum and steel, has begun to push up world prices of these commodities.

The pattern of FDI inflows in China is likely to change from the past. Inflows in China's protected manufacturing industries are likely to slow, while investment in services industries is expected to pick up. Even in services industries, the gradual phasing out of restrictions will moderate the pace of investment inflow. Overall, FDI inflows to China will increase, but unlikely dramatically. It is also important to remember that in competition for attracting FDI, China does not have advantage versus other Asian developing countries in every aspect. For example, it will probably take China a long time to catch up with some ASEAN countries in the areas of banking and legal institutions.

When it comes to FDI, it is important to note that China is also a larger investor overseas, and its FDI outflows are expected to grow further (OAAP, 2002b). By the first half of 2001, Chinese companies had set up 6,439 firms in 160 countries and committed to investing 7.7 billion dollars in projects in trade, natural resources exploration, transportation, labor services, and agriculture (OAAP, 2002b). Many Chinese companies are investing more overseas to bypass quotas and other trade barriers, secure the supply of raw materials, and gain access to foreign technology. In many cases, Chinese investors use manufacturing equipment as equity to form joint ventures with local partners, which usually provide land and infrastructure.

Will China be able to comply with the WTO commitments?

Foreign investors will watch closely how China will implement its WTO comments, especially in the areas of market access in services, the legal framework, the judiciary system, and accounting and auditing practices. These pose difficult challenges to the Chinese government. Enterprises, urban workers, professionals, and farmers will also have to adjust to new economic circumstances. The government's nature and role will have to change. Outdated regulations and laws will have to be abolished or revised, and new ones will have to be introduced to improve consistency and transparency.[4] These are daunting tasks given China's size. Based on the past record on structural adjustment, however, there is a good chance that China will continue to make progress in compliance with its WTO commitments (OECD, 2002).

Conclusion

It is important to bear in mind that China's opening up has been going on for more than two decades; developing countries have in general benefitted from this process. China's WTO accession was just an extension of this long-term process and should further benefit both industrialized and developing countries. In addition, China's WTO accession has been designed to be gradual and less disruptive to itself and other member countries. This is reflected in the phased-in approach to market access to China and its partner countries, buttressed by safeguard measures, even though some of them are discriminatory against China and are likely to damage the interest of countries that invoke such measures.

The emergence of any large economy of China's size will inevitably have significant implications for world production, trade and investment, and hence employment.[5] China's increasing openness will pose challenges to other developing countries. To meet these challenges, they must restructure their industries and enhance their export competitiveness where they have comparative advantage, and exploit new opportunities in China's increasingly open market. China's opening up is not a zero-sum game; it will provide unprecedented market opportunities for its trading partners as well as increased competition in the world market.

China itself also has enormous tasks ahead for further reform. China needs to reform its banking system, restructure state-owned enterprises and farm businesses, establish a viable social security system, and develop its western regions. In the long run, the real competition between China and other developing countries lies in the pace of domestic reform. What will happen in trade and foreign direct investment will be simply an outcome of that competition.

Notes

1 For further details, see Lardy (2002) and Suppachai and Clifford (2002).
2 The estimated losses for these countries are largely attributed to the elimination of quotas on Chinese textile and clothing exports, which tend to replace products from less competitive exporting countries (Yang, 2003). Without this one-off impact, China's increasing openness is more likely to benefit other developing countries, as was the case historically (Yang and Vine, 2000).
3 Including Hong Kong, China now takes 70 percent of all FDI in Asia (OAAP, 2002b).
4 The State Council abolished 221 laws before and around China's WTO accession, but more needs to be done under the country's WTO commitments.
5 Based on 2000 data, China is the sixth largest market (GDP); seventh leading exporter and eighth largest importer of merchandise trade; also tenth leading importer and twelfth leading exporter of services.

References

Adhikari, R. (2001) "China's openness – implications for other countries in the region", presentation at Asian Development Bank Institute, 28 November 2001, Tokyo.

Adhikari, R. and Yang, Y. (2002) "What will WTO membership mean for China and its trading partners?", *Finance and Development*, 39(3): 22–25.

Asian Development Bank (2003) *Asian Development Update 2003*, presentation slides, Economics and Research Department, Asian Development Bank, Manila, December.

Fernald, John G., Hali Edison, and Prakash Loungani (1999) "Was China the first domino? assessing links between China and the rest of emerging Asia", *Journal of International Money and Finance*, 18(4): 515–536.

Ianchovichina, Elena and Will Martin (2001) "Trade liberalization in China's accession to the World Trade Organization", unpublished, World Bank, Washington DC, June.

Li, Yuefin (2003) "Economic implications of China's accession to the WTO", *China and the World Economy*, No. 2 (November): 7–16.

Kwan, C.H. (2002). "Complementarity and composition between China and Japan – an empirical analysis based on US import statistics", presentation at the Asian Development Bank Institute, Tokyo, January.

Lardy, Nicholas R. (2002) *Integrating China into the World Economy*, Washington, DC: Brookings Institution.

Loungani, Prakash (2000) "Comrades or competitors? Trade links between China and other East Asian countries", *Finance and Development*, 37(2): 1–5.

Organization for Economic Cooperation and Development (OECD) (2002) *China in the World Market – The Domestic Policy Challenges*, Paris: OECD.

Oxford Analytica Asia Pacific Daily Brief (OAAP) (2001) "ASEAN – Brunei Summit", 9 November.

Oxford Analytica Asia Pacific Daily Brief (OAAP) (2002a) "China challenge", 8 January.

Oxford Analytica Asia Pacific Daily Brief (OAAP) (2002b) "China: changing investments", 14 May.

Prasad, E. and Thomas Rumbaugh (2003) "Beyond the Great Wall", *Finance and Development*, 40(4): 46–49.

Ramli, Rizal (2002) "Lessons for Indonesia", *Jakarta Post*, 12 January, Jakarta.

Roland-Holst, David, Iwan Azis, and Li-Gang Liu (2003) "Regionalism and globalism: East and Southeast Asian trade relations in the wake of China's WTO accession", Discussion Paper, ADB Institute, Tokyo, January.

Rumbaugh, Thomas and Nicolas Blancher (2004) "China: international trade and WTO accession", IMF Working Paper, WP/04/36, Washington, DC.

Suppachai P. and Mark L. Clifford (2002) *China and the WTO – Changing China, Changing World Trade*, Singapore: John Wiley and Sons (Asia).

Wang, Zhi (2001) "The Impact of China's WTO Accession on Trade and Economic Relations Across the Taiwan Strait", *Economics of Transition*, 9(30): 743–785.

Yang, Yongzheng (2003). "China's Integration into the World Economy: Implications for Developing Countries", IMF Working Paper, WP/03/245, Washington, DC.

Yang, Yongzheng and David Vines (2000) "The Fallacy of Composition and the Terms of Trade of Newly Industrializing Countries", paper presented at a seminar in the Department of Economics, Oxford University, November 9.

10 China's position and role in the WTO

Xinquan Tu

Since China applied for membership of the World Trade Organization (WTO) in 1986 there have been many concerns about its future position and role in the WTO. The reason for these concerns is that although China is a developing country, it is also a large and fast growing economy. What position would China take in the WTO? What role could China play in the WTO? The size and dynamics of the Chinese economy make China's entry to the WTO different from that of any new members in past decades.

This chapter analyzes China's position and role in the WTO. It is clear that any country joining the WTO does so to maximize national interests through membership. The position and role played by a country depends primarily on its economic (and political) characteristics. In the case of China, its developing country status is obvious, but this does not mean it would oppose developed country members. Based on an analysis of China's trading conditions and its international historical performance, we conclude that China is likely to support developing members as well as cooperate with developed members in further trade liberalization within the WTO framework.

China as a large open developing country

China's situation is very complicated, in that many contradicting features coexist, thus it is not easy to set a simple standard for positioning China. Here we attempt to use income level (GDP per capita) and country size (GDP) to evaluate China, which is an important consideration in defining China's role and strategy in the WTO.

China as a developing country

China's status as a developing country took center stage during its accession negotiations. This debate was provoked mainly by the US for the purpose of its own interests. However, China as a developing country has changed very little in a long period of time.

The essential and distinct index weighing one country's economic level is GNP per capita. As shown in the world development report released by the World Bank (2003), the GNP per capita of China in 2001, the year of China's accession is $890 (see Table 10.1), accounts for 2.55 percent of the US, 2.47 percent of Japan, 12.8 percent of Argentina, 29 percent of Brazil, and 17.3 percent of the world average. According to the PPP method, however, GNP per capita for China in 2001 was $4,260, accounting for 12.2 percent of the US, 15.5 percent of Japan, 36.4 percent of Argentina, 57.2 percent of Brazil, and 56.3 percent of the world average. In view of the criteria set by the World Bank, China is slightly higher than India among the large countries. In recent years, there has been a wave among western scholars of doubting the viability of China's economic statistics.[1] Lardy (2002) held that the real development of China was apparently lower than what was published officially in the past two decades. In light of their estimation, China's economic development level should be even lower, which further proves China is indeed a developing country. The Strategy Research Team of DRC (2001) concluded that China is still in the process of industrialization and modernization, and there is some considerable distance to go before it achieves developed country status, after a thorough review of its developmental stage at the beginning of the twenty-first century in terms of the following eight aspects: GDP per capita, structure and quality of input factors, output structure, occupation structure, consumption patterns, income-allocation structure, urbanization and education level, trade patterns.

In fact, there is no need to prove China's status as a developing country. What this chapter is concerned with is how a country's economic level can decide its attitude to multilateral trading. During the evolution of the

Table 10.1 GNP per capita of major economies, 2001 (US$)

Economy	GNP per capita		PPP GNP per capita	
	2001	Rank in the world	2002	Rank in the world
Japan	35,990	4	27,430	13
US	34,870	7	34,870	3
Argentina	6,960	52	11,690	50
Brazil	3,060	89	7,450	81
Russia	1,750	107	8,660	79
China	890	138	4,260	121
India	460	161	2,450	149
Low income	1,240	–	5,020	–
Middle income	1,850	–	5,710	–
High income	26,710	–	27,680	–
World average	5,140	–	7,570	–

Source: *World Development Report 2003* (World Bank, 2003).

GATT/WTO, there has always been friction and conflict between developing and developed countries. Developed countries like the US, EU, and Japan generally have a positive attitude towards multilateral trading in spite of certain differences. Developing countries such as India keep looking with suspicion at the WTO, which was considered to be a tool for the US to establish its global economic hegemony (Srinivassan and Tendulkar, 2003). How then could China understand and participate in a multilateral trading system as a developing country?

The GATT/WTO by nature is a tool created by the US to realize its global political and economic interests, whereas the remaining countries take part in it for their own economic interests. It is understandable for developing countries to approach the multilateral trading system with distrust when the long colonial history of domination is taken into account. However, it doesn't mean their choice to be an onlooker is correct. The case is that developing countries cannot develop without cooperation from those that are already developed. An international division of labor and exchange are absolutely essential for industrialization and modernization, while self-closeness leads to a dead end, as demonstrated in India. As an Indian-born economist Bhagwati (2000) points out, that what was reckoned in the past – that developing countries were in need of different policy frameworks and special exemptions such as trade restriction to meet the balance of BOP and also exemptions from removing trade barriers in reciprocal trade – is now believed to be like cutting off their nose to spite their face.

The GATT/WTO set reciprocity as a fundamental principle, i.e. no pay, no gain. Developing countries managed to use morality to achieve non-reciprocal preferential treatment in the GATT, which were actually still reciprocal in essence. Because developed countries gave preferential treatment on the basis of their own interests and didn't lower their trade barriers to developing countries on certain sensitive products given that developing countries didn't make substantial market access. The case in point is agricultural products as well as textiles and apparel where developed countries kept holding high trade protectionism outside the GATT package. Even after the Uruguay round, tariffs and other trade barriers remained high in developed countries for imports from developing ones. For instance, products worth $26 billion exported from developing countries to the rest of the world were levied more than 50 percent in 1999, which made the real export volume to the Quad countries just $5 billion, compared with $21 billion to developing countries. Moreover, there's no preferential treatment in developed countries for sensitive products (World Bank, 2001).

What developing countries got from their morality was merely moral comfort and psychological satisfaction (Zhang, 2001). It was naive of them to expect mercy from developed countries. Taking part in a multinational trading system is to some extent essential for developing countries as it is the only access to foreign markets. On the other hand, developing countries' transformation and reconsideration in their development strategies in the 1980s were based on the basic economic laws. Trade liberalization would make their dreams come true. However, developing countries held that trade liberalization should be in accordance with their economic developmental levels. Free trade was neither unconditionally accepted by developed countries from the very beginning but anti-free trade was more prevalent (Yu, 1997). But now developed countries were constantly asking developing ones to progressively open up their markets. The competing nature of trade liberalization between developed and developing countries means it will last for a long time, and this has already been reflected by the failure of the Seattle Ministerial and the Cancun Ministerial.

China's attitude towards trade liberalization is similar to those of other developing countries, and this has been reflected by the minimum concessions tactics used during its accession negotiation (Sheng, 2002). This ensures that China will stand together with other developing countries in the WTO, and not only ask developed countries to carry out the Uruguay Round agreements and offer developing countries more flexibility in enforcing TRIPS, but also ensure that steps are taken to enlarge market access for developing countries' special products and improve the WTO's decision-making mechanism thus making it more transparent. China used to redress the scales for developing countries in world affairs as it held it was a member of them (Economy and Oksenberg, 1998). Excusing itself from G8 suggested that China was quite aware that it was still a developing country.[2] When it comes to conflict between developing and developed countries, China will continue trying to make the WTO offer developing countries more help. Cooperation with other developing countries is quite crucial in order for China to play its full role in the WTO.

China as a large fast growing economy

The US taking China as a developed country blurred the concepts of economic scale and developmental level. Although China has a rather backward developing level, it has never denied that it is a large country. A huge population and a vast territory destined China to play an important role on the world stage of politics and economy. In 2001, the population of China's mainland was as much as 1.5 times that of G8, consisting of US, England, Canada, Japan, France, German, Italy, and Russia. Its sheer size has enabled it to participate fully in international organizations such as the UN.

As discussed earlier, GDP is a good indicator of economic levels. In 2001, China was already in the top six in terms of exchange rate GDP in the world. In terms of PPP GDP, China was the second largest economy after the US (Table 10.2). From 1979 to 1999, China's actual GDP rate was higher than the world, the US and the developed countries by

Table 10.2 Top six countries in GDP and GDP (PPP) in 2001

Rank	Country	GDP	Rank	Country	GDP (PPP)
1	US	99,007	1	US	99,020
2	Japan	45,742	2	China	54,150
3	Germany	19,480	3	Japan	34,870
4	UK	14,514	4	India	25,300
5	France	13,774	5	Germany	20,980
6	China	11,310	6	France	14,950

Source: *World Development Report 2003* (World Bank, 2003).

6.13 percent, 6.90 percent, and 7.03 percent respectively. According to a Goldman Sachs's research reporting in 2003, China is not only likely to surpass German exchange-rate GDP in the next four years, but also to overtake Japan in 2015, and to exceed the US in 2039. Lin *et al.* (1999) have a different view on China's economic development suggesting that: "If China can maintain its rapid growth, it will become the world's largest economy in the first half of the 21st century."

Though the function of international institution tends to be of more importance in international economic relationships, a country's actual strength remains the number one factor in deciding its negotiation power. A large GDP reflects a large domestic market, therefore it has the power to bargain with other countries in market access negations. Moreover, to exert a stronger influence in the WTO, a country's position in foreign trade and international investment is also an important decisive factor. As shown in Tables 10.3 and 10.4, in 2003 China ranked among the fourth biggest trading countries in terms of imports and exports. More crucially China had the fastest development among the top five countries during this period with its increase in both exports and imports surpassing 30 percent. Despite with a less-developed service industry, which accounted for less than 32.3 percent of its national economy,[3] China had already nudged into the top five for service trade, and similarly with the fastest development rate. Meanwhile, China was also among the countries that absorbed the most foreign direct investment (FDI). In 2002, it actually attracted $52.7 billion in FDI, ranking second in the world, which is nearly the same was the total amount of FDI being used in Latin America (56 billion dollars).[4] And China has ranked first among developing countries for ten years. In 2003, China's foreign direct investment continued to rise, and amounted to 53.5 billion dollars, while the utilization of foreign investment by contract increased to $115.1 billion. By the end of 2003, the number of accumulated authorized foreign investment corporations had reached 465,277, with $943 billion of FDI contracts and $501 billion of realized FDI.[5] No wonder Panagaria (2000) suggested that in the new round of negotiations developing countries should not discuss FDI until

Table 10.3 Leading exporters and importers in world merchandise trade, 2003 (US$ billion/%)

Rank	Exporters	Value	Share	Growth	Rank	Importers	Value	Share	Growth
1	EU	1,105.3	14.7	7	1	US	1,303.1	16.8	9.0
2	US	723.8	9.6	4	2	EU	1,119.0	14.4	20.0
3	Japan	471.8	6.3	13	3	China	413.1	5.3	40.0
4	China	437.9	5.8	34	4	Japan	382.9	4.9	14.0
5	Canada	272.7	3.6	8	5	Canada	245.0	3.2	8.0

Source: *International Trade Statistics 2004* (WTO, 2004).

Note
The rank does not include intra-EU (15 countries) trade.

Table 10.4 Leading exporters and importers in world trade in commercial services, 2003 (US$ billion/%)

Rank	Exporters	Value	Share	Growth	Rank	Importers	Value	Share	Growth
1	EU	361.5	27.1	17	1	EU	336.4	25.4	16
2	US	287.7	21.5	5	2	US	228.5	17.3	8
3	Japan	70.6	5.3	9	3	Japan	110.3	8.3	3
4	China	46.4	3.5	18	4	China	54.9	4.1	19
5	Hong Kong	44.6	3.3	4	5	Canada	50.0	3.8	12

Source: *International Trade Statistics 2004* (WTO, 2004).

Note
The rank does not include intra-EU (15 countries) trade.

China's accession to the WTO, because China is the biggest country utilizing FDI among developing countries. China's accession to the WTO could enhance developing countries' negotiation ability in areas such as trade and investment. Huefbauer (1998) even said that without China's participation, the international agreement on FDI would be a mere scrap of paper.

So as a country with a significant trading economy and inward FDI, China should have an equivalent influence in the WTO. Furthermore, China can also make full use of its negotiation power to safeguard its national interests in the WTO.

China's integration into the world economy

Usually a country's economic development relies more on its domestic market and resources, making the international economic activities comparatively less important (Table 10.5), however, China is the exception. Since 1979, its opening-up policy has formed part of its basic development strategy. The Strategy Research Team of DRC (2001) summarizes China's more than two decades opening-up experience, and points out that it was this policy that sustained China's two decades of rapid development. Ever since the Third Plenum of the 14th Central Committee of the CPC, the theme of "developing an open economy" had been increasingly deemed as an internal demand and inevitable result as China progressively realizes modernization and the establishment of a socialist market economy system. Though self-independence is still a principle to insist on, continuous opening-up is already mainstream for China. Even in the automobile industry – which was seen as an off-limits area to foreign investment by many other developing countries – China has adopted a very welcoming attitude. In fact, nowadays domestic investment and foreign investment have an equal share in China's automobile industry. So the extent, speed and resolution of China's integration into the world economy demonstrate that China is not hostile to multinational trading systems. In past years

Table 10.5 Trade/GDP ratios of main economies, 2001 (US$ billion/%)

Rank	Economy	GDP	Merchandise trade volume	Trade/GDP ratio
1	US	9,900.7	1,911.4	19.3
2	EU	8,430.0	1,786.9	21.2
3	Japan	4,574.2	754.8	16.5
4	China	1,131.0	509.7	45.1
5	Brazil	528.5	116.5	22.0
6	India	474.3	94.4	19.9

Source: *World Development Report 2003* (World Bank, 2003); the data about EU excluding intra-EU trade comes from *International Trade Statistics 2003* (WTO, 2003).

prior to China is accession to the WTO, it had already begun to reduce tariffs and relieve its restrictions to imports and foreign investment. Therefore, the need for self-determination and the gradual opening-up policy can also be seen as the key factors that made China confident with the challenges it would face after entering the WTO.

Impact of China's accession on the WTO

While Chinese people were looking at the WTO with some doubt, the WTO and the rest of the world were also feeling excited as well as concerned about China's entry. For the WTO, China's accession meant that a new balance would be established for, as a big actor, it was thought that China would be able to significantly influence the function and development of the WTO regime. For other WTO members, China's accession will transform the current pattern of international economic competition because it will become more deeply integrated into the world economy. Therefore, China's entry will bring both opportunities and challenges for China as well as for the WTO and its current members (Lardy, 2002)

The WTO regime

There were two assumptions about China's influence on the WTO regime. One was that China would not sincerely and resolutely carry out the accession commitments and would destroy the WTO accession. It would destroy the WTO's efficiency and authority (Scott, 2000). Another supposed that China would be a troublemaker by right of being a big actor. The *Wall Street Journal* had an editorial asserting that it was reasonable to worry that Beijing's entry into the WTO might cause disruption.[6]

However, China has never acted as a troublemaker in the international community, nor has it challenged the current international regime. The Chinese government reiterated that China as a responsible country would actively perform its WTO commitments at the time of accession. What has happened in the last three years since accession has made it clear that even though abiding by WTO rules is a great challenge for all developing countries (Finger and Schuler, 2002), China has been persistently implementing its commitments as faithfully as possible which are far broader and deeper than those of other developing members. In fact, some objective western observers have also acknowledged the political sincerity and efforts of the Chinese government (Lardy, 2002). In the transitional trade policy reviews on China by the General Council, China praised for its wiliness to cooperate with the WTO regime.

China's standpoint was crucial when it attended the Cancun Ministerial as a formal member and according to statements by the government,[7] its basic goal was to promote the Doha Development Agenda. A major reason for the failure of the Cancun Ministerial was the conflict between developed and developing members. As an important member of G-21 led by Brazil and India, China's proposals were different from those of developed members. It was therefore assumed that China would lead any counterwork with developed countries in the WTO. In fact, in the Doha Round China always claimed that the needs of developing countries should be given priority, however, this does not mean that China intends to hold back the wheels of progress As a matter of fact, China shares common interests with developed countries on further trade liberalization and hopes that the WTO can find more of a balance between its developed and developing members. China's entry serves to enforce the negotiating capability of developing countries in the WTO and to help balance the structure of the WTO, however, this does not mean that it intends to drastically the WTO system. China will not prevent trade liberalization of the WTO by countries that want to actively participate in the process.

The WTO members

China's accession undoubtedly has an impact on its trading partners as well as the entire world trade (Yang, 2000). Econometrical research has been undertaken analyzing the economy-wide impact of China's accession on world economies. It was generally considered that industrialized and newly industrializing economies and developing economies directly trading with China would benefit from China's trade liberalization commitments while those Southeast Asian, South Asian and Latin American countries competing with China in the world market would be losers. As an example, Vietnam might be most hurt because it has a similar comparative advantage and export structure to China (Ianchovichina and Martin, 2002).

The US is most concerned about China's accession to the WTO because integrating China into the world trading system could impact greatly on the US economy. USITC (1999) estimated that China's tariff concession would increase American exports to China by 10 percent while American imports from China would increase by 7 percent, exacerbating the trade imbalance. However imports from China would be substituted for imports from other countries, affecting the overall trade balance of the US. China's phase-out of non-tariff barriers would further promote American export to China and liberalization in foreign investment and service industries would provide more opportunities for American companies which are competitive in those fields. Viewed over the last two years since entry, China's surplus over the US has continued to increase reaching US$42.7 billion in 2002 (52.1 percent growth) and US$58.6 billion in 2003 (37.2 percent growth). Nevertheless, the US and China had divergent explanations for the reason for this trade imbalance. Some scholars believe that it was caused by the difference between the economic structure and development level between the two countries (Feenstra *et al.*, 1998). It can be presumed that the US will constantly put pressure on China to further open its market.

In fact for the US, the most serious challenge brought by China's accession to the WTO is that China may rival the US as leader of the developing members. No doubt, China will side with developing members as a whole, and if there is any conflict between developed members and developing ones, China will stand by the latter, but its prime goal will be to protect its own national interests rather than those of the developing countries. To sustain the steady development of the WTO benefits China most. China has never intended to drastically reform the WTO system. As Jeffrey Schott from the Institute for International Economics said: "If China's goal is just to cripple and even destroy the WTO, it is illogical for China making so much effort to enter the organization."[8] Undoubtedly, developed countries headed by the US are the basis of the WTO's evolvement and rivalry would lead to the WTO existing in name only or falling apart. Moreover, for China, it is irrational to challenge the authority of the US in a power-oriented world therefore, just like in other international political and economic affairs, China will cooperate with the US in the WTO. Even though in the foreseeable future it is unlikely that China will be an ally sharing common values with the US, they certainly would not want to be enemies.

China's accession to the WTO may damage the competitive countries of Southeast Asia, which has been a concern for some time. A former Singapore Premier once warned: "The top challenges we face are whether we can take our place when so many attractive and reasonably priced Chinese products flood into the world market. China's potential economic scale is almost ten times as large as Japan. How can we compete with the industrialization and export from ten Japans after World War II?"[9] Such views are mainly generated from fear of the infinite and low-cost labor supply in China. They believe that China will squeeze all the Southeast Asian countries out of the third countries' (developed countries such as the US and Japan) markets and that China will become a black hole absorbing all the foreign investment that should belong to them. Using the CGE model, Ianchovichina and Walmsly (2003) reckon that as China becomes more competitive in the advantageous sectors, developing countries of Southeast Asia would suffer a modest decline in real GDP and welfare. But Supachai and Clifford (2001) suggested that after the accession to the WTO, China would be the engine of the regional economic development and that Southeast Asia would form a new economic order around China so that all the neighbors would benefit from it. Shafaeddin (2002) thought that because of the constriction of the commitments (such as the transition period safeguard measures), the accession to the WTO did not mean that the export potential could be fulfilled, so the fear of China's increasing exports has always been exaggerated. In terms of the conditions two years after China's accession, almost all exports to China have increased substantially (Table 10.6). In 2002, China's imports reached 295.2 billion

Table 10.6 Leading import sources of China in 2002 and 2003 (US$ billion/%)

| Source | 2002 | | | |
	Imports	Growth	Share	Change in share
Japan	53.47	25.0	18.1	0.5
EU	38.54	7.9	13.1	−1.6
Chinese Taiwan	38.06	39.2	12.9	1.7
ASEAN	31.20	34.4	10.6	1.1
Korea	28.57	22.2	9.7	0.1
US	27.23	3.9	9.2	−1.6
Hong Kong, China	10.74	14.0	3.6	−0.3
Russia	8.41	5.6	2.8	−0.5
Australia	5.85	7.8	2.0	−0.2
Canada	3.63	−10.0	1.2	−0.5
World	295.2	21.2	100.0	−

| Source | 2003 | | | |
	Imports	Growth	Share	Change in share
Japan	74.15	38.7	18.0	−0.1
EU	53.06	37.7	12.9	−0.2
Chinese Taiwan	49.36	29.7	12.0	−0.9
ASEAN	47.33	51.7	11.5	0.9
Korea	43.13	51.0	10.4	0.7
US	33.86	24.3	8.2	−1.0
Hong Kong, China	11.12	3.7	2.7	−0.9
Russia	9.73	15.7	2.4	−0.4
Australia	7.30	24.8	1.8	−0.2
Brazil	5.84	94.6	1.4	0.4
World	412.84	39.9	100.0	−

Source: Ministry of Commerce of China, mofcom.gov.cn.

dollars (an increase of 21.2 percent). In 2003, imports broke through 400 billion dollars (an increase of 39.9 percent), much more than exports for the same year (34.6 percent). Among these, the exports from developing countries to China increased much faster, especially the ASEAN countries. And the ratio of import from ASEAN to China continues to increase 2 percentage points every two years. Obviously, projections are very different from the reality, and attempts to predict China's future is a fare more complex affair.

China as vindicator and promoter of a multilateral trading system

China is a large country in its upward period, which will inevitably disturb the existing economic system. The role China plays in the WTO will be a reflection of its attitude it prefers progress as it attempts to increasingly advance its global status. Whether it will maintain the status quo or reconstitute the institution for its national interests has been a major concern (Supachai and Clifford, 2001). Without question, as a large developing country, China has considerable influence in international trade and investment. The WTO is a global organization run by members, whose institution gives its members authority to fulfill their interests and most other countries, China's accession in WTO is to realize its own interests. Historically developing countries have always been in the outermost positions of the GAWW/WTO, mainly because of their lack of strength but also because of their poor economic development strategy. Nowadays, China still falls behind comparatively, but its opening-up strategy and allows it to play a positive and effective role in the WTO. On the one hand, China will apply itself to vindicate and promote the multilateral trade system that is proposed by the WTO, while on the other hand, it will persist in establishing a more balanced economic system to aid the further development of developing countries. As a matter of fact, developing countries have taken more than two out of every three seats. In this case, only a multilateral trade system that is balanced and in favor of the economy development could function permanently and smoothly.

The multilateral trading system and China's interests

China's efforts to accede to the WTO are well known. It's hard to conceive of China joining the WTO just because the WTO needs China. As Lardy (2002) points out, China attempted to realize its interest through accession to the WTO, the same as most countries. Long Yongtu, the former chief negotiation representative of China's accession, also said that China's accession proceeds from the national interest. A much more stable international market and promotion to the national market economic reform is the dominating national interest that China gained from the accession.

However, the development of a multilateral trading system is not plain sailing. Limited by its institution and the international economic environment, the GATT/WTO is under continuous threat from trade protectionism (Bhagwati, 1991). Bergsten (2000) suggested that once the multilateral trading system stagnated, trade protectionism would become resurgent so multilateral trading should keep going forward, just like a bicycle, or it will fall over. In fact, China has always been the victim of trade protectionism. For example, the MFA has confined the production and capacity utilization of the textile industry; invidious distinctions in anti-dumping has impaired the international competitive capacity of China's advantageous industries; tariff escalation and tariff peak still hinder Chinese products from entering developed countries. Hence, vindication of the stability of the multilateral trading system and the stimulation of the multilateral trade system developing gradually conforms to China's interests.

Cooperation rather than rivalry: China's experiences

From a historical perspective of China's participation in international regimes, it can be observed that it has always been cooperative and true to its words. China's general objective is to protect its own basic interests, rather than to be leader or to transform existing systems. Some foreign scholars have even considered that China has often played a relatively negative and passive role in international institutions. Free-riding and Small-for-Big are strategies often taken by China (Johnston, 2003). Although one of the main concerns of the US is China's compliance with WTO rules, the US actually has a much worse record in terms of carrying out its international obligations. Odell and Eichengreen (1998) point out, for instance, that the US has the worst record of abiding by the WTO's dispute settlement rulings; it refused its contributions to the UN and vetoed resolutions about the Israel–Palestine issue again and again; it was convinced that unilateralism was the best course of action in the Iraqi war; and that it retreated from the Kyoto Protocol showing its ignorance of international obligations. Economy and Oksenberg (1998) highly praise Chinese leaders' wisdom while criticizing implicitly US leaders' unilateralism in world and regional affairs.

Although it is still a new member of the WTO, China's integration into the international trading and investment system took place at the same pace as its reform and opening-up. Pearson (1999) notes that China has never brought disruption to international trade and investment systems, but has always been the one to adapt. China has always appeared to be a modest learner and partner, and has not aroused other developing countries' hostility even when it became the top FDI destination. According to China's performance in the IMF and the World Bank, Jacobson and Oksenberg (1990) believe that this came about by China not challenging the world economic mechanism but adapting itself to the existing regime. However, China's complacent attitude towards Taiwan's human rights affair was quite serious, even arousing criticism from other developing countries (King, 1998). But, with economic development, China has become progressively more active in international affairs and is increasingly aware of its strengthening role in international society (Wang, 2003).

China as a bridge between developed and developing members

Multinational trade liberalization is important for China's industrialization, but an open market is essential for its economic development. All of these factors determine that China will stand by developing members and impel the WTO to be more development-oriented. On the other hand, China also has much in common with developed countries. Both developing and developed countries therefore need China's cooperation and China needs their support at the same time and because of its special status it is seen as the bridge between developed and developing countries. Supachai (2003), the WTO's first Director-General to come from a developing country, expected China to set up a connection between developing and developed members by virtue of its influence. He was convinced that China's unique position in the WTO would not only improve its own national interests but also promote the WTO's development.

China's exports after the WTO accession

Yang (2000) points out, the primary goal of China's entry is to obtain a more stable and open export environment for its rapidly increasing number of products. What has happened in the last three years shows that this goal has been achieved. Chinese exports for 2001 was $266.2 billion an increase of 6.8 percent.[10] In 2002, the year after WTO entry, exports increased to $325.6 billion with a growth rate of 22 percent. The increase in 2003 is more astonishing (37.1 percent), with export value reaching $438.4 billion. Since the reform of export drawback policy and the increase of anti-dumping legislation and other trade barriers to China's exports, by early 2004 many people began to worry about the growth of the export market. But the result is still very optimistic. The export value of 2004 exceeded $500 billion for the first time reaching $593.36 billion (double that of 2001). China's surprising export-driven expansion has seen it emerge as an important force in the world economy.

While China's export market began to quickly enlarge, other economies found it difficult to keep pace with China. Different annual growth rates have gradually altered the structure of the world merchandise export market (Table 10.7). China's share has risen from 5.6 percent in 2001 to 5.8 percent in 2003 till eventually in 2004, it exceeded Japan as the third largest merchandise exporter although Japan has made a strong recovery in recent years. This suggests that China's effect on the pattern of world trade will remain while it continues to have a voice in the WTO forum.

But it should be noticed that processing trade still accounts for more than half of total trade volume, which means higher exports must be accompanied by higher imports. Factually, the growth of imports in recent years is higher than that of export. For instance, in 2004 China's exports rose by 35.4 percent while the imports went up by 36 percent. This means the rest of the world also benefitted from China's rapid growth. Meanwhile, foreign investment enterprises have become the main force of trade. In 2004, FIEs exported $338.6 billion which accounted for 57 percent of total exports. So China's performance is closely linked to that of other countries in the world and its development benefits both China and its economic and trading partners.

Table 10.7 Top four merchandise exporters between 2001–2004 (US$ billion/%)

Economy 2001			2002			2003			2004		
	Value	Annual percentage change	Share	Value	Annual percentage change	Share	Value	Annual percentage change	Share	Value	Annual percentage change	Share
EU15	874.1	0	18.4	939.8	6	19	1,105.3	17	14.7	n.a.	n.a.	n.a.
US	730.8	−6	15.4	693.9	−5	14	723.8	4	9.6	807.6	13.3	n.a.
Japan	403.5	−16	8.5	416.7	3	8.4	471.8	13	6.3	565.1	20.3	n.a.
China	266.2	7	5.6	325.6	22	6.6	437.9	34	5.8	593.4	35.4	n.a.

Sources: WTO, International Trade Statistics (WTO, 2002–2004); the Japanese data of 2004 comes from the JETRO; the Chinese data of 2004 comes from the Ministry of Commerce; the US data of 2004 from US Department of Commerce.

Conclusion

China's accession was one of the most important events in the history of the WTO. As the largest developing member, China's entry changed the existing political structure of the WTO. What position and role China chooses and plays in the WTO becomes a crucial issue for its members.

China's position and role in the WTO depends on its own national interests, not simply its developmental status. China is undoubtedly a developing country because of its fairly low GNP per capita and because developing and developed countries have different standpoints on trade liberalization, China shares many viewpoints with developing countries. China has been integrating into the world economy on her own initiative for over 20 years and further trade liberalization is seen as a necessity rather than a burden for China.

So, China's entry may not have negative effects on the WTO but make it more dynamic and balanced. On the one hand, China will cooperate with developed members to encourage multilateral trade liberalization. China will not challenge the existing power structure dominated by the US in the WTO because it is not strong enough, and more importantly, it has many common interests with the US. On the other hand, China will support developing members by drawing more attention on their interests in the WTO. Besides, China's success in economic reform and opening-up will encourage other developing countries to follow suit, which must be good news for the WTO and the US.

Based on China's current development level, trade strategy and trade, we can conclude that China will comply with the multilateral trading system and cooperate with developed members. China is willing to bridge the gap between developed and developing countries and capable of playing the role of vindicator and promoter of the WTO.

Notes

1 See *Symposium of China's GDP statistics* in Jingjixue jikan (*China Economic Quarterly*), vol. 2, No. 1, 2002.
2 Zhongguo yu baguo jituan de weimiao guanxi (The delicate relation between China and G-8), *Singapore United Morning Daily*, 27 May 2003.
3 See 2003 guomin jingji he shehui fazhan tongji gongbao (Statistical gazette of national economy and social development 2003), China State Statistics Bureau.
4 UNCTAD (2003), *World Investment Report 2003*. Table 1.2.
5 The Ministry of Commerce, http://www.fdi.gov.cn/common/info.jsp?id.
6 See Lardy (2002), p. 195.
7 Former Minister of Commerce Shi Guangsheng's speech at International Symposium on the WTO and China 2003 and Then-Minister of Commerce Lu Fuyuan's speech at Cancun Ministerial shows this point. See the WTO Tribune No. 10 and No. 10, 2003.
8 Quoted from Zhang (2002), p. 114.
9 Quoted from Supachai and Clifford (2001), p. 105.

10 Unless specialized, all data about China's trade value come from the website of China's Ministry of Commerce.

References

Bergsten, C. Fred (2000) "Fifty Years of the GATT/WTO: Lessons from the Past for Strategies for the Future," in WTO Secretariat (ed.), *From GATT to WTO: The Multilateral Trading System in the New Millennium*. The Hague: Kluwer Law International.

Bhagwati, Jagdish (1991) *The World Trading System in Risk* (in Chinese), Beijing: Commercial Press 1996.

Bhagwati, Jagdish (2000) "Fifty Years: Looking Back, Looking Forward," in WTO Secretariat (ed.), *From GATT to WTO: The Multilateral Trading System in the New Millennium*, The Hague: Kluwer Law International.

Economy, Elizabeth and Michel Oksenberg (eds) (1998) *China's Integration into the World: Progress and Prospects* (in Chinese), Beijing: Xinhua Press.

Feenstra, Robert C. *et al.* (1998) "Trade imbalance between China and the U.S.: Scale and determinants," China Center for Economic Research of Peking University, working paper No. C1998009.

Finger, J. Michael and Philip Schuler (2002) "Implementation of WTO Commitment: The Development Challenge," In Hoekman, Mattoo, and English (eds), *Development, Trade, and WTO: A Handbook*. Washington, DC: The World Bank.

Huefbauer, Garry (1998) "China's role in the world economy," in Fredrick M. Abbott (eds), *China in the World Trading System* (in Chinese), Beijing: Law Press.

Ianchovichina, Elena and Will Martin (2002) *Economic Impacts of China's Accession to WTO*. Paper presented to conference on China's Accession to WTO, Policy Reform and Poverty Reduction, Beijing, June 28–29, 2002.

Ianchovichina, Elena and Terrie Walmsley (2003) "Impact of China's Accession on East Asia," *World Bank Policy Research Paper 3109*. Washington, DC: The World Bank.

Jacobson, Harold K. and Michel Oksenberg (1990) *China's Participation in the IMF, the World Bank, and GATT: Toward a Global Economic Order*, Ann Arbor: The University of Michigan Press.

Johnston, A.I. (2003) "China and international regimes: from an outside perspective," in Wang Yizhou (ed.), *The Relations between China and International Organizations* (in Chinese), Beijing: China Development Publishers.

Khor, Martin (2002) *Multilateral Trading System: Future Development*, Pinang, Malaysia: Third World Network.

King, Samuel (1998) "China and the United Nations," in Economy, Elizabeth and Michel Oksenberg (eds), *China Joins the World: Progress and Prospects*, Beijing: Xinhua Press.

Lardy, Nicholas (2002) *China in the World Economy* (in Chinese), Beijing: Economic Science Press.

Li, Yuefen (2002) *China's Accession to WTO: Exaggerated Fears?* UNCTAD Discussion Papers No. 165.

Lin Yifu, Cai Fang, and Li Zhou (1999) *China's Miracle: Development Strategy and Economic Reform* (in Chinese), Shanghai: Shanghai Sanlian Publisher.

Odell, John and Barry Eichengreen (1998) Meiguo, "The U.S., International Trade Organization and WTO," in Anne O. Krueger (ed.), *WTO as an International Organization* (in Chinese), Shanghai: Shanghai People's Press.

Panagaria, Arvind (2000) *The Millennium Round and Developing Countries: Negotiating Strategies and Areas of Benefits*, G-24 Discussion Paper Series, New York: UNCTAD.

Pearson, M.M. (1999) "China and international trade and investment system," in Elizabeth and Michel Oksenberg (eds), *China Joins the World: Progress and Prospects* (in Chinese), Beijing: Xinhua Press 2001.

Scott, Robert E. (2000) "The highest cost of the China-WTO deal," *EPI Issue Brief No. 137*, Washington DC: Economic Policy Institute. http://epinet.org.

Shafaeddin, S.M. (2002) *The Impact of China's Accession to WTO on the Exports of Developing Countries*, Discussion Papers No. 160, New York: UNCTAD.

Sheng Bin (2002) *The Political Economy of China's Foreign Trade Policy* (in Chinese), Shanghai: Shanghai Sanlian publisher.

Srinivasan, T.N. and Suresh D. Tendulkar (2003) *Reintegrating India with the World Economy*. Washington, DC: Institute for International Economic.

Strategy Research Team of DRC (2001) *Chinese Economy in the Early 21st Century* (in Chinese), Beijing: The People's Press.

Supachai, Panitchpakdi and Mark L Clifford (2001) *China and WTO: Changing China, Changing World Trade* (in Chinese), Beijing: Mechanical Industry Press.

Supachai, Panitchpakdi (2003) *Importance and Prospect of Bringing Doha Round back into its Track* (in Chinese), WTO Tribune, No. 12, 2003.

UNCTAD (2003) *World Investment Report* 2003.

USITC (1999) *Assessment of the Economic Effects on United States of China's Accession to WTO*. Publication 3229, Washington, DC: USITC.

Wang Yizhou (2003) "Beginning multi-dimensional research on the relations between China and international organizations," in Wang Yizhou (ed.), *The Relations Between China and International Organizations* (in Chinese), Beijing: China Development Publishers.

World Bank (2001) *Global Economic Perspective 2001* (in Chinese), Beijing: China Financial and Economic Press.

World Bank (2003) *China Country Economic Memorandum: Promoting Growth with Equity* (in Chinese), Beijing: Tsinghua University Press.

WTO (2002) International Trades Statistics 2002: Geneva: World Trade Organization.

WTO (2003) International Trades Statistics 2003: Geneva: World Trade Organization.

WTO (2004) International Trades Statistics 2004: Geneva: World Trade Organization.

Yang, Yongzheng (2000) "China's WTO Accession: The Economics and Politics," *Journal of World Trade* 34 (4): 77–94.

Yu, Pingen (1997) *Trade Systems of Newly Industrializing Economies* (in Chinese), Beijing: The Commercial Press.

Zhang, Xiangchen (2001) *Political and Economic Relations between Developing Countries and WTO*, (in Chinese), Beijing: Law Press.

Zhang, Xiangchen and Liang Sun (2002) *US-China Relationship after WTO Entry: Dialogues with American Scholars* (in Chinese), Guangzhou: Guangdong People's Press.

11 Policy traps and the linkage between China's financial and foreign exchange systems

Thomas F. Cargill, Federico Guerrero, and Elliott Parker

Introduction

In the past quarter of a century, China has made rapid and significant progress towards becoming an important part of the world economy. With a quarter of the world's population, China now produces at least 3.5 percent of the world's GDP, which makes it the world's sixth largest economy.[1] In its drive for growth, China has followed a development strategy that was previously charted by some of its Asian neighbors, particularly Japan and South Korea. Like South Korea (hereafter, Korea) before the 1990s, China exhibits many of the features of the early postwar Japanese financial regime (Cargill and Parker, 2001), and China shares an export orientation that is helped by a fixed and, many perceive, undervalued exchange rate. As a result, China now accounts for almost 5 percent of the world's exports. China's recent admission to the World Trade Organization (WTO) and its rapid growth record suggest its economic importance will only continue to increase.

One manifestation of China's development strategy is the increasing conflict over trade imbalances between China and the US, reminiscent of the conflicts in the past with Korea and Japan. Though China purchases less than 4 percent of US exports, it provides 11 percent of US imports and accounts for 20 percent of the US trade deficit.[2] As Figure 11.1 demonstrates, the US bilateral trade deficit with China has been steadily growing as a share of GDP. In the past year, China has overtaken Japan to become the third largest exporter to the US, behind Canada and Mexico, and together these three economies account for over half of US imports. In some specific labor-intensive sectors such as toys and textiles, China is a dominant player, and China has even begun to make inroads into some high-tech sectors and in services.

China is thus increasingly blamed for the rising US current account deficit, which reached $500 billion in 2002 and is currently projected to exceed that amount in 2003 (though economists tend to argue that this deficit may be better explained by the rising fiscal deficits of the US federal government and a falling rate of domestic private savings). China

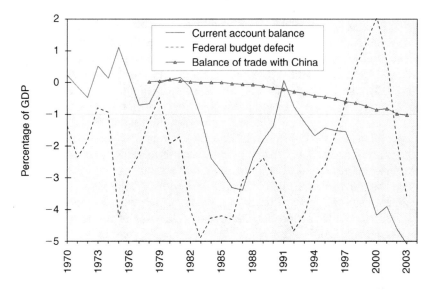

Figure 11.1 US current account balance (relative to bilateral trade balance with China and the federal budget deficit) (source: US Bureau of Economic Analysis; data for 2003 is estimated).

is also being blamed for the decline of 2.5 million jobs (or 16 percent) in the US manufacturing sector between 2000 and 2003.[3] Of course, Japan, France, Norway, Switzerland, and Canada, among other nations, continue to run equal or larger overall current account surpluses than China; yet China is also a net recipient of capital inflows and was the largest accumulator of foreign reserve assets in the world in both 2001 ($47 billion) and 2002 ($75 billion).

In this chapter, we argue that China's financial structure and its export orientation are both connected to its gradual transition from a reliance on socialist institutions and state-owned enterprises, but that its experience also mirrors some of the past experiences of Japan and Korea. China is a financially repressed economy with a high savings rate, and like Japan's *keiretsu* and Korea's *chaebol*, China's large firms have had privileged access to bank lending, which has in turn created a *vicious* policy trap of forgiveness, forbearance, inefficient investment, and bad debt. Like Japan before the 1970s and Korea before the 1990s, China has a fixed and under-valued exchange rate regime with a largely closed capital account, resulting in current account surpluses, rapid growth, and the accumulation of foreign exchange reserves. We argue in this chapter that this development strategy creates policy traps which make it difficult for the government to change policies; the financial system creates a *vicious* trap, while the exchange rate regime creates a *virtuous* trap that provides the government with both the opportunity to address the problems of the financial system as well as a means of delaying meaningful reform.

This chapter consists of five sections. In the next section we review the experiences of Japan and South Korea to draw lessons for economic policy in China. That is, we show how their financial and trade strategies created policy traps, and how this led to an "accident waiting to happen" scenario, particularly once they began financial liberalization. Then we review China's economic reforms that commenced in the early 1970s and focus on the problems created by the relationship between the state-owned enterprises and the banking sector. The next section reviews China's exchange rate regime and consider the implications of an undervalued yuan, and we argue that undervaluation combined with other export-led policies has created a virtuous policy trap that makes significant change unlikely in the near future. We then discuss general principles of shifting to a regime of capital account convertibility and apply those principles to China. We argue that if China is to avoid the "accident waiting to happen," in the best interest of both China and the world economy, then external liberalization is not desirable until the non-performing loan and state-owned enterprise problems are resolved, both of which will require significant changes in China's corporate governance structure and a transitional increase in unemployment. The final section closes the chapter by drawing together the main points on both the policy dilemma faced by Chinese policy makers and specific policy recommendations to prevent the type of economic and financial distress experienced by other Asian economies in the 1990s.

Lessons from Japan and Korea

China's emphasis on export-led growth and an exchange rate regime that intentionally or unintentionally encourages exports while limiting capital flows is a strategy that follows a well-established development pattern of other Asian economics. This strategy was considered successful through the early 1990s. In both Japan and Korea, for example, this development strategy was supported by a rigidly regulated and administratively controlled financial sector and central bank policy focused on exchange rate objectives. Both of these countries eventually embarked on a path of financial liberalization and exchange rate liberalization, to varying degrees, at different points in time, for different reasons, and with different policy outcomes. During the periods where one could reasonably regard the won and yen as undervalued because of either fixed exchange rates and or heavy intervention (Korea, 1960s to early 1990s and Japan, 1949 to 1973), Korea and Japan exhibited impressive growth, as Figure 11.2 demonstrates. Japan was regarded as "Asia's Giant" and Korea was "Asia's Next Giant." China appears to be following the same strategy. In the first 25 years after their rapid growth began, both Japan and Korea

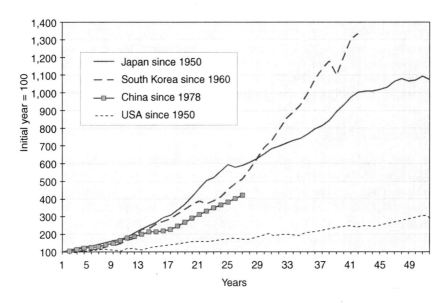

Figure 11.2 Rising per-capita GDP in China, Japan, Korea and the US (each relative to base year).

increased their per-capita GDP six fold; China's growth, however impressive, has only increased per-capita GDP four fold.

Significant differences exist. Neither Korea nor Japan were concerned with the particular problems of maintaining the legitimacy and political power of the Communist Party. While Korea lagged in democratic reforms, both countries now possess functioning democratic governments. In contrast, China's development agenda is as much political as it is economic, and the economic objectives are themselves a means to a political end that is something less than a functioning democracy. Both Korea and Japan were also able to sustain economic growth for several decades without significant unemployment; in contrast, despite China's rapid real GDP growth, there is a serious unemployment problem because the more efficient and dynamic urban centers cannot absorb the increasing number of workers leaving the agricultural sector and because of the decline in employment in the state-owned enterprises (SOEs).

The differences, though important, do not reduce the lessons that China can learn from the experiences of Korea and Japan with export-led economic growth development strategies. Korea and Japan show that under-valued exchange rates and other export-led strategies are beneficial to developing economies only to the extent they utilize the time to establish a transparent and competitive domestic financial system, establish a regulatory framework that limits deposit guarantees and deals with any existing non-performing loans (NPLs), non-performing borrowers, and insolvent financial institutions. This is the virtuous aspect of the policy. Only until these conditions are satisfied can a country seriously consider allowing its currency to become market sensitive. Unfortunately, there is a temptation to postpone these reforms and either postpone external liberalization or permit external liberalization in the context of a weak domestic financial structure. This is the vicious phase of the policy.

Lessons from Japan

In 1949, the Dodge Line established the exchange rate of 360 yen to the dollar, which Japan adhered to until 1971 when the Bretton Woods fixed-exchange rate regime began to unravel. By the 1960s, this yen rate was generally regarded as significantly undervalued because of Japanese productivity growth and the completion of the reindustrialization process,[4] and there is little doubt that it played a major role in Japan's reindustrialization success and emergence by 1975 as the world's second largest economy. These achievements, however, had a price. The rapid growth of the Japanese economy from 1950 to the early 1970s permitted Japan to maintain an inherently inefficient financial system with pervasive deposit guarantees unsuitable for a more liberated external environment.

Japan thus had good reason to resist revaluation of the yen against the dollar, even after President Nixon's 1971 announcement that the "gold window" was closed. Dunn (1973) argues that both Japan and Germany, another country at the time with an undervalued currency and persistent current account surpluses, had powerful political coalitions supporting the exchange rate regime, and significant capital investments in export sectors. Japan also had accumulated significant foreign exchange reserves, mostly in dollars, which presaged a significant fiscal loss once the dollar was devalued. Though Japan was the last major country to admit that the Bretton Woods system had failed, by 1973 the yen appreciated to 260 per dollar, which many analysts consider to have been its parity value at the time.

After the yen floated, financial liberalization became official policy in Japan, and financial liberalization from 1976 to 1989 was gradual, incremental, and administratively directed. By 1989, Japan had achieved progress when judged against the pre-liberalization structure and the absence of the type of financial disruptions exhibited by the US and Scandinavian countries. Loan rates and large deposit interest rates were liberalized, with complete liberalization achieved by 1994. Short- and long-term capital flows were relaxed and foreign financial institutions were permitted a small, but significant, presence in the domestic system, mainly in the securities market. Corporate flow of fund patterns reflected enhanced reliance on money and capital markets, both domestic and international, and reduced reliance on bank finance. Short and long-term capital flows became increasingly liberalized until 1997, when the yen was completely liberalized. These changes initiated the unraveling in the *keiretsu* relationship between large businesses and banks or main bank system. Households had greater access to consumer and mortgage credit, and there was generally more competition between markets and securities companies.

These changes, however, paled in comparison to the reforms that would be required to render Japan's financial system compatible with the new economic, technological, and political environment that favored more open and competitive financial regimes. Japan's macroeconomic performance and growing export sector masked the underlying problems through the mid-1980s. The macroeconomic environment, however, began to unravel in the second half of the 1980s. In 1986, Japan entered into a period now referred to as the "bubble economy." Real GDP grew around 4–6 percent per year, inflation was low and steady, and Japan appeared to have achieved financial liberalization progress without any of the disruptions experienced by many other industrial countries. At the same time, equity and land prices increased beyond underlying economic fundamentals. The increase in asset prices in 1985 and 1986 could be justified by fundamentals, but after 1986, asset price inflation took on all of the characteristics of a speculative bubble. The asset inflation can be traced to two factors: an easy Bank of Japan policy after 1985 and structural characteristics of the banking system rooted in the pre-liberalization financial regime.

The collapse in equity and land prices in 1991 and 1992 was initiated by the Bank of Japan in May 1989 and brought an end to Japan's impressive postwar economic and financial performance. Japan's "burst of the bubble economy" period commenced. Japan permitted banks to accumulate NPLs, resisted closing large banks, and resisted policies that would increase the number of bankruptcies in the real sector. As a result, the economic and financial distress continued to accumulate after 1990 which the result that in 1998, Japan came close to collapse manifested by negative real GDP growth and deflation, and continues to struggle through an extended "lost decade."

The basic lesson from Japan is that rapid export-led GDP growth can mask serious financial distress, provide a basis for forgiveness and forbearance policies in dealing with the financial distress, and provide a false sense of security to regulatory authorities and foreign investors about the stability of the financial system. As time passes, the system becomes more susceptible to a shock, which in Japan's case came in the form of a sudden collapse of asset prices. Japan did not, however, experience a sharp fall in the yen due to the large accumulation of international reserve assets, the larger role the yen played as an international reserve and transactions asset, the less-intense political problems of a hostile country just 30 miles away from the country's capital, and the lack of external debt. Unlike Korea, Japan had neither a significant external debt nor a large NPL problem at the start of the collapse. These factors have made it possible for Japan to postpone reform and engage in a forgiveness and forbearance policy. Yet Japan's economic and financial distress continues through 2003, while Korea recovered from its economic collapse in late 1997 in less than two years. Indeed, Japan's economy appears to have begun a recovery in the second half of 2003 and while recovery continues as of mid-2004, the recovery is narrowly based on exports and dependent on China's growth.

Lessons from Korea

Like China and Japan, Korea followed an export-oriented development strategy that relied for several decades on a currency that was thought to be undervalued in real terms, and Korea also created a state-owned banking system that devoted its lending to large, government-favored firms. Korea thus illustrates the case where a troubled financial system was permitted to remain in place for over two decades, but rapid GDP growth led by exports masked the financial distress until the 1990s. Despite a growing NPL problem starting in the early 1970s, Korea was able to procure considerable external lending. Rapid GDP growth, and projections that Korea would be Asia's next giant after Japan, supported confidence among foreign investors that Korea would be able to generate the income to service the debt.

Korean economic and financial development from the end of the Korean War through the 1970s was uneven and unstable at times, but overall, Korea's growth was impressive. Korea's financial reforms[5] started in the early 1980s in response to poor macroeconomic performance attributed to inefficient government influence over the allocation of resources in both the real and financial sectors, especially in the chemical and heavy industrial sectors. Liberalization proceeded in two stages: first, policy from 1981 to 1988 focused on improving macroeconomic performance, and second, once macroeconomic performance improved, policy was directed towards liberalization of the real and financial sectors.

Though financial liberalization became official policy and some changes were enacted, the pace of reform prior to 1997 was slow and often more rhetoric than substance. What achievements were made were often in response to outside pressure from the US, the World Bank, and the OECD as the price of reducing tensions over trade imbalances and/or to gain admittance to the OECD in 1995. Despite a number of institutional changes, such as denationalization of the banking system in the early 1980s, initiation of interest deregulation in 1988, and further interest rate deregulation policies in 1991–1992 designed to completely phase out interest rate ceilings by 1997,[6] the pace of liberalization was incomplete and flawed. Denationalization was incomplete, for example, because the Ministry of Finance and Economy continued to play a heavy role in bank decisions and liberalization was flawed because the implicit deposit guarantees and no-failure policy of large institutions remained in place thus enhancing moral hazard incentives. The most serious flaw was pursuing liberalization without addressing the NPL problem estimated at 10 to 20 percent of total loans that had been embedded in the banking system since the early 1970s.[7] Despite denationalization, the Ministry of Finance and Economy continued to influence bank operations ranging from credit allocation policies to management promotions with predictable results. The banking system for all practical purposes was regarded as a guaranteed and passive source of low cost funds to the *chaebol*.

By the early 1990s, however, many observers warned that Korea's financial structure was weak and the won susceptible to rapid depreciation if foreign investors changed their views on Korea's ability to service its debt. Any sharp depreciation would exacerbate the external loan problem. The shock came from internal and external sources. In 1996 and 1997, Korea's macroeconomic performance slowed. GDP growth slowed from 8.9 to 7.1 percent in 1996 and to 5.5 percent in 1997. Regulatory authorities paid insufficient attention to the degree banks and non-bank institutions were dependent on foreign borrowing and to the increasing financial weakness of major *chaebol*. The economic and financial distress intensified as the Asian financial crisis (AFC) spread and uncertainty surrounded both the presidential election of Kim Dae-jung in late 1997 and the subsequent lame duck period of his predecessor. The won depreciated rapidly in the face of increasing capital flight and recognition that the Bank of Korea's international reserve assets were insufficient to prevent a major depreciation. Korea came close to a complete economic and financial collapse by the end of 1997 and was forced to seek the assistance of the IMF with the promise of an austerity program to prevent further won depreciation and a promise to accelerate reform in the financial system, corporate governance, and the *chaebol*.

The new reform process has proceeded on a broad front and macroeconomic activity recovered after 1999. Korea moved aggressively to deal with the weak banking system by essentially nationalizing many banks, however, reform of corporate governance and labor union activity has been much slower. In addition, the political situation with North Korea has worsened adding a new dimension to the reform of the Korean economy.

The basic lesson from Korea is that rapid export-led GDP growth can mask serious financial distress in the form of large amounts of NPLs, provide a basis for forgiveness and forbearance policies in dealing with the financial distress, and provide a false sense of security to regulatory authorities and foreign investors about the stability of the financial system. As time passes, the system becomes more susceptible to a shock and in the case of Korea, increasingly an "accident waiting to happen."

China's economic development strategy since 1972

When Nixon went to China in 1972, China was a closed, mostly rural society run by a Chinese Communist Party (CCP) obsessed with socialist ideology. Industrial output was generally produced by SOEs, and was growing rapidly due to high investment rates of 30 percent or more channeled through investment grants from the state-owned banking system and directed by a centralized planning system that never quite achieved the degree of control seen in the Soviet Union. Outside of the state banking system, the economy was largely non-monetized, as rural areas were self-sufficient (other than providing cheap food for urban workers), markets were absent, rationing was widespread, and state-owned firms tended to be large and autarkic.

After the death of Chairman Mao Zedong in 1976, and the ascendancy of Deng Xiaoping as the paramount leader of the CCP by the end of 1978, China began to slowly reform its economy. The reforms initiated a process of significant transition for China's economic institutions, often in directions that were not always anticipated. In the following discussion, we focus on four aspects of the transition: (i) the changing objectives of economic reform; (ii) the emerging problems of the SOEs and the state banking system; (iii) the emergence of unemployment, NPL problems, and conflicts for central bank policy; and (iv) the monetization of transactions in the context of relatively undeveloped money and capital markets.

Economic reform and changing objectives

Naughton (1995) divides China's reform process into three distinct stages. The first "bird in the cage" stage, to cite Chen Yun's famous axiom, began with an effort to shift from ideological to practical economic thinking, decollectivization of the agricultural sector, permitting rural markets in agricultural products, and a small degree of internationalization. The policy of rapprochement with the west encouraged participation in international organizations, study abroad, and tourism as well as international trade and investment. Special economic zones and policies allowing minority foreign ownership in joint ventures were implemented to attract foreign direct investment (FDI), technology, and management.

The second stage of reform followed in the mid-1980s under the direction of Zhao Ziyang, and attempted to extend these reforms to the SOEs, including the state-owned banking sector. A major objective was to force both the state-owned banks and their state-owned borrowers to rely on bank loans rather than government grants in order to generate a more efficient allocation of resources. Despite these reforms, the CCP continued to view economic reform as a temporary stage on the road to socialism and full communism. The Tian'anmen demonstrations of 1989 put a halt to the reform process and forced Zhao from power, and conservatives in the

CCP began a three-year period of retrenchment. Efforts to scale back reform created more problems for the CCP leadership than it solved, and the leadership eventually chose to abandon the socialist goals through the traditional route of control and state planning. In 1993, the CCP instead announced a new objective of creating a "Socialist Market Economy." That is, the goals of socialism could be achieved with market forces and internationalization. Parker (1995) argued that the party thus came to rely on its economic management and the nation's economic performance for its legitimacy, rather than its adherence to the thought of Marx, Engels, Lenin, and Mao. The success indicators of this new policy included high growth, low inflation, low unemployment, and social stability.

Among the many reforms that followed in this third stage, the official exchange rate was unified and devalued to match the black market rate and further efforts were made to improve the performance of SOEs. Exports became increasingly important to the government as a means to achieve this performance, particularly in light of the export-driven growth of Japan, South Korea, Taiwan, and other countries in the region. Because the banking sector remained inefficient and largely tied to propping up the declining and inefficient SOEs, China came to rely on FDI for funding the production of a large portion of these exports.

State enterprises and the state banks

Initial reforms in the foreign trade sector were targeted at improving the incentive to export in SOEs (Lardy, 2002). However, by the end of the 1980s it was clear that these reforms were not very successful, and SOEs were beginning to face real competition. Most of China's rapid export growth was in the non-state sector, from new rural township and village enterprises often funded with overseas Chinese funds, and from joint ventures between Chinese and foreign enterprises. By the early 1990s, private enterprises and firms fully funded with foreign investment were legal and increasingly common. The non-state-owned enterprises continue to account for most of Chinese exports.

Not only were the traditional SOEs not responsible for China's export growth, but they were declining in profitability and market share. In 1978, SOEs accounted for almost 80 percent of Chinese industrial output (the remainder was produced by small quasi-state firms called urban collectively-owned enterprises). By 2002, the non-state sector accounted for 75 percent of industrial output and half of industrial employment.

The reasons for this decline are still under debate, but considerable evidence has accumulated that SOEs are significantly less efficient than non-stated-owned enterprises (Zhang, Zhang and Zhao, 2003). In the 1980s, state firms improved their average total factor productivity at very respectable rates, but the non-state sector improved faster. The Chinese economy became increasingly competitive, but for state-owned firms this meant a loss of monopoly power along with falling relative output prices and rising wages. State-owned firms were more likely to bear a high social cost burden in providing housing, schools, medical care, and retirement to their workers, while non-state firms typically employed younger employees and lacked the historical obligations to provide support beyond wages. State-owned firms had less incentive to be efficient since they had soft budget constraints and the lack of effective bankruptcy policies until the 1990s which led in turn to the accumulation over time of vast disparities in performance and significant inefficiencies.

However, SOEs continued to receive the major share of capital investment. Prior to economic reforms in the 1980s, the primary source of investment for state firms was in the form of grants from the state budget, and in return, profits were delivered to the state as the primary source of government revenue. In the industrial reforms that followed the strategy of the agricultural sector's household responsibility system, firms were allowed to keep an increasing share of their own profits for self-investment and bonuses, and investment grants were gradually replaced by loans from the state-owned banking sector. As the Chinese savings rate grew in response to the opportunities now afforded by economic reform, the relative size of the government's budget declined. The result, however, was rapidly rising borrowing, high investment rates, and falling rates of return. In one sample of large state-owned industrial firms, Parker (1999) estimated that the marginal product of capital declined steeply throughout the 1980s, and became negative by 1992. Other studies have found similar results. The state-banking system played an important support role by providing credit to these inefficient state-owed enterprises. Jefferson (2001) suggested that banks served as an unsupervised "commons" for state enterprises, with predictably "tragic" results.

Efforts were made to reform the banking system to address the lending problems. In the 1980s, China's monobank was divided into four large banks: the Bank of China, the Agricultural Bank of China, the Industrial and Commercial Bank of China, and the Construction Bank of China. These four banks were given different missions and placed under the administration of the People's Bank of China, which in turn became China's central bank and chief banking regulator. In the 1994 reforms which followed the Party's announcement of the Socialist Market Economy, the state banking sector was divided into commercial and policy banks, with the goal of having the commercial operations become market-driven and financially sound.

Despite these institutional changes, the state banking sector continued to focus its lending on the older SOEs, many of which were relatively inefficient, increasingly unprofitable, and often insolvent. Brandt and Li (2003) find evidence that this discrimination against non-SOEs forced the growing private sector into more expensive forms of credit. By the early 1990s, the investment hunger of state firms led the government to look for new sources of funding outside of the banking sector.

The creation of the Shanghai and Shenzhen stock markets coincided with the early plans to create a Socialist Market Economy. Government restrictions on which firms could offer stock, however, effectively prevented non-state firms from entering the market. Instead, larger and more successful traditional SOEs recreated themselves as holding companies and spun off the relatively profitable portions of their operations using corporate structures with limited liability but continued to maintain effective state control through majority ownership. Though non-state firms have now been allowed to participate in the stock markets, 95 percent of all firms listed on the two stock exchanges continue to be majority controlled by the state and its sanctioned agencies.

Emerging problems in the financial sector

These and many other efforts at reform attempted to improve the incentives of state enterprises and force harder budget constraints on them. Time and again, these efforts were frustrated, and by the end of the presidency of Jiang Zemin, the government announced a policy of *jua da, fang xia*o (release the small, retain the large), pushing for the creation of a relatively small number of large, *chaebol*-like state firms and the elimination or privatization of most of the remainder. Between 1997 and 1998 alone, the number of state-owned firms dropped by over 40 percent, while the number of foreign-invested, private, and joint-venture firms rose dramatically (Jefferson, 2001). As the smaller state firms were gradually dismantled or converted into new forms of ownership, it was hoped the new, mostly export-oriented firms would take up the slack in the labor force. Estimates of the number of workers in SOEs who lost their jobs by 1999 ranged from 30 to 50 million. China's official urban unemployment rate has generally remained below 5 percent – about seven million people – though official sources also said that up to 24 million urban job seekers would be disappointed in 2003. Of course, this figure excludes the many millions of rural workers who migrate to urban areas in search of jobs; one source noted that the government expected the number of surplus rural workers to reach 100 million people (CIIC, 2002).

The inefficient SOEs and the lack of effective credit evaluation and monitoring by the state-banking system have generated an enormous bad debt problem that shows no signs of being resolved in the near future. While official reports place the NPL ratio at an enormous figure of around 25 percent of loans, other estimates suggest that it may be closer to 40 percent. In the absence of the implicit state guarantee, the four major state banks are insolvent under any reasonable independent accounting system. The problem has serious implications for monetary policy. In the mid-1990s, monetary policy was required to restrain bank lending to reduce inflationary pressures, while simultaneously providing funds to prevent a worsening of bad debt problems. This generates a conflict between the central bank and the state banks, which find they can improve the bad debt ratio in the short run through new lending, even if that new lending may eventually lead to more bad debts.

Yet the state banking sector has continued to benefit from rising money demand, which has led to rapidly rising deposits due to the state's implicit guarantees and the lack of real alternatives to the state banks. Economic development has led to an increasing monetization of transactions between firms, high savings rates to finance large consumer purchases and self-investment, and the development of new financial assets and services. At the end of the Maoist period of self-reliance and limited markets, currency in circulation was about 6 percent of GDP. By 1984, after the first stage of reform, this ratio almost doubled as more goods became available, bank savings became less politically risky, rural markets expanded, and the absence of consumer credit led to a rapidly rising personal savings rate. China began reporting its M2 money stock in 1984, which at the time added up to about half of its GDP. As China's economy increasingly relied on market processes, real money demand continued to grow, primarily in the form of bank deposits. While currency in circulation has stabilized at about 16 percent of GDP, M2 grew rapidly with China's market development: by 1993, it was equal to GDP, and by 2002 it rose to a ratio of 174 percent of GDP. In the 17 years from 1984 to 2002, the total nominal Chinese M2 money stock grew 50-fold, an annual growth rate of over 25 percent. This is demonstrated in Figure 11.3, which also includes the ratios

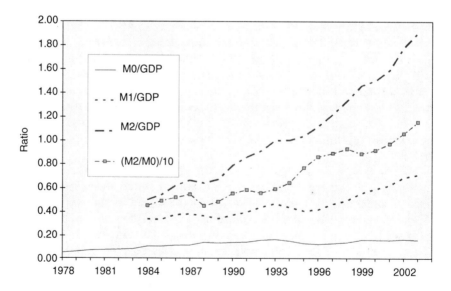

Figure 11.3 China's money ratios (source: People's Bank of China; data for 2003 is as of September).

for M1 (currency and demand deposits) and M0 (currency) as well as the M2/M0 ratio (since the monetary base is unavailable). This rapid increase in money demand made it possible for China's government to use the banking sector to finance both its own budget deficit and the credit demand of its own enterprises without a corresponding increase in the rate of price inflation. Yet while M2 monetization has been significant, other financial instruments are still underdeveloped.

China's exports and its exchange rate regime

Chinese exports in the last decade appear to have had a significant effect on economic growth, not only through aggregate demand and comparative advantage, but also through technology transfer and spillovers (Liu, 2002; Tseng and Zebregs, 2002). Zhang (1999) provides evidence that FDI inflows in China (and several other Asian economies) were significantly correlated with long-run growth. By the early 1990s, the export sector was relying primarily on FDI for funding rather than the domestic state-owned commercial banks (Huang, 1995), in spite of a domestic savings rate of almost 40 percent primarily channeled into the banking system, and foreign affiliates produced almost half of China's exports (Zhang and Song, 2000). Zhang and Felmingham (2001) find evidence of bidirectional causality between exports and inward FDI in China, particularly in provinces that receive relatively more, while Liu, Wang, and Wei (2001) find evidence of a virtuous cycle in which more imports lead to inward FDI, which leads to more exports, which leads to more imports.

As a result, Chinese leaders have come to see the export sector as the solution to China's looming unemployment problems, as millions of urban workers are released from inefficient SOEs. This export sector has come to rely heavily on FDI, particularly from the economies of the "greater China" sphere, e.g. Taiwan and Hong Kong. While FDI from the US and Western Europe is larger, Lardy (2003) points out that it is focused primarily on supplying the Chinese domestic market, a fact that helps explain why the bilateral trade deficit overstates the bilateral current account balance.

China's exchange rate regime

China's foreign exchange regime in the 1980s used what the World Bank called an "airlock" system and exports were not very responsive to changes in the real exchange rate. This situation began to change by the 1990s. Export quotas were dismantled, trade decisions were decentralized, exporters were allowed to retain increasing shares of their foreign exchange earnings, and exchange rates were unified (Lardy, 2002: 55). As a soft currency, the Chinese currency was considered significantly overvalued, and as foreign trade and tourism grew the black market increased.

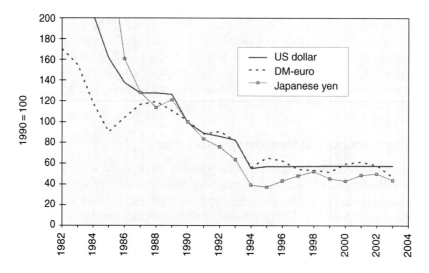

Figure 11.4 China's nominal exchange rate (source: St Louis Federal Reserve Bank, Federal Reserve Economic Data; data for 2003 is as of third quarter).

In 1980, the official exchange rate was 1.5 yuan (Renminbi) per US dollar, as Figure 11.4 shows. The yuan was gradually devalued until by 1993 the official rate fluctuated around 5.5 yuan per dollar. The real exchange rate did not fall at the same rate, since China's inflation rate exceeded that of the major economies by a significant margin by the early 1990s. In 1993 the black market rate for converting the Renminbi (RMB), the "People's money," into convertible Foreign Exchange Certificates (FEC) was roughly 1.5:1, for an equivalent rate of 8.3 RMB per dollar.

In 1994, the official exchange rate was set for all transactions to roughly 8.6 yuan (RMB) per dollar, and the FEC and other such instruments were eliminated. Overnight, the black market in changing money was virtually eliminated, though the nominal exchange rate was allowed to appreciate back to around 8.28 yuan per dollar, and rapid inflation in the mid-1990s quickly eroded some of the effects on the real exchange rate, as Figure 11.5 shows.

By 1996, the current account achieved full convertibility, though the government continued to restrict foreign exchange transactions for capital account. China's equity markets have been largely closed to foreign investors, except in the foreign-currency-denominated B-share exchanges in Shanghai and Shenzhen, though the government is now considering changing this through Qualified Foreign Institutional Investor (QFII) rules. Foreign direct investors were given promises that they could repatriate their profits, though some firms insured against this by relying on debt rather than equity to finance their investments. Throughout the 1990s,

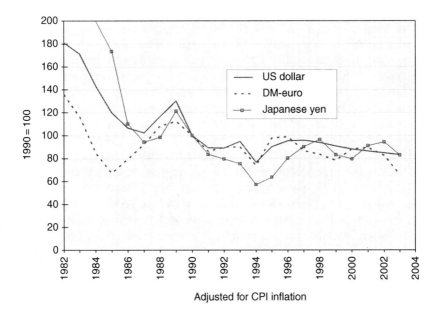

Figure 11.5 China's real exchange rate.

illicit capital flight by Chinese firms was achieved through underinvoicing exports and overinvoicing imports, among other methods (Gunter, 1996). The omissions and errors in China's balance of payments have been significant and negative, indicating a continued and significant outflow of funds into other major currencies in spite of official prohibitions and the lower exchange rate. By the late 1990s, there were reports of a resurging black market in currency transactions.

As Lin and Schramm (2003) discuss, the main goal pursued by the Chinese authorities when they devalued the yuan in 1994 was not to under-value the domestic currency, but rather to eliminate (or at least substantially mitigate) the allocative inefficiencies stemming from both overvaluation and widespread black market activity in foreign exchange. While markets regarded the devaluation as a move towards market-clearing, the lack of convertibility for capital transactions led to relatively less demand for the yuan than purchasing-power parity would indicate. In 1997, when many other Asian exporters devalued their currencies in response to their balance of payments crises, China's government stood firm in maintaining its dollar peg, much to the relief of the rest of Asia since many feared that a further competitive devaluation would set off a race to the bottom. The fact that China did not devalue their currency amid such pressures not only increased political goodwill towards China in the rest of the region, it also increased the credibility of its dollar peg for foreign and domestic investors.

The desirability of the yuan changed after 1997. A policy of disinflation by the People's Bank of China combined with increased competition led to price deflation after the AFC (Cargill and Parker, 2004). Direct foreign investments in the early 1990s began to pay off and led to rapidly expanding exports, while China's WTO accession led to improved confidence in the future for both domestic and international investors. The deflation in China led to a falling real exchange rate against the dollar, but the effects were initially disguised as the dollar rose against other currencies. Recently, however, lower interest rates in the US have helped to set off a significant drop in the US dollar against other major currencies, and the yuan fell with it; though the dollar did not depreciate against the yuan, as US exporters would have hoped, the yuan has depreciated against the euro and the yen. Firms in US import-competing sectors are frustrated that the dollar's decline is not helping them with the Chinese competition, while Japan and the Euro countries are concerned about their export sectors.

Is China beggaring its neighbors?

When President Bush met China's president Hu Jintao at the APEC summit in Bangkok during the last week of October of 2003, he was under intense pressure from manufacturers and politicians back home to persuade China to revalue its currency. Critics claimed that by keeping an undervalued yuan, China's firms are increasing their share of the world market, increasing unemployment in the US and causing a record US trade deficit. China-bashing is also popular in Japan where China is not only facing the same charges made by the US, but in addition, is blamed for causing deflation, as cheap imports of Chinese origin are said to push down prices. In the euro area, politicians and businessmen have complained that because of China's undervalued currency, the euro suffers an unfair share of the burden of dollar depreciation. This has only been exacerbated in the past months as the yuan has accompanied the dollar's slide.

Is the yuan undervalued? Undervaluation was clearly not the objective of the official exchange rate adjustment in 1994, when the exchange rate was set essentially at the black market rate. But has a policy of unintended undervaluation emerged almost ten years later? From the US perspective, of course, the growing bilateral trade deficit with China is evidence of a distorted exchange rate. Figure 11.6 demonstrates that from China's perspective this bilateral surplus has grown to over 4 percent of GDP, and now exceeds China's overall current account surplus (both because China has a current account deficit with the rest of the world and because it has a deficit in bilateral trade in services and factors with the US).

FDI has also been high for the past decade, though Wei (2000) argues that this is still low given the size of China's economy. China is now the largest recipient of FDI among the developing nations; in 2001 it received

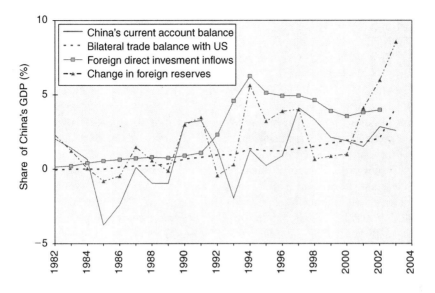

Figure 11.6 China's international transactions (sources: IMF International Financial Statistics; US Bureau of Economic Analysis; 2003 data, where available, is estimated).

$47 billion in inward FDI, over 6 percent of the world total, and in 2002 inward FDI increased to $49 billion.

Since China has borrowed relatively little from abroad and has yet to allow for significant international equity flows, China's balance of payments remains in surplus, and by the end of 2003 its holdings of foreign exchange reserves exceeded $400 billion, roughly a third of its GDP at current exchange rates. Most of this was held in US securities. This has provided a non-trivial downward pressure on short-run interest rates in the US in spite of the growing US federal budget deficit. While the interest rate spread between US securities and China's long-term borrowing (which contains a risk premium) generates a large opportunity cost for China (Kwan, 2003), the fact that China is long in dollars provides a significant disincentive for the Chinese to allow the dollar to depreciate.

The answer to the question of undervaluation also seems clear if we use the purchasing-power parity (PPP) approach. At official exchange rates China's per-capita GDP is currently almost $1,000, but if we use the World Bank's reported PPP estimates, China's per-capita GDP is almost $5,000. If accurate, this would suggest a significant undervaluation relative to the dollar, though most scholars believe that these PPP estimates are significantly overestimated, and there are many good reasons why price levels tend to be significantly lower in less developed economies (e.g. Balassa, 1964; Samuelson, 1964; Bhagwati, 1984; Kravis and Lipsey, 1983).

This argument is problematic for three reasons. First, China's currency is not fully convertible, its financial system is weak, and its banking system is essentially insolvent, so it is not clear how desirable the currency would be at PPP given the risk premium. Second, while China is running large trade surpluses with the US it is also running deficits with other Asian economies. As a result, China's overall current account surpluses are not so large, and are expected to be heading towards an overall deficit soon. Third, Zhang (1998) and others have noted that the Chinese exports are not very sensitive to changes in the real exchange rate, so it is not clear that a revaluation would reduce any remaining trade surplus.

It should also be noted that in the last five years China's imports have grown even faster than exports, so China's net demand for the goods and services of the industrial economies has increased. This pattern has accelerated recently: for example, in the period January–September 2003 exports increased by 32 percent and imports by 41 percent, a gap that when compounded over five years exceeds that prevailing in the period 1998–2003 (a period in which imports multiplied by three and exports by 2.3).

John Snow, the US Secretary of the Treasury, has suggested the Chinese currency may be undervalued by as much as 40–50 percent, but this amount can really only be supported by considering the bilateral trade relationship in isolation, and not the other elements of the current account nor China's trade with other countries. A report by the Federal Reserve Bank of Cleveland (2003) suggests skepticism of the claim that the yuan is undervalued to such a significant extent.

Lardy (2003) estimated that a 20 percent revaluation would be appropriate, while the general manager of Goldman Sachs Asia was quoted as saying the yuan was undervalued by only 10–15 percent (Interfax, 2003). According to Lardy's estimates, a revaluation of this magnitude would probably reduce China's current account surplus by $40 billion but reduce the US current account deficit by only a quarter of that, an amount so small relative to the overall US current account that it would only reduce its rate of growth. In testimony before the US Senate, Lardy even raised the possibility that if it floated the value of the yuan might even depreciate once it floats (SCMP, 2003).

What of the oft-used claim that China's artificially undervalued yuan has exported deflation to Japan? This charge can be dismissed by noting that imports from China represent only 1.5 percent of Japan's GDP; even with complete pass-through to other goods and services traded in Japan, it is implausible to suggest that Chinese imports are significantly responsible for deflation in Japan. This is not to deny that some prices have clearly fallen in Japan due to cheaper imports, but the effect is far too small to be the source of Japan's overall price deflation. The allegation can only be interpreted as an effort to divert attention away from the position that deflation is a monetary phenomenon and that the Bank of Japan's tight monetary policy is the main suspect, not China. A similar line of reasoning applies to explaining the low level of economic activity in Europe. The blame should not be placed on China, but rather on the European Central Bank for not being more aggressive in cutting interest rates.

Even in the absence of upcoming elections, blaming external sources is an argument deficit countries often allege to avoid discussing domestic factors that contribute to external imbalances. China is not the real issue, since it is not yet big enough to explain what has happened to the US economy anymore than China is responsible for Japanese deflation. The US and other industrial countries have made their own policy tradeoffs and decisions that generate external deficits. It is easier to blame China rather than to recognize US trade and current account imbalances are the result of a low overall saving rate (a fact that has recently been aggravated in the US by an overly expansionary fiscal policy that transformed a budget surplus of 1.5 percent of GDP into a budget deficit of more than 4 percent in just three years). Similarly, Japan and the European countries would be better advised to reform their own domestic systems rather than focus on China as an excuse to postpone those much needed reforms.

Vicious and virtuous policy traps

In Figure 11.7, we diagram two policy traps for the Chinese government, one vicious and one virtuous. In the first policy trap, which we find in the financial sector, the magnitude of the bad debt problem in the state-owned banks combined with concerns over urban unemployment from shutting down insolvent SOEs leads to policies which seek to delay meaningful changes in corporate governance or lending behavior. Policies of forgiveness and forbearance, protectionism and favorable regulation for large state firms, and an unwillingness to sell off state shares to truly privatize them, combined with resistance to allowing international banks to compete in the banking sector on a level playing field in spite of China's WTO commitments, all lead to a growing non-performing loan problem and a drag on economic growth.

But there is a virtuous trap too. In this scenario, which we think explains China's situation in the last three years or so, the perception that the yuan is undervalued by the market has unintended, positive, consequences which make it difficult for the government to change policies. Not only does the low price of the yuan help Chinese export growth, and thus allow for increased employment and incomes along with improved productivity from the shift of resources, but it also creates an asymmetric expectation of revaluation that provides implicit insurance for domestic and foreign investors alike. Expectations of a possible revaluation of the yuan have increased investors' willingness to hold Chinese assets despite poor projected performance in the stock market, bad loans, and a troubled banking system (Bradsher, 2003). This leads to rising FDI, which is needed

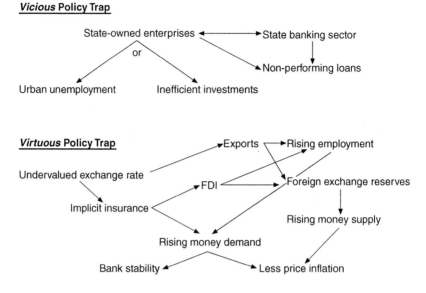

Figure 11.7 Vicious and virtuous policy traps.

to fund export growth because the banking sector devotes too much of its resources into inefficient domestic firms. Illegal capital flight turns from an outflow into an inflow, as Chinese savers and speculators alike become more willing to keep their money in yuan. Because stocks and other non-monetary asset markets are still poorly developed, money demand rises. Depositors are willing to keep their money in the big state banks, in spite of their high bad debt ratios, because of the government's implicit guarantees and the insurance that the undervalued exchange rate provides them, and the government's guarantees become more credible as their foreign exchange reserves rise.

Finally, though the accumulation of foreign reserves has led to rapid growth in the money supply (M2 money supply has grown at an annual rate of almost 15 percent since 1997, while nominal GDP has grown at an annual rate of almost 7 percent), high money demand transitorily dampened inflationary pressures: the price level has *fallen* by an average of 1 percent per year in the period 1997–2002, and as Cargill and Parker (2004) argue, lower price inflation has a further positive and marginally significant effect on money demand. This becomes a policy trap because a change in the exchange rate regime now has real and significant costs. Once the revaluation occurs, money demand may fall back and price inflation may result – even though foreign exchange accumulation would slow or reverse. Capital flight out of China may occur, inward FDI could slow, and depositors may lose some faith in the value of their yuan-denominated assets. This in turn could exacerbate the banking problem. Moreover, China's government lacks incentives to revalue the yuan, because China is now holding large amounts of US dollar-denominated securities. Much as the Bank of Japan, the Deutsche Bundesbank, and other central banks tried to prop up the dollar before the collapse of the Bretton Woods regime in 1971, China has an additional strong interest in the current valuation because the losses from a falling dollar would be significant.

The policy trap previously discussed runs contrary to Hume's famous specie-flow mechanism, and standard expectations that a surplus in the balance of payments will quickly result in inflation. It did not happen quickly, but eventually the standard adjustment mechanism occurred; as of December 2003, inflation, which was dormant for most of the year, reached the 6 percent *monthly* rate. The sudden appearance of price inflation coupled with a credit boom (bank credit grew by 21 percent in the year to the first quarter of 2004) and other signs pointing to an overheated economy (GDP growth of almost 10 percent and investment growth of more than 40 percent in the year to the first quarter of 2004) triggered concerns about a possible hard landing.

The way forward

As in Japan and Korea, the Chinese financial regime has created a vicious policy trap that makes it difficult to implement significant financial liberalization and address the corporate governance issues that were created as a legacy of China's socialist past. But China has also followed, however unintentionally, an exchange rate regime that has recreated the strategy followed by Japan and Korea in their initial decades of postwar development, and in China's case at least this has created another (virtuous) policy trap. This virtuous policy trap has temporarily addressed some of the problems created by the financial regime, and as a result of this and other factors it now provides China's leadership with two choices. First, the government can continue to rely on this mechanism and delay much needed reforms. Second, the government can use the opportunity provided by the current situation to address long-standing problems and begin the process of real reform in domestic and international financial markets.[8]

The accident waiting to happen scenario

China's undervaluation, whether intentional or unintentional, is part of a larger strategy to encourage export-led economic growth. Other parts of the strategy include capital account controls, regulations designed to encourage FDI, and a financial system protected by the government. To the extent the strategy is successful, rapid export and GDP growth masks inefficiency in the financial system and allows China's financial system to continue to build up high levels of NPLs. The success of the strategy is manifested in trade and current account surpluses which in turn, generate international reserve assets, primarily in the form of dollars which in turn provides China with the ability to maintain an undervalued currency and at the same time provides an incentive to maintain an undervalued currency because of the large exchange rate loss that would occur with a higher value of the yuan. This in turn provides incentives for FDI since foreign investors judge the probability of revaluation low.

All good things must come to an end. Eventually, of course, money supply will outstrip money demand, and price inflation will then begin to cause real exchange rate appreciation. This could in turn start a cascade of events, and the virtuous policy trap could turn into a vicious cycle. A rising exchange rate could lead to a fall in money demand and FDI, which could be a severe problem, setting off financial distress, inflation, and rising unemployment.

Eliminating the asymmetry affecting how exchange rate movements are being currently perceived could lead once again to capital flight. In addition, the effects on the US economy could be unexpected. US producers subcontract with China and this could affect their profits and prices. Chinese holdings of US dollar assets not only provide a disincentive for the Chinese to allow their currency to appreciate, but they also dampen interest rates in the US at a time when federal deficits are projected to be large for the next several years. Rising interest rates, if significant, could slow the US recovery and cause the US deficit to grow larger.

The longer the undervaluation and other export-strategies continue, the more financial distress is likely to accumulate in the Chinese banking system. Not only does the undervaluation and export strategy in general mask accumulating financial distress, the success of the strategy in terms of rapid GDP growth supports a "forgiveness and forbearance" policy on the part of government in dealing with the financial distress. Foreign investors adopt a similar perspective as long as the export sector and GDP are increasing at rapid rates.

At some point, however, the financial system distress reaches a level that induces capital flight, financial instability, and lost output. Thus, long-term undervaluation and other export-led growth strategies generate an "accident waiting to happen" scenario. China thus needs to resolve the NPL and SOE problem immediately. The longer this is postponed, the further China moves down the steps of an accident waiting to waiting scenario. While other domestic financial reforms and external liberalization are desirable, Chinese authorities need to carefully consider the sequence of reforms in both the domestic and international sectors. In particular, China should reject pressure to revalue the yuan and/or liberalize the capital account.

Domestic and international financial liberalization

The Chinese government recently announced that it would use $46 billion of its foreign exchange reserves to bail out the banking sector. As this demonstrates, the current situation provides an opportunity to address China's financial problems, if it accompanies real reform in corporate governance for both firms and banks, and liberalization in domestic and international financial markets. What would this entail?

China's capital account liberalization has been focused on encouraging inflows of FDI and most restrictions on FDI have been lifted, however, China maintains tight controls on other components of the capital account such as restricting outflows of capital and closely regulating capital and money market transactions and foreign borrowing. In general, outflows remain more tightly regulated than inflows.[9] Regarding inflows of foreign capital, the domestic capital and money markets remain tightly controlled: inflows of capital to the domestic capital market are permitted only through purchase of shares or securities issued by Chinese institutions abroad. In December 2001 several steps were taken to relax controls on foreign exchange transactions. Importantly, requirements for domestic firms to establish foreign exchange accounts in the previous year or the total amount of foreign exchange spending in the previous year. China's capital account, however, remains tightly controlled and no timetable for its liberalization has been announced to date.

The potential for capital flight is only one element of the costs of capital controls. Other costs (see Gao 2000) include: (i) insufficient diversification of portfolios; (ii) costs of enforcing control regulations, investigating suspected violations of controls, and prosecuting violators of the capital controls code; (iii) associated rent-seeking activities induced by capital control regulations themselves; and (iv) adjustment costs, if capital controls induce private agents to believe that the government is using capital controls as a short-term fix for more fundamental problems connected with the balance of payments, monetary policy, or the prudential regulation of banks.

In light of these problems intrinsic to capital controls, should China remove controls on the capital account? This would certainly be the policy recommendation from standard economic models where trade occurs across all different time periods (and across all different states of nature). In this context, the rationale for the opening up of the capital account is the same as the rationale for free international trade.

Because international investment is intertemporal trade, trade between periods and trade between countries have the same welfare effects in an Arrow-Debreu framework. In other words, in a first-best world, maintaining restrictions on capital flows is not recommended; yet it is a well known result of the theorem of the second best that removing one distortion may not be welfare enhancing if other distortions are in place. Clearly, then, in a second-best world the immediate unconditional opening up of the capital account is not necessarily an optimal policy, and indeed, it will more likely be suboptimal (see the section below on the speed and sequencing of capital account liberalization in a second-best scenario).

Different forms of financial liberalization have different implications for financial stability. As stressed by Eichengreen (2001), permitting banks access to off-shore banking but not simultaneously permitting foreign access to domestic equity and bond markets may be more destabilizing than doing the reverse because it allows foreign funds to flow through the banking system, the weakest link in the financial chain. In recent crises episodes the liberalization of off-shore bank funding came before foreign investors were granted access to domestic securities markets. This factor seems to have played a prominent role in the Venezuelan banking crisis of 1994, and it was also an issue in Korea's banking crisis.

The sequencing of external and internal liberalization is critical to financial stability, and Chile during the late 1970s illustrates the danger of dismantling capital controls before commencing domestic financial liberalization and strengthening financial supervision. The elimination of controls on capital inflows should come at a relatively late stage in the liberalization process. Chile learnt from its mistakes and subsequently followed a cautious strategy that avoided dismantling controls on capital inflows and indeed, imposed steep marginal reserve requirements on very short-term capital inflows.

Interventionist approaches to allocating credit to privileged sectors and export-promoted activities in the context of no bankruptcy among exports and financial institutions have a short life (Cargill and Parker, 2002). Once enough inefficiencies have been accumulated economic growth slows down, inefficiencies become harder to hide, the marginal product of capital declines, investors' optimism falls, and political support erodes. At some point, effective bankruptcy policies will have to be enforced in both the real and financial sectors and in the case of China, especially among the SOEs. The example of Japan during the 1990s neatly shows the consequences of ignoring this important lesson.

Implicit and/or explicit deposit guarantees that were pervasive in Korea, Japan, and other Asian and South American economies need to be an integral part of the reform process. Failure to reduce these guarantees in the face of financial liberalization creates a fundamental flaw that renders the financial system unstable. Moral hazard problems are exacerbated if implicit guarantees operate combined with a lack of appropriate financial supervision, as discussed by Gao (2000) for the case of Thailand in the late 1990s and by Diaz Alejandro (1985) for the case of Chile in the early 1980s. The experiences of virtually every country in the past three decades illustrates the danger of pursuing liberalization without a corresponding redesign and reduction of government deposit guarantees.

The speed and sequencing of capital account liberalization

This section elaborates further on the critical issue concerning the timing of external versus domestic financial liberalization, by discussing a framework where policy makers are uncertain about the outcomes of the reforms they introduce, and thin markets prevent contingent contracts that cover policy makers against risk. In those circumstances the benefit of a gradualist approach is that it keeps the option of (early) reversals open to the policy makers.

Dewatripont and Roland (1995) presented a general second best framework for studying the effects of uncertainty (both aggregate and idiosyncratic) on the speed and sequencing of reforms. For the case without political constraints and no binding majority rule (the most relevant case in the present context, since the CCP faces no formal opposition) the framework stresses the key role played by the option value of early reversal at the time of determining the optimality of gradualism versus a Big Bang approach.

The cost of gradualism is simply the current-period loss from implementing partial reform rather than immediate full reform (that is, the opportunity cost of being unable to reap off all the benefits from reform). The gain from gradualism comes from the possibility of learning about the negative expected outcomes of full reform, and thus the possibility of reversing the reform process at a lower cost than otherwise possible.

Regarding the speed of reforms, if policy makers' learning is fast enough and the probability of early reversals of reforms is positive, then gradualism is proved to be optimal, relative to Big Bang, in the face of aggregate uncertainty. Regarding the optimal sequencing of reforms, the reforms with higher expected benefits should be implemented first, as long as the policy makers display a positive rate of time preference.

When comparing two different reforms, one riskier than the other (the fixing of the banking problem versus the sudden opening up of the capital account, for example), abstracting from risk aversion – and given identical expected outcomes and reversal costs – the riskier reform should be implemented first.[10] This is so, because starting with the riskier reform increases the option value of reversibility and hence the expected outcome. When both gains and losses from reform grow, a reform becomes more attractive if losses can be avoided by reversal.

This abstract framework has important implications for China. The reforms with the highest expected return and also the riskiest if delayed or not properly implemented involve the resolution of the banking problem, establishing a transparent regulatory and supervisory framework, and reducing further the number and importance of SOEs. Of the three, the bank problem is the pivotal element. Not only should banking reform be accomplished first, but policies closer to a Big Bang rather than a gradualist approach are preferred. This is because the longer the period of resolution, the larger the problem of moral hazard. Lardy (1998: 17) considers a sound banking system as a prerequisite for capital account convertibility, particularly given the relative importance of banks in China's financial system and the high degree of state ownership in the banking sector.

The international evidence regarding the GDP costs of banking crises leaves no room for doubt about the potential risks and benefits stemming from a reform of the banking system. Estimates of these costs for recent crises are provided in Frydl and Quintyn (2000) and Dziobek and Pazarbacioglu (1997). Likewise, the international evidence about the costs of opening up the capital account without having fixed weaknesses in the domestic banking system beforehand is also unambiguous (e.g. Edwards, 1984 regarding Southern Cone countries).

The AFC alerted Chinese authorities of the risks of a rapid liberalization of the capital account without sufficient preparation. Indeed, there seems to be a consensus in Chinese policy circles about the wisdom of adopting a cautious, gradualist approach in regard to the issue of capital account liberalization. In particular, there seems to be agreement around a well-defined set of preconditions for a successful implementation of capital account liberalization. These preconditions include the following: (i) prudent macroeconomic management (sound fiscal and monetary policies, in particular the need to ensure a proper coordination between the two); (ii) an adequate real exchange rate (in particular the need to avoid dangerous overvaluations that proved to be very costly in the cases of the Southern Cone countries during the late 1970s; (iii) continuing development of the domestic financial markets and institutions including the need to put a modern, effective and efficient framework of prudential regulation and supervision in place, and the need to complete domestic financial liberalization; and (iv), resolving the banks' balance sheet problems, including the weakness of the four state-owned banks that currently hold NPLs estimated at 20 percent of their outstanding loans (Lin and Schramm, 2003).[11]

Policy dilemmas

Policy dilemmas for China can be classified from a domestic and international perspective. Domestically, interest rate and financial liberalization in general need to be balanced against the fragility of inefficient SOEs and insolvent big four state-owned banks, that account for 90 percent of all assets and 70 percent of deposits held by financial institutions, respectively. Two factors play a crucial role. First, domestic financial liberalization increases the fragility of the four big state-owned banks, as they will have to pay higher interest rates to depositors and charge lower rates to creditors if domestic competition is increased. Second, if domestic banks also face competition from abroad, this could pose a serious threat to China's financial stability. However, foreign banks also introduce competition, the use of international best practices, etc. Chinese authorities will need to balance the tradeoffs very carefully. Because the banking system is usually regarded as the "weakest link in the financial intermediation chain" (Eichengreen, 2001), access by foreign banks to the domestic market should probably be permitted only after the process of cleaning domestic banks' balance sheets is well underway.

As noted by Lardy (1998), Gao (2000), Cargill and Parker (2001), and others, a key link in the reform process is the one connecting the performance of SOEs, the NPL problem, and fiscal policy. Fiscal policy will have to generate the fiscal surpluses that will be required to support both a transitory safety net to deal with the excess labor currently hoarded by inefficient SOEs, and also the recapitalization of banks.

The international perspective emphasizes that in a world of perfect capital mobility, countries cannot maintain control of the exchange rate and monetary policy at the same time. One monetary tool must inevitably be surrendered. So far China has virtually maintained a fixed exchange rate arrangement and, given the prevalence of a wide range of capital controls combined with a degree of imperfect asset substitutability between domestic and international assets, has also been able to use monetary policy for countercyclical purposes. This is clearly illustrated by the expansionary monetary policy following the AFC and the continued fixed exchange rate. This type of flexibility to accommodate shocks will clearly be lost once China liberalizes the capital account significantly. At this stage, policy makers will have to adjust for the loss of degrees of freedom. Deeper financial markets, a more effective framework for prudential regulation, and the generalization of market strategies for risk management will all act as functional substitutes for the loss in flexibility stemming from a reduced number of policy tools that will inevitably accompany the opening up of the capital account.[12] A corollary of this principle is that the liberalization of domestic interest rates will have to wait until China moves towards a more flexible exchange rate regime to take place or the price to be paid by Chinese policy makers would be the complete loss of monetary independence.

To complicate things more from an international perspective, the move towards a more flexible exchange rate regime and the associated need to resort to more indirect methods of monetary control (i.e., open market operations) the Chinese authorities should promote the creation of markets for government bonds of different maturities, currency denominations, etc. At the same time, Chinese authorities need to pursue a firm fiscal policy that reduces public debt (including pressing implicit commitments as well as explicit ones) as a share of GDP. In this sense the experience of Chile after 1985 provides a very interesting example on how to manage this tension in a successful way (Johnston, Darbar, and Echeverria, 1997).

Implications

China's exchange rate regime has created conditions that currently mitigate the problems caused by the vicious policy trap created through the
interaction of state firms and the domestic banking sector, but this may in
turn create a virtuous policy trap if it induces China's leadership to avoid
needed financial reforms. Delaying the completion of the reform agenda is
costly, and Japan and South Korea are good examples of the costs
involved. As Japanese regulators avoided addressing their troubled banks,
non-performing loans grew, and Japan's economy suffered. Korea's
unwillingness to address these issues rendered the Korean financial system
increasingly susceptible to shocks, as the Asian financial crisis so clearly
demonstrated.

China has acted on the presumption that delay in the context of high
GDP growth would permit the economy to outgrow the problems, but this
policy of forgiveness, forbearance, and delay has proved to be non-optimal
in the long run. Chinese authorities should more closely study the experiences of Korean, Japan, other Asian countries as well as the US and many
of the European countries. China's export strategy has thus generated an
accident to waiting sequence and the longer China delays meaningful
reforms, the more likely the real and financial sectors will experience
serious difficulties. Drawing the various issues discussed in this chapter,
the following four policy recommendations are offered.

First, China should not rush to opening up its capital account nor give
in to external pressure to revalue the yuan. While there are costs to delaying capital account liberalization, the costs of a massive banking crisis
likely outweigh the allocative, efficiency, and enforcing costs of capital
controls. In general, domestic liberalization should proceed external liberalization.

Second, the most immediate focus of reform is the interconnected twin
problems of inefficient state-owned enterprises and non-performing bank
loans. This will involve a high fiscal commitment to recapitalize banks and
to provide emergency assistance to the large number of unemployed
workers that will result from the implementation of bankruptcy procedures.

Third, resolving the banking problem needs to be accompanied by a
broad set of reforms to enhance human capital in the financial sector and
to design a regulation and supervisory regime. Financial expertise needs to
be developed along with an effective framework for financial regulation
and supervision that limits systemic risk.

Fourth, this broad range of financial liberalization reforms can accompany resolution of the banking and the state-owned enterprise problems,
however, other reforms of the financial sector cannot proceed until this is
accomplished. These two problems present the most serious threat to
China's financial stability and most be addressed immediately. Once

accomplished, the following financial reforms can then be pursued. The development of capital and money markets is an important part of broadening the financial asset base of the economy, which in turn require flexible interest rates and interest rate deregulation of the banking sector. If China is to eventually move to more indirect methods of monetary control (policy instruments, high powered money, and the economy), an appropriate array of government instruments need to be developed to give the monetary authority a variety of options to conduct open market operations. Without sufficiently developed market for government bonds indirect ways of monetary control will be inadequate to stabilize the price level, as the experience of so many developing countries illustrates. The move towards a more flexible exchange rate system is conditional on the development of a market for foreign exchange, since it is well known that floating the currency in the face of a shallow market tends to produce excess price volatility that is in turn transmitted to the real sector of the economy through the so-called balance sheet effect.

In conclusion, China's export strategy and unintentional undervaluation has generated a serious policy dilemma. On one side, the export-led growth has been responsible for significant economic growth, but on the other side, the narrow focused strategy has weakened the financial sector and rendered China susceptible to shocks with serious adverse effects on the real and financial sectors. Revaluation of the yuan and/or capital account liberalization is not the solution and would only make the situation worse. Chinese authorities should stand firm in rejecting the demands for the revaluation of the yuan and/or for a move towards immediate capital account convertibility and should instead move immediately to tackle the reforms with the highest expected payoff as outlined above.

Notes

1 Using official exchange rates, China ranks behind the US, Japan, Germany, France, the UK, and France. If China's currency is undervalued by 40 percent, as the US government has recently claimed, then it would be the world's fourth largest economy, behind only the US, Japan, and Germany. If the purchasing power parity (PPP) estimates published by the World Bank are used instead, then only the US remains a larger economy. These comparisons however, are for the level of GDP. With an official GDP per capita of roughly $1,000 ($5,000 in PPP terms), China remains a less developed economy, particularly outside its prosperous coastal cities.

2 Many observers point out that this bilateral trade deficit significantly overstates the US bilateral current account deficit, both because of measurement differences and, more significantly, because the US has a bilateral surplus in services and investment income receipts, as many US firms produce goods in China for the Chinese domestic market.

3 It might be worth noting, however, that since 1955 US manufacturing employment has gradually declined from 32 to 11 percent of total non-farm employment, and it has been declining in absolute terms since 1980, from 19.4 million in 1979 to 16.8 million in 1993, 17.2 million in 2000, and 14.7 million in 2003.

Meanwhile, between 1995 and 2002 China lost 16 million manufacturing jobs, 15 percent of its total. The net gainers of manufacturing jobs appear to be Canada, Mexico, Spain, Taiwan, and the Philippines, though the absolute numbers are relatively small (Baum, 2003).

4 Gowa (1983: 143) cites a public statement to this effect by Philip Trezise, the Assistant Secretary of State for Economic Affairs, four months prior to President Nixon's 1971 announcement to no longer support the dollar price of gold.

5 Korea's reform process is reviewed in the followed selected sources: Cargill (1997/98, 1998a, and 1998b), Greenwood (1986), KEIA (2000), Krause (2000), and SERI (2000).

6 The government encouraged the development of non-bank financial institutions, money and capital markets began to develop, foreign financial institutions were permitted greater access to the domestic financial system, restrictions on inflows and outflows of capital were relaxed, and the won was permitted more market sensitivity.

7 Official estimates understated the magnitude of the problem according to many outside observers, for example, Huh and Kim (1994) found higher NPL rates for Korean than Japanese banks over the period from 1971 to 1991. NPLs ranged from 12–25 percent of total loans in the late 1980s with no apparent downward trend during the entire period studied. Chung (1991) found similar results based on examination of NPLs for eight major Korean commercial banks in 1988 based on internal Bank of Korea data.

8 As one example of the opportunity that the foreign exchange regime presents for addressing the problems of the banking sector, China just announced a transfer of $45 billion from its international reserves to two of its state-owned commercial banks, the third large bailout in less than six years (Bradsher, 2004). Rating agencies such as Standard & Poor and Moody's welcomed the bailout as a sign that Chinese authorities were addressing difficult and pressing problems in the financial sector. What Chinese banks badly need, however, is not only the additional resources to recapitalize themselves, but the right set of incentives that lead them to reform their lending practices and stop making bad loans. In this respect, introducing credit-risk management procedures should be a key ingredient of the reform package. Unless this system is introduced, the banks will continue to be pressed to make politically connected loans, whether at the provincial and municipal levels as has been the case so far, or at the national level if they centralize their lending decisions in Beijing as recent developments seem to indicate.

9 For a detailed documentation of China's Foreign Exchange Policies since 1979, see Lin and Schramm (2003).

10 The riskiness of the reform refers to the risk to the economy if the objective of the reform is left unresolved.

11 See the comprehensive discussion contained in BIS Papers #15, in particular the reflections in Zhang (2003) included in that volume.

12 We are ruling out the possibility of China moving right away to a purely clean float here, simply because it is not a plausible scenario. The basic requirement of deep financial markets is not met.

References

Balassa, B. (1964), "The purchasing power parity doctrine: A reappraisal," *Journal of Political Economy* 72: 584–596.

Baum, C. (2003), "Commentary: Who is stealing China's manufacturing jobs?" *International Herald Tribune*, Oct. 14.

Bhagwati, J. (1984), "Why are services cheaper in the poor countries," *Economic Journal* 94: 279–280.

Bradsher, K. (2003), "Rating agencies see danger in yuan float," *International Herald Tribune*, 16 September.

Bradsher, K. (2004), "China announces new bailout of big banks," *New York Times*, 6 January, p. C1.

Brandt, L. and H. Li (2003), "Bank discrimination in transition economies: Ideology, information, or incentives?," *Journal of Comparative Economics* 31(3): 387–413.

Cargill, T.F. (1997/1998), "Central bank restructuring and independence in Korea and Japan: A solution to current financial problems?," *Central Banking*, Winter.

Cargill, T.F. (1998a), "Financial crisis, reform and prospects for Korea," *Financial Regulator* 3 (June): 36–40.

Cargill, T.F. (1998b), "Korea and Japan: The end of the 'Japanese Financial Regime'," in G. Kaufman (ed.), *Bank Crises: Causes, Analysis and Prevention.* London: JAI Press, Inc.

Cargill, T.F. and E. Parker (2001), "Financial liberalization in China: Limitations and lessons of the Japanese regime," *Journal of the Asia-Pacific Economy* 6(1): 1–21.

Cargill, T.F. and E. Parker (2002), "Asian finance and the role of bankruptcy: A model of the transition costs of financial liberalization," *Journal of Asian Economics* 13(3): 297–318.

Cargill, T.F. and E. Parker (2004), "Price deflation, money demand, and monetary policy discontinuity: A comparative view of Japan, China, and the United States," *North American Journal of Economics and Finance* 15(1): 125–147.

CIIC (2002), "Analysis of China's current unemployment rate," China Internet Information Center, www.china.org.cn/baodao/english/newsandreport/2002june2/12-5.htm.

Chung, U.C. (1991), *Financial Market Reform*, (in Korean), Seoul: Bupmum-sa. Cited in Huh and Kim (1994).

Diaz Alejandro, C.F. (1985), "Goodbye financial repression, hello financial crash," *Journal of Development Economics* 18 (September): 1–24.

Dewatripont, M. and Roland, G. (1995), "The design of reform packages under uncertainty," *American Economic Review* 85, 1207–1223.

Dunn, R.M. (1973), "Exchange rate rigidity, investment distortions, and the failure of Bretton Woods," Princeton University Essays in International Finance 97.

Dziobek, C. and C. Pazarbacioglu (1997), "Lessons from systemic bank restructuring: A survey of 24 countries," IMF Working Paper WP 97/161. December.

Edwards, S. (1984), "The order of liberalization of the external sector in developing countries," Princeton Essays in International Finance no. 156. New Jersey, International Finance Section, Princeton University, December.

Eichengreen, B. (2001), "Capital account liberalization: What do cross-country studies tell us?," *The World Bank Economic Review* 15(3): 341–365.

Federal Reserve Bank of Cleveland (2003), "Is China's currency undervalued?," June. Accessed from: www.clevelandfed.org/Research/ET2003/0603/china.pdf.

Frydl, E.J. and M. Quintyn (2000), "The benefits and costs of intervening in banking crises," IMF Working Paper WP/00/147. August.

Gao, H. (2000), "Liberalizing China's capital account: Lessons drawn from Thailand's experience," Visiting Researchers Series 6. February. Institute of Southeast Asian Studies.

Gowa, J. (1983), *Closing the Gold Window*. Cornell University Press.

Greenwood, J.G. (1986), "Financial liberalization and innovation in Seven East Asian Countries," in Y. Suzuki and H. Yomo (eds), *Financial Innovation and Monetary Policy: Asia and the West*. Tokyo: Tokyo University Press.

Gunter, F. (1996), "Capital flight from the People's Republic of China: 1984–1995," *China Economic Review* 7(1): 77–96.

Huang, F. (1995), "China's utilization of foreign capital and the related policies," *Journal of Asian Economics* 6(2): 217–232.

Huh, C. and S.B. Kim (1994), "Financial regulation and banking sector performance: A comparison of bad loan problems in Japan and Korea," *Economic Review*, Federal Reserve Bank of San Francisco, 2: 18–29.

Interfax (2003), "Renminbi undervalued by 10–15% says head of Goldman Sachs Asia," *Interfax China*, 15 September.

Johnston, R.B., S.M. Darbar, and C. Echeverria (1997), "Sequencing capital account liberalization: Lessons from the experiences of Chile, Indonesia, Korea, and Thailand," Working Paper WP/97/157. International Monetary Fund, November, Washington, DC.

Jefferson, G.H. (2001), "China's state-owned enterprises did their job – Now they can go," *Transition Newsletter*, World Bank, pp. 31–32.

KEIA (2000), *The Korean Economy in an Era of Global Competition*, Korea Economic Institute of America: Washington, DC, 17–18 September.

Kravis, I.B. and R.E. Lipsey (1983), *Toward an Explanation of National Price Levels*, Princeton Studies in International Finance 52.

Krause, L.B. (2000), "The Aftermath of the Asian Financial Crisis for South Korea," *Journal of the Korean Economy*, 1 (Spring): 1–21.

Kwan, C.H. (2003), "The more foreign reserves the better?," *China in Transition*, 14 February.

Lardy, N.R. (1998), *China's Unfinished Economic Revolution*. Brookings Institution Press.

Lardy, N.R. (2002), *Integrating China into the Global Economy*. Brookings Institution Press.

Lardy, N.R. (2003), "United States–China ties: Reassessing the economic relationship," Testimony before the House Committee on International Relations, U.S. House of Representatives, October 21, accessed from www.iie.com/publications/papers/lardy1003.htm.

Lin, G. and R. Schramm (2003), "China's foreign exchange policies since 1979: A review of developments and an assessment," *China Economic Review* 14(3).

Liu, X., C. Wang, and Y. Wei (2001), "Causal links between foreign direct investment and trade in China," *China Economic Review* 12(2–3): 190–202.

Liu, Z. (2002), Foreign direct investment and technology spillover: Evidence from China," *Journal of Comparative Economics* 30(3): 579–602.

Maddison, A. (2003) *The World Economy: Historical Statistics*. Paris, France: Organisation for Economic Co-operation and Development.

Naughton, B. (1995), *Growing out of the Plan*. Cambridge University Press.

Parker, E. (1995), "Prospects for the state-owned enterprise in China's socialist market economy," *Asian Perspective* 19(1): 7–35.

Parker, E. (1999), "Are wage increases in Chinese state industry efficient? A study of productivity in the Nanjing machine-building industry," *Contemporary Economic Policy* 17(1): 55–68.

Samuelson, P. (1964), "Theoretical notes on trade problems," *Review of Economics and Statistics* 46: 145–154.

SCMP (2003), "A question of the right balance," *South China Morning Post*, 13 October.

SERI (2000), *Two Years after the IMF Bailout: A Review of the Korean Economy's Transition*, Samsung Economic Research Institute, March.

Tseng, W.S. and H.H. Zebregs (2002), "Foreign direct investment in China: Some lessons for other countries," IMF Policy Discussion Paper, PDP/02/03.

Wei, S.-J. (2000), "Why does China attract so little foreign direct investment?," in T. Ito and A.O. Krueger, *The Role of Foreign Direct Investment in East Asian Economic Development*. NBER-East Asia Seminar on Economics, vol. 9, University of Chicago Press.

Zhang, A., Y. Zhang, and R. Zhao (2003), "A study of the R&D efficiency and productivity of Chinese firms," *Journal of Comparative Economics* 31(3): 444–464.

Zhang, K.H. (1999), "Foreign direct investment and economic growth: Evidence from ten East Asian economies," *Economia Internazionale* 52(4): 517–535.

Zhang, K.H. and S. Song (2000), "Promoting exports: The role of inward FDI in China," *China Economic Review* 11(4): 385–396.

Zhang, Q. and B. Felmingham (2001), "The relationship between inward direct foreign investment and China's provincial export trade," *China Economic Review* 12(1): 82–99.

Zhang, X. (2003), "Capital Account Management and its outlook in China," in BIS Papers no. 15. China's capital account liberalization: international perspectives. Monetary and Economic Department, April, Bank for International Settlements, Basel, Switzerland.

Zhang, Z. (1998), "Does devaluation of the Renminbi improve China's balance of trade?," *Economia Internazionale* 51(3): 437–445.

12 FDI and labor reforms in Guangdong Province

Minquan Liu, Luodan Xu, and Liu Liu

Introduction

Since the end of the 1970s, China has adopted a wide range of market-oriented economic reforms, including "opening up" to the outside world. As part of this "opening up," foreign direct investment (FDI) was first sanctioned and then actively encouraged by the Chinese government. Over the period since they first appeared, foreign-invested enterprises (FIEs)[1] have played an especially important role in China's rapid economic growth through technology and knowledge spillovers as well as contributions to China's exports. They have also contributed directly to China's market-oriented economic reforms. In China's overall reform program, labor market reforms have perhaps been the most important and protracted part. Among the contributions that FIEs have made to China's economic reforms what stands out is their role in promoting China's labor market reforms.

Even at the very early stages, FIEs in China were institutionally guaranteed the right to make production and investment decisions according to market rules, including a much greater power in respect of wages and labor recruitment decisions. In the dualistic structure of the state vis-à-vis non-state sectors that emerged in the reform years, FIEs indisputably belonged to the latter group, representing a nascent market force but also quickly becoming a model to the state-sector enterprises in their market-oriented reforms. In labor practices, FIEs have exerted strong competitive pressures on China's domestic enterprises (both state- and non-state-owned) by paying better wages to skilled and well-educated new recruits who may well have job-hopped from domestic enterprises. In terms of wage differentiations, since skilled labor has been a relatively scarce resource to the unskilled labor in China throughout the reform years, an enterprise operating much more in line with market practices would presumably have had greater internal wage differentials between skilled and unskilled labor, and hence provided better returns to human capital.

In addition to the impact on wages and wage reforms (i.e. towards much more market-determined wages), China's FIEs have also contributed to the formation of a unified national labor market by helping breaking down many former bureaucratic, sectoral and geographic segmentations. Under the pre-reform labor regime,[2] workers of state-owned enterprises (SOEs) were recruited according to whether they had an urban *hukou*, were from the same city, and sometimes were from particular units of the same city (e.g. if a job change were involved).[3] Indeed, more often than not, workers were "allocated" to an enterprise by government bureaus, often irrespective of the enterprise's need or a person's wish (this was especially true of the allocation of new cohorts of school and college graduates each year). When reforms began, FIEs, driven by profit-motives, were understandably the first to break away from this labor recruitment practice and to win the right to hire workers and staff irrespective of their bureaucratic, sectoral and geographical segmentations. In part necessitated by the competitive relationship they had with the FIEs, domestic enterprises subsequently also moved in this direction. In turn, this greater labor mobility – which FIEs had done so much to contribute to – has sometimes enabled Chinese domestic enterprises to benefit from a reverse flow of workers from FIEs, with their better job-specific skills and knowledge.

While it may generally be accepted that FIEs have contributed to China's labor reforms by remunerating workers more closely in reflection of human capital variations and adopting more flexible and market-oriented labor recruitment practices than domestic enterprises, there is a dearth of empirical studies estimating the role of FIEs in these respects in China's labor reforms over the reform decades. Many studies of wage determination in transitional China have addressed the issues of wage differentials and returns to human capital generally. Some reported positive but low returns to human capital (Byron and Manaloto, 1990; Gregory and Meng, 1995; Knight and Song, 1991); others even found negative returns (Gelb, 1990; Meng, 1993), while still others have reported a rise in the returns in the 1990s compared with in the 1980s (Lai, 1998; Zhao *et al.*, 1999). Researches on labor mobility and labor market segmentations have usually focused on rural–urban migration and the migrant population (Forbs and Linge, 1990; Lin, 1993; Du, 1994; Yang, 1997; Knight *et al.*, 1999; Roberts, 2001). Most of such studies, however, do not relate to FIEs.

In this chapter, we empirically examine wage determination and labor recruitment practice in FIEs by analyzing a data set from a survey of 405 FIEs. The survey was carried out in 1998 in Guangdong Province in southern China. This is where FDI first took hold in the late 1970s after China had begun to accept and actively seek for FDI, and where FDI subsequently expanded by leaps and bounds and by the late 1990s accounted for close to a third of total accumulated FDI inflow in China. Our findings demonstrate that wholly foreign-owned enterprises (WFOEs) tended to provide higher returns to education and were more inclined to recruit workers from provinces outside Guangdong than non-wholly foreign-owned enterprises

(NWFOEs).[4] This we take to be evidence in support of the hypothesis that FDI has contributed to China's market-oriented labor reforms.[5] However, from our findings, it also emerges that the extent of this contribution depended on some other factors. One factor found to significantly influence an FIE's wage level and the extent of its recruitment of workers from outside Guangdong is its degree of export orientation, which can be interpreted to indicate an FIE's investment strategy. In addition, we find important differences in wage levels among FIEs by source of investment (overseas Chinese, US, EU, and Japan), which we interpret to mean that wages in FIEs were also significantly influenced by the levels in their home countries.

The rest of the chapter proceeds as follows. In order for the reader to have a clear picture of the enormous problems China's pre-reform labor regime had, the protracted nature of the reforms, and the role FIEs have played in promoting the reforms, in Section 2 we provide a brief description of the main features of the pre-reform labor regime in China and the principal reform measures the Chinese government has undertaken since then. This is then followed by an account in Section 3 of the rise of the FIEs in China and a discussion of their role in promoting labor reforms in China. A brief review of some secondary evidence on the differences in returns to human capital and in labor recruitment practices between FIEs and non-FIEs is also provided. In Section 4, we turn to the Guangdong survey, where we describe the survey sampling, data set, and our empirical estimation strategy. Section 5 presents the estimation models and interprets the results. Section 6 concludes the chapter.

The pre-reform labor regime and labor reforms in China

The pre-reform labor regime

China began its economic reforms and the "open door" policy in 1978. The objective was to transform the previous centrally planned economy into a market-oriented one. Labor reforms have since been an important but also an especially protracted part of the overall reform program. Before the economic reforms, there was essentially no "labor market" in China in the strict sense of the word. The labor regime then had the following features. To begin with, a rigid rural–urban divide separated the rural sector from the urban state sector (state-owned enterprises or "work units"). Two completely different systems governed job allocation, remuneration and other labor practices in these two sectors. In the urban state sector, as noted, irrespective of the actual needs of an enterprise or work unit, each year cohorts of young urban workers would routinely be allocated to them. Employment was for lifetime, once a worker was given a job in an enterprise or work unit, there were few chances to change that job.[6]

All officially recognized and approved urban residents were given an official local urban residency status (*hukou*). Strictly, urban state sector job allocation only applied to people with an urban *hukou*. In addition to *hukou*, each worker was also given a work-related personal file (*dang'an*). When a person was allocated a job, their personal file would be placed with the labor office of the local government bureau responsible for the enterprise. Should they seek a job transfer to another unit, they would have to obtain the consent of both their existing work unit and their new work unit. Job transfers between work units subordinate to the same local government bureau could already be hard enough; job transfers between work units of different government bureaus would be even harder, as it was considered at the time that this would disrupt the state's manpower allocation plan. In any case, administratively this would have to require the consent of two local government bureaus. Finally, job transfers between two cities would be still harder, as this would imply a change of a person's urban residency status from one city to another, and in many large cities restrictions were in place limiting the influx of immigrant manpower from other cities (and, of course, from the rural areas).

Thus while an urban worker received lifelong employment, there was no choice for a preferred job, even if one was offered. The iron-rice-bowl employment system, while providing full job security for workers, gave workers few opportunities of changing jobs should they become dissatisfied with their existing jobs.

On the other side of the divide was the rural sector. As a rule, rural workers were denied state sector jobs, a privilege reserved only for urban residents. Rural workers were organized into agricultural collectives and worked jointly on collectively owned land. Their remuneration depended on their collective's income as well as on their personal labor contribution. Indeed, rural workers were not even able to move between collectives except in such cases as marriage.[7]

One further feature of the pre-reform system was that wages for state-sector workers were determined by the central government. A national wage scale existed that determined the wages for each skill rank, and there were altogether only eight different skill ranks. Wage differentials between these ranks were narrow and tightly compressed, with the highest wage only around five or six times that paid to a worker in the lowest skill rank. This followed the egalitarian principle guiding income distribution in China at the time. Note that neither an enterprise nor a worker was in a position to negotiate wages.[8]

Labor reforms in transitional China

It is clear from the above that the pre-reform "labor market" (if we can call it that) was heavily sectorally, regionally, and institutionally segmented. Workers could not freely choose their preferred job, and did not have the right to a negotiated wage. One would of course expect both such severe market segmentations and the extreme egalitarian wage remunerations to undermine the efficiency of human resource allocation and the efficacy of wage remuneration as an incentive for better work performance. Indeed, this was true, and it provided the initial impetus to market-oriented labor reforms in China.

The subsequent labor reforms were aimed at rationalizing the system of job allocation and wage remuneration so as to improve efficiency. Specifically the reforms focused on dismantling the lifetime employment system, removing major market segmentations and linking individual remuneration to performance.[9]

Dismantling the lifetime employment system

In 1983, the government began to introduce a labor contract system for new employees in some SOEs. However, this met with strong resistance from both enterprises and workers, and disagreement among policy makers subsequently delayed its wider adoption until 1986. The system was later extended to all eligible employees in SOEs. In 1995, a new Labor Law came into force requiring all workers to be employed under a formal, written contract, which could be entered into by workers individually or *en masse* collectively.

The labor contract system symbolized an important departure from the old system of guaranteed lifetime employment by introducing the threat of contract non-renewal. In principle, the system should give an enterprise the power to recruit and dismiss workers as it deemed fit. In practice, however, restrictions on such power were commonplace. Nevertheless, the new system did give an enterprise greater freedom to do so. At the same time, it also gave workers greater freedom to leave their existing jobs and choose better ones. The contract system redefined the responsibilities and rights of both the workers and enterprises, and reduced the rigidity of the relationship.

Removing major hindrances to labor mobility

Even with the labor contract system, however, major hindrances to labor mobility remained. The principal ones were the residency (*hukou*) system and the personal record files. The role of residency qualification in determining a person's employment and job allocation was gradually de-emphasized since the mid-1980s. Not having a local urban *hukou* would no longer automatically disqualify a person from taking up an urban job, be they from another city or a rural village. By the mid-1990s, rural workers could even buy an urban *hukou* in some small and medium-sized cities, and rural migrant workers had become common in China's large cities. When an urban worker left the state sector, his personal record files were placed with a Personnel Exchange Center that looked after such files for workers in the non-state sector.[10]

Wage reforms

The way wages are set in the state sector has gone through a series of reforms since the late 1970s. The objective of these reforms has been twofold: (i) to move away from the highly egalitarian wage structure – the eight-skill rank system; (ii) to increase the power of an enterprise to set wages. The ultimate objective was to introduce a performance-based wage remuneration system.

In 1978, bonuses and piece rates were first introduced into state enterprises. In 1984, SOEs were given the power to set bonuses according to their financial performance, while the central authorities levied a progressive tax on these bonuses. In 1985, a system of determining an enterprise's total wage bill according to its economic performance was introduced. This allowed the state to control the total wage bill in the economy (an incomes policy) while allowing SOEs to have greater freedom in setting wages. This system was subsequently revised in 1989, 1993, and 1995. These revisions, however, mainly concerned methods of implementation and not the principle. Starting in 1990 a more radical wage reform program – the so-called post-and-skill wage system – went through a period of experimentation and was subsequently popularized by the Ministry of Labor. Under this system, a worker's wage is based on both their "skill" and "post." The post-related part serves to reflect the arduousness of a worker's individual duty and performance and may vary markedly as and when a worker's individual duty and performance change. In contrast, the skill-related part is stable, more like the regular wage under the former eight-skill rank system. It closely reflects a person's years of service.

FIEs and labor reforms in China

The emergence of FIEs in China

Before the reforms, China was a closed, centrally planned economy. Trade was regarded as a means of acquiring the necessary foreign exchanges for imports, state-owned enterprises (SOEs) dominated the industries, and FDI was completely banned. Trade and FDI have since been two inseparable planks to China's "opening up" to the outside world. Between 1992 and 1998, the average annual rate of growth of exports and combined trade were 24.84 percent and 22.85 percent, respectively, a truly phenomenal rate of growth. The expansion of FDI in China underwent three broad stages. Throughout the 1980s, realized FDI inflow increased only moderately. This was then followed by a period of rapid expansion in the early 1990s when the realized inflow soared and by 1993 China had become the second largest recipient country in the world only next to the US. Since then this booming trend has slowed down. Table 12.1 provides data on annual realized FDI inflows for selected years. As of 1998 (the year of our

Table 12.1 Growth of FDI in China since the economic reforms (selected years)[a]

Year	FDI (bn USD)	FDI annual growth (%)	Exports by FDI (bn USD)	Share of FDI in total export (%)	Employment in FIEs (mill persons)	Share of FDI in total industrial output (%)
1985	1.66	32.03	0.30	1.10	n.a.	n.a.
1990	3.49	2.80	n.a.	n.a.	n.a.	n.a.
1991	4.37	25.21	n.a.	n.a.	n.a.	n.a.
1992	11.01	152.11	17.36	20.44	0.66	n.a.
1993	27.52	149.98	25.24	27.51	2.21	n.a.
1994	33.77	22.72	34.71	28.68	4.06	9.47
1995	37.52	11.12	46.88	31.51	5.13	11.67
1996	41.73	11.20	61.51	40.72	5.40	12.17
1997	45.26	8.46	74.90	40.98	5.81	12.66
1998	45.46	0.46	80.96	44.05	5.87	14.91
1999	40.32	−11.31	88.63	45.47	6.12	15.92
2000	40.71	0.97	119.44	47.93	6.42	27.39[b]
2001	46.88	15.16	133.24	50.06	6.17	28.52[b]

Source: *China Statistical Yearbook*, various issues, China National Statistical Bureau.

Notes
a All values are in current prices converted into US$ at the official exchange rate prevailing at the time. FDI's growth rates are calculated using the previous year's value as the base.
b Beginning in 2000, the coverage of "industrial output" is changed from industrial output of all categories of industrial enterprises to industrial output of all state-owned industrial enterprises and other industrial enterprises above scale.

Guangdong survey), the realized value of FDI stood at 45.46 billion US dollars, total exports 183.76 billion US dollars, and combined trade 323.93 billion US dollars.

Over the last two decades the contribution made by FDI to trade, industrial output and employment rose rapidly with increased FDI inflows (Table 12.2). The share of total exports accounted for by FIEs rose from a mere 1.1 percent in 1985 to 44.1 percent in 1998, and again to 50.06 percent in 2001. The role of FIEs in international processing activities explained a great part of this increase. Between 1994 and 1998, FIEs' processing activities were by far the most dynamic component of China's trade, and they accounted for 38 percent of China's total exports and 34 percent of total imports in 1998 (CSP, 1999). The share of FIEs in China's industrial output rose from 9.5 percent in 1994 to around 15 percent in 1998.

FIEs in China are, by and large, biased in favor of labor-intensive sectors where China has a comparative advantage. Consequently, they also have made a significant contribution to employment creation in China. The number of employees (managerial and technical staff and production workers) working in FIEs in urban areas increased from 0.66 million in 1990 to 5.87 million in 1998, accounting for 2.84 percent of the total urban employment in the country in 1998 (CSP, 1999). This does not yet include employment generated by FIEs in rural areas. When that is included, the total employment created was 20 million in 1998 (CSP, 1999). These employment opportunities provided by FIEs made a major contribution to the absorption of the surplus manpower laid off from the state sector in urban areas, and of the abundant unskilled surplus labor in rural areas. According to Ma (1999), if jobs indirectly related to FIEs are further included, the total employment created by FDI would increase to over 30 million in 1998.

Of all FIEs in China, around half were invested by overseas Chinese (these investments principally came from Hong Kong, Macao, and Taiwan). Besides the geographical, cultural, and language proximity that favors China, and Guangdong in particular, as the location of these investments, cost reduction has been an important motive. Overseas Chinese investments in China have mostly involved transferring traditional labor-intensive operations from their home economies to labor-abundant China, thereby saving on labor costs, a close reflection of Vernon's (1966) product cycle theory. Other FIEs of Asian origins, mainly Japan, have also pursued a largely cost reduction objective and have mostly located their labor-intensive stages of production in China as part of their global production network. Both these and overseas Chinese investments were mainly export-oriented.

Although actively encouraging FDI, in the early years China also placed major limits to it in the form of various restrictions that were erected regarding the sectors open to FDI, export quotas, and local content requirements. During this time (much of the 1980s and the early 1990s), China's FDI inflow was dominated by overseas Chinese investments. Beginning in the early 1990s when an increased number of sectors were opened up to FDI and restrictions on export quotas and local content requirements were relaxed, FDI from non-overseas Chinese backgrounds, principally the US and European countries, also began to arrive in significant amounts. These investments were principally market seeking, and were largely concentrated in capital-intensive manufacturing and service sectors, producing products mainly to serve China's own emerging market. According to our own Guangdong survey (Liu *et al.*, 2000), FDI from US and European countries in Guangdong have adopted characteristically market-seeking investment strategies, while those of overseas Chinese and Japanese origins have mainly pursued cost-reduction objectives producing much of their output for export.[11]

The role of FIEs in labor reforms

FIEs have not only radically altered China's economic landscape and contributed to its rapid economic growth, but also have played an important role in facilitating and indeed even "leading" China's labor reforms. While the Chinese government has adopted a series of major labor reform measures, many of these were in fact "led" by the practices already existing in FIEs in China. And even after their adoptions in SOEs, by no means have all these measures always been readily welcomed and accepted by the SOE workers and managers. FIEs have again played an important role in exerting pressures on the reluctant domestic SOEs to comply with the new practices.

Leading by example

First FIEs have led by example. In fact, if one looks at the enactment of the various regulations on labor practices culminating in the passing of the 1995 Labor Law, one can see a direct role played by FIEs in leading the reform. When FDI first began to arrive in China in the late 1970s and FIEs (principally joint ventures at the time) appeared in any significant numbers, the Chinese government issued a set of key regulations, the Sino-Foreign Equity Joint Venture Labor Management Provisions, in 1980 to govern labor practices in FIEs. At that time, there were no formal regulations governing labor practices in domestic firms anywhere in the economy. The provisions stipulated certain basic rights for both the employers and employees with regard to hiring, firing, wages and bonuses, work schedule, paid leave of absence, labor insurance and welfare benefits, labor protection, labor discipline, written employment contracts, and trade union membership. In 1984, when other forms of FIEs than joint ventures appeared in large numbers, the Auxiliary Implementation

Procedures to the 1980 Provisions was issued. Under this document, all forms of FIEs in China were brought under the 1980 provisions. These provisions initially did not apply to domestic firms but there were subsequently a series of experimental regulations that brought domestic firms closer to the standards governing FIEs. In 1994, a Labor Law was passed (i.e. the 1995 Labor Law) which went into effect in the following year. This law took precedence over all previous varied and confusing sets of regulations governing FIEs and domestic firms, and for the first time brought all enterprises, FIEs and non-FIEs, under a common set of rules. After examining the main terms of the 1995 Labor Law, Markel (1994) notes that the effect of this law was to bring SOEs in line with FIEs in labor practices.

Competitive pressures

Through various backward linkages, FIEs have also exerted competitive pressures on domestic enterprises, principally SOEs, to change their labor-related practices. The main source of such pressures was, of course, the greater freedom enjoyed by FIEs in recruiting workers and in setting wages. In this case SOEs were often disadvantaged by their own past in having a high level of incumbent labor force, low technology, poor management, few financial resources, and a poor prospect of expansion. Nevertheless, when young, educated, and skilled workers were enticed to FIEs by better wages, better working conditions and better prospects of career advancement (for example, as a result of better training and greater exposure to new technology and new management methods), this generated pressures for SOEs to improve their wage remunerations and labor practices generally, even if these do not entirely match those of an FIE.

Breaking down labor market segmentations

We emphasize in particular FIEs' role in breaking down various labor market segmentations. Given their greater freedom in recruiting workers and staff and in setting wages, a privilege enjoyed from very early on, FIEs have played the role of a vanguard in breaking down major labor market segmentations characteristic of the pre-reform labor regime. When SOEs were still constrained in their choice of recruitment of workers and staff to locally registered urban residents, FIEs had already begun to recruit workers and staff from across China's cities and from rural areas. When an SOE worker still had to face bureaucratic hindrances in obtaining a transfer from one work unit to another, FIEs had already begun to recruit workers from across bureaucratic divides. Needless to say, a major factor that enabled FIEs to do so was the better wages and labor practices they offered.

To be exact, in the very early stages FIEs came up against much the same institutional restrictions in their recruitment of workers and staff as

SOEs: they were forced to recruit workers and staff with the "right" local urban residency status and personnel record files. However, in order to encourage FDI inflows, both the central and various local governments soon relaxed these restrictions for FIEs, effectively putting FIEs out of the purview of those policy restrictions.[12]

The role of FIEs in breaking down the rural–urban divide and regional segmentations deserves special emphasis. FIEs in effect led the process of recruiting workers and staff from outside the local city and from across the rural–urban divide. The reason is simple; it enabled them to recruit more able and better-qualified workers and staff, often for the same wage. Nowhere was this role more pronounced than in Guangdong, the province that led FDI growth in China. Beginning from the early 1980s, each year hundreds and thousands of rural migrant workers from across China flocked to the province to seek employment there, mostly in FIEs (principally those overseas Chinese-invested enterprises producing labor-intensive products for exports). Although labor standards in many of these FIEs were appalling and close to sweatshop conditions, on the whole they provided rural migrant workers with an employment opportunity they could only have dreamt of before. As well as rural migrant workers, throughout the 1980s and the 1990s Guangdong also attracted numerous urban workers from other cities in China. According to the 1995 Pilot Census (based on 1 percent of the population), Guangdong recorded the highest ratio (5.2 percent) of "migrant population" in China,[13] much higher than the second highest ratio (4.8 percent) recorded for Beijing. In the Special Economic Zones of Zhuhai and Shenzhen (both in Guangdong) where FIEs dominated local industries, the ratio of migrant population to total population was as high as 25.3 percent and 61.3 percent, respectively.

Wages, returns to human capital and labor recruitment practice in FIEs and non-FIEs

Below we briefly review some secondary evidence on differences in wage levels, returns to human capital, and labor recruitment practices between FIEs and non-FIEs in China.

Wages

Both the publicly available macro data and micro survey data show that, on average, workers in FIEs tend to be paid higher wages than their counterparts in indigenous firms. According to data published in the China Statistical Yearbooks, since 1985 when wages of FIEs were first reported, the average wages of both overseas Chinese (CN) FIEs and non-overseas Chinese (non-CN) FIEs have been consistently higher than the two main types of indigenous firms, SOEs and collective-owned enterprises (COEs) (Table 12.2).[14] What is more, the absolute gaps in average wages between

Table 12.2 Average annual per worker wage income (yuan) by ownership, all China, selected years

Year	SOEs	COEs	FIEs	CN-FIEs	FIE/SOE	CN-FIE/SOE	FIE/COE	CN-FIE/COE	FIE/CN-FIE
1985	1,213	967	1,847	2,143	1.52	1.77	1.91	2.22	0.86
1992	2,878	2,109	4,347	4,740	1.51	1.65	2.06	2.25	0.92
1993	3,532	2,592	5,315	5,147	1.50	1.46	2.05	1.99	1.03
1994	4,797	3,245	6,533	6,376	1.36	1.33	2.01	1.96	1.02
1995	5,625	3,931	8,058	7,484	1.43	1.33	2.05	1.90	1.08
1996	6,280	4,302	9,383	8,334	1.49	1.33	2.18	1.94	1.13
1997	6,747	4,512	10,361	9,329	1.54	1.38	2.30	2.07	1.11
1998	7,668	5,332	11,767	10,027	1.53	1.31	2.21	1.88	1.17
1999	8,543	5,774	12,951	10,991	1.52	1.29	2.24	1.90	1.18
2000	9,552	6,262	14,372	11,914	1.50	1.25	2.30	1.90	1.21
2001	11,178	6,867	16,101	12,544	1.44	1.12	2.34	1.83	1.28

Source: *China Statistical Yearbook* and *China Labor Statistical Yearbook*, various issues.

Note
CN-FIEs are overseas Chinese-invested enterprises and FIEs refer to non-CN FIEs.

FIEs and each type of indigenous firms have been increasing overtime, although the relative gaps have been stable on the whole. Within FIEs, since 1993 non-CN FIEs on average have consistently paid higher wages than CN FIEs, and the ratio of the average wage of non-CN FIEs to that of CN FIEs increased over time from 0.86 in 1985 to 1.28 in 2001, reflecting a slower rate of wage increase in CN FIEs than in non-CN FIEs in most years.

A sample survey of wages in 44 cities across China in the year 2000 by the Ministry of Labor and Social Security (MOLSS, 2001) confirms the above trends (Table 12.3). The average wages of workers in FIEs in 1999 were 1.44 times (12,627 yuan) that in indigenous firms (8,794 yuan). Both CN and non-CN FIEs paid higher average wages than SOEs and other indigenous firms. CN FIEs, however, recorded a slower rate of increase of wages (8.1 percent) in 2000 than non-CN FIEs (12.64 percent). Indeed, because of this, the rate of wage increase for FIEs as a whole (12 percent) fell below that for indigenous firms taken together (12.12 percent).

It needs to be pointed out that, in addition to wages, a worker may receive other benefits from their enterprise. According to a labor cost survey of 5,280 enterprises in 11 major cities in Hebei Province as of 1998,[15] making up the total labor costs of an enterprise were wages, employer' social security and welfare contributions, training and education costs, and other (Table 12.4). Not only did FIEs on average pay higher wages (6,849 yuan) than both COEs (3,354 yuan) and SOEs (5,328 yuan), the share of wages in their total per-worker labor costs was also the lowest among the three enterprise types. If one includes all labor costs as, in some sense, remunerations for workers, then FIEs paid a total of 10,291 yuan per worker in the year, 36.6 percent and 1.3 times higher than SOEs and COEs, respectively. Note that while FIEs paid the highest remuneration per worker, they also recorded the highest average value added per yuan of labor costs among the three enterprise types. This indicates that FIEs on average had higher labor productivities, part of which was then used to pay to workers in terms of a higher level of remuneration.

Wage differentials and returns to education

While FIEs on average pay higher wages and possibly provide a higher level of other benefits to workers than all types of indigenous firms, both anecdotal observations and in-depth empirical studies show that wage differentials, and probably differentials in non-wage benefits as well, are much larger within FIEs than for indigenous firms. The issue of wage differentials (and perhaps non-wage benefit differentials as well) relates closely to returns to education. Where the differentials are unduly narrow, returns to education are likely to be depressed.

Using data from an extensive labor force survey in China, Dai (1997) found that workers in FIEs were on average paid higher wages with much

Table 12.3 Annual market wages in 44 cities, China (2000)

	Sample wage (yuan)	1999 average wage (yuan)	2000 average growth (%)	2000 average wage
Total	704,349[a]	8,967	10,070	12.30
Indigenous firms	661,912	8,794	9,860	12.12
State-owned enterprises	455,115	9,308	10,536	13.19
Collective-owned enterprises	80,051	7,058	7,642	8.27
Cooperative units	29,050	7,384	7,748	4.94
Joint-owned units	2,256	10,599	11,359	7.17
Limited liability corporations	87,591	8,256	9,159	10.93
Private-owned enterprises	4,752	6,479	7,443	14.88
Others	3,106	8,805	10,072	14.39
Foreign-owned enterprises[a]	42,428	12,627	14,142	12.00
Overseas Chinese (CN) FIEs	17,463	11,607	12,547	8.10
Non-CN FIEs	24,965	13,350	15,037	12.64

Source: MOLSS (2001).

Note

a The total sample is obtained by adding together the sub-samples for indigenous firms and foreign-owned enterprises. Figures for "all FIEs" are in reach case weighted averages of the corresponding figures for CN FIEs and non-CN FIEs, with the respective sample sizes being the weights.

Table 12.4 Per worker labor costs by type of enterprise, Hebei Province (1998)

	FIEs yuan	FIEs %	SOEs yuan	SOEs %	COEs yuan	COEs %
Average per worker labor costs	10,291	100	7,534	100	4,486	100
Wage cost	6,849	66.55	5,238	69.52	3,354	74.77
Social security cost	1,734	16.85	1,110	14.73	654	14.58
Welfare cost	863	8.39	602	7.99	259	5.77
Education cost	50	0.49	50	0.66	17	0.38
Other cost	795	7.73	534	7.09	202	4.50
Value added per yuan of labor cost	2.23		1.59		1.19	

Source: www.ld.hebnet.gov.cn.

larger wage differentials than in SOEs. In another study, relying on survey data on incomes in 1988 and 1995, Lai (1998) computed human capital returns by the Mincerian equation, and found the coefficient for human capital returns in FIEs to be much higher than in SOEs. What is more, although both FIEs and SOEs showed increased returns to human capital over time, the rate of the increase was higher for the former group. Both these studies ignore non-wage benefits. In another study, using data from the *China Statistical Yearbook 1995* and the *China Industrial Economic Statistical Yearbook 1995*, Gordon and Li (1999) convert non-wage compensations into equivalent wage income and find substantial compressions of the "wage" scale within the state sector. The enterprises in the state sector effectively paid substantial income subsidies to the least skilled workers. There was little pay differential by education, and the wages for more educated workers were much lower than their marginal value product. Non-wage compensations were generally paid according to seniority and based on egalitarian principles. Their study, however, did not relate to FIEs.

Based on a study of evolving wage differentials in Zhejiang Province, Zhuang *et al.* (1998) observe that the size of wage differentials within an enterprise was positively correlated with profits and the wage level of an enterprise, and they speculate that as an enterprise's profits increase, its wage differentials will be on the rise. They base their observations on a study of wage differentials in SOEs, COEs, and "other" enterprises (including FIEs). In their study, FIEs are generally found to have paid higher wages, earned greater profits, and had wider wage differentials.[16]

Equality of employment opportunities and labor mobility

SOEs in China today are, to an extent, still under the shadow of their past. Workers may now leave their existing work units and move to an FIE, or to an indigenous private firm, or indeed into self-employment, with greater ease.[17] However, while exit may have been eased, entering the state sector is still fraught with difficulties, especially for certain social groups. For various reasons, SOEs have still tended to reserve jobs for people with local city residency status. Outside workers, including rural workers, may find employment in an SOE, but typically only as "temporary" workers, without the full range of social security and welfare benefits available to a "regular" worker.[18] If an SOE were forced to downsize, these "temporary" workers would be the first to be laid off, irrespective of their work performance.

In fact, in many cities even these "temporary" positions have been difficult to come by for outside workers. In fear of social unrest that may follow a large-scale job loss in the state sector, in some places local governments have required SOEs in their jurisdictions to give priority to recruiting newly laid-off former local SOE workers, rather than outside workers.

Indeed, as a result of these policies, in some places even young workers with local city residency status may not be able to obtain a state sector job. Equality of employment opportunities in the state sector is still only a distant prospect.

As noted, in contrast, FIEs, even in the very early stages, were granted a greater freedom of choice in recruiting workers and staff. Recruitment has generally been on a competitive basis, irrespective of a candidate's residency status. There are no particular social groups of workers to protect in this sector, and quitting is, of course, without restriction.[19]

The Guangdong survey, data set, and estimation strategy

The Guangdong survey and the data set

The Guangdong survey was carried out in the summer of 1998; the information collected pertains to 1997. A total of 405 FIEs were interviewed with the aid of a questionnaire. Of these, 276 were of overseas Chinese investment (CN) from Hong Kong, Macao, and Taiwan, 35 of Japanese (JP), 50 of US (US), and 41 of European (EU) investment. The exact source of investment of three other firms was not known. Of the whole sample, 320 are manufacturing firms, 83 service sector firms, and two agricultural and mining firms. The data set we use for empirical examination in this chapter pertains to only the manufacturing firms.

Sampling was based on a population data set provided by the Data Management Center of the Guangdong Research Institute, the Commission of Foreign Economic and Trade Relations of Guangdong Province, and used a combination of stratified and systematic sampling methods.[20] The population data set contained all the officially registered FIEs in Guangdong as at the end of 1997. Six hundred target firms were initially selected for interview by investment source (US, JP, EU, and CN). At completion, 405 firms were successfully interviewed,[21] producing a sample that is, insofar as the industrial sector composition is concerned, reasonably representative of the population (Liu *et al.*, 2000).

Table 12.5 presents the composition of the manufacturing sample firms by source and form of investment and firm size. Form of investment refers to whether an FIE is a wholly foreign owned enterprise (WOFE), or a non-wholly foreign owned enterprise (NWFOE), which includes joint ventures (JV), cooperative ventures (CV), and other. Following a widespread practice, firms employing 300 workers and above are classified as large enterprises (LEs), and those with less than 300 workers small and medium-sized enterprises (SMEs). (In regression estimations, though, we use the total number of workers and staff of a firm for firm size.) Note that CN firms have the lowest ratio of WFOEs, while US firms have the highest, followed by JP and EU firms. Table 12.6 reports the average annual sales, registered capital, total investment, numbers of employees,

Table 12.5 Form of investment and firm size by source of investment, manufacturing sectors (1997)

	CN	EU	JP	US	Total
WFOE	56 (25.23)	9 (29.03)	8 (30.77)	12 (37.5)	85 (27.33)
NWFOE	166 (73.77)	22 (70.97)	18 (69.23)	20 (62.50)	226 (72.67)
JV	118 (52.15)	21 (67.74)	16 (61.54)	15 (46.88)	170 (54.66)
CV	39 (17.57)	1 (3.23)	2 (7.69)	5 (15.63)	47 (15.11)
Other	9 (4.05)	0 (0)	0 (0)	0 (0)	9 (2.89)
Obs.	222 (100)	31 (100)	26 (100)	32 (100)	311 (100)
SMEs	131 (59.28)	19 (65.52)	13 (50)	12 (41.38)	175 (57.38)
LEs	90 (40.72)	10 (34.48)	13 (50)	17 (58.62)	130 (42.62)
Obs.	221 (100)	29 (100)	26 (100)	29 (100)	305 (100)

Note
The numbers of sample firms for CN, EU, JP and US sources are 228, 31, 27 and 32, respectively. Figures in parentheses are percentages. Obs indicates number of respondents. JV, CV, SMEs, and LEs stand for joint venture, cooperative venture, small and medium-sized enterprises and large enterprises, respectively.

Table 12.6 Average sales, registered capital, total investment, number of employees and capital intensity by source, manufacturing sectors (1997)

	CN	EU	JP	US	Total
Annual sales	136.35	400.61	209.26	668.62	215.89
Registered capital	45.53	164.65	97.47	150.46	68.57
Total investment	130.86	267.77	263.74	272.3	164.27
Employees	548.59	451.31	693.46	1,208.59	611.57
Capital intensity	556.57	1916.8	352.93	702.85	664.27

Note
The units for annual sales, registered capital and total investment are million RMB yuan. Capital intensity is given by the ratio of total investment, in thousand RMB yuan, to the number of employees of an enterprise.

and capital intensity (total investment per employee) of the manufacturing sample firms by source group. These provide a broad picture of the type of manufacturing firms included in our sample by source.

Estimation strategy and variables

Our data set contains only firm-level data, and consequently it does not permit us to examine wage differentials or returns to human capital within a firm. However, it permits an empirical examination of firm-level average hourly wages and the geographic origin of production workers (percentage of production workers from outside Guangdong) by form of investment, their educational level (percentage of production workers with high-middle school education and above), source of investment, the ratio of export to total sales (proxy for investment strategy), industrial sector, and the size of a firm.[22] The first two variables (firm-level average hourly wages and the geographical origin of workers) are to be our endogenous variables, while the rest are explanatory variables. The use of form of investment as an explanatory variable enables us to assess whether, other things being equal, WFOEs perform better than NWFOEs in respect of workers' hourly wages and geographical origin (the latter as represented by a greater share of workers hired from outside Guangdong, implying a greater degree of geographical labor mobility). The inclusion of workers' average educational level (percentage of workers with high-middle school education and above) as an explanatory variable allows us to evaluate returns to education and its impact, if any, on workers' geographical origin. These are two principal explanatory variables. In addition, to allow for the possible influence of source of investment and a firm's investment strategy (as represented by its share of export in total sales) on the endogenous variables, we include variables pertaining to these in our estimating equations. Finally, we control for the possible influence of the industrial sector and the size of a firm (total number of employees) on the endogenous variables. Detailed hypotheses and models of estimation are given shortly.

Because there was not a comparable contemporaneous survey of SOEs or, more generally, non-FIEs in Guangdong, we will, in fact, be unable to compare FIEs and non-FIEs in respect of workers' hourly wages and geographical origins. However, if FDI indeed promotes the performance of a firm in these respects and if the relationship is also monotone, then one would expect, other things being equal, WFOEs to outperform NWFOEs in these respects. Conversely, if as a group WFOEs outperform NWFOEs, then other things being equal this can be seen as evidence of a positive effect of FDI in these respects.

The point just made requires some explanation. Let the percentage of a firm's investment that is foreign funded measure the extent of a firm's FDI. Then if the relationship between FDI and a given endogenous variable is monotone positive, one will expect, other things being equal, WFOEs to outperform NWFOEs in that variable. Of course, if the relationship between FDI and a given endogenous variable is non-monotonic, the picture can be complex. We shall, however, assume such a situation not to occur.

Table 12.7 lists the variables used in our estimation with definitions. ln(WAGE) is the natural logarithm of workers' average hourly wages of a firm, and OPORIN the percentage of production workers of a firm hired from outside Guangdong.[23] FM is a dummy variable denoting form of investment, with FM = 1 for WFOEs, and FM = 0 for NWFOEs. HEDU

Table 12.7 Description of variables

Variables	Description
FM	Form of investment: WFOEs = 1; NWFOEs = 0.
EU, JP, US	Source of investment dummies, with overseas Chinese firms as the reference group.
ln(WAGE)*	Average hourly wage of a firm in RMB yuan, in natural logarithm.
OPORIN	Percentage of workers recruited from other provinces than Guangdong in a firm (%).
HEDU	Percentage of workers with high-middle school education and above in a firm (%).
SECTD	Industrial sector dummy: capital intensive sectors = 1; labor intensive sectors = 0. Capital intensive sectors include machinery, mechanic products, metallic and non-metallic products. All other manufacturing sectors are labor intensive sectors.
EMPLOY	The number of employees of a firm, proxy for firm size.
EXR	Ratio of exports to total sales of a firm (%).

Note
* One firm reported an hourly rate of 50 yuan for wage, which is tested to be an outlier. In regression estimations the outlier is excluded.

indicates the percentage of a firm's production workers who received high-middle school education and above. The higher is HEDU, the better educated the workers are on average. To assess the possible difference in returns to education and the impact of education on workers' geographic origin by form of investment, an interaction term (FM*HEDU) is included in some of the regression models we estimate. EU, JP, and US are three dummy variables indicating source of investment (EU = 1 for European investment, and EU = 0 for non-European investment, etc.), the reference group being the overseas Chinese FIEs. EXR is the ratio of a firm's export to its total sales in a year and is used, as already noted, as a proxy for a firm's investment strategy. SECTD is an industrial sector dummy dividing the sample firms into two groups by industry: SECTD = 1 for capital-intensive and SECTD = 0 for labor intensive industries.[24] Finally, EMPLOY is a non-dummy variable measuring the number of employees of a firm, and is used here as a proxy for firm size.

Table 12.8 presents summary statistics of the mean, median, range, and standard deviation for hourly wages, the percentage of production workers hired from outside Guangdong, and for each non-dummy explanatory variable by form and source of investment.[25] Table 12.9 reports results of the tests of the equality of the means of these variables by form and source of investment. In the absence of any knowledge of factors other than source and form of investment affecting the variables in question, and under the normality assumption, these results would indicate whether there exist statistically significant differences for each variable by form and source of investment. Table 12.10 reports correlation coefficients for each possible pair of the variables, and the results of the tests of their statistical significance under the normality assumption.

Labor practice in FIEs in Guangdong: empirical results

In this section we present our models of estimation and the results. We first consider hourly wages and then workers' geographic origin. Finally we summarize our findings.

Hourly wages and returns to human capital

The arguments advanced in Sections 2 and 3 would imply that, other things being equal, returns to human capital are higher in FIEs than in non-FIEs. Subject to the qualifications made at the beginning of this section, one would also expect them to be higher in WFOEs than in NWFOEs. We want to test if this hypothesis is true by regressing the natural logarithm of firms' average hourly wages, ln(WAGE), on workers' educational level, HEDU, and an interaction term FM*HEDU. The result obtained on this latter term can tell us differences, if any, in returns to education between WOFEs and NWFOEs.

Table 12.8 Descriptive statistics, manufacturing sectors (1997)

		CN	EU	JP	US	WFOE	NWFOE
Wage	Average	4.35 (4.84)	6.3	5.26	7.62	3.92 (5.16)	5.14
	Median	3 (3)	6.4	3.5	3.75	3 (3)	3.5
	Maximum	22 (50)	13	20	25	20 (50)	25
	Minimum	0.97	2	2.5	1.1	2	0.97
	Std dev.	3.81 (6.06)	2.94	5.02	8.16	3.07 (8.16)	4.58
	Obs	92 (93)	10	11	7	36 (37)	86
Origin	Local city	35.91	40.68	29.05	37.09	20.11	41.09
	Guangdong	17.83	31.84	24.16	24.81	15.17	22.41
	Other province (OPORIN)	46.25	27.48	46.79	38.09	64.71	36.5
	Median	50	12	45	20	75	30
	Maximum	100	98	100	98	100	99
	Minimum	0	0	0	0	0	0
	Std dev.	34.22	31.02	35.23	37.04	30.43	32.85
	Obs	202	25	24	27	72	208
HEDU (high-middle school and above)	Average	55.38	71.19	72.57	65.95	50.19	61.94
	Median	50	80	84	70	40	70
	Maximum	100	100	100	100	100	100
	Minimum	0	0	11	0	0	0
	Std dev.	32.1	31.09	31.13	29.89	32.52	31.79
	Obs	204	24	25	27	71	211
Employment	Average	549	451	693	1,209	612	611
	Median	200	212	293	328	285	200
	Maximum	9,000	3,000	3,350	20,000	6,800	20,000
	Minimum	8	15	11	57	8	10
	Std dev.	1,223	741	950	2,661	1,094	1,716
	Obs	221	29	26	29	83	224
EXR	Average	56.35	24.09	46	29.79	69.61	43.77
	Median	74	7.5	32.5	15	96	22
	Maximum	100	100	100	100	100	100
	Minimum	0	0	0	0	0	0
	Std dev.	43.09	32.45	44.10	34.03	39.38	42.23
	Obs	196	22	22	26	67	201

Note
Figures in parentheses are calculated by including the outlier reporting an average hourly wage of 50 yuan. Two firms in the sample reported form of investment but not source of investment. Hence, the total number of observations by form and by source of investment may not be equal in some cases.

Table 12.9 Tests of the equality of the means by form and source of investment, manufacturing sectors (1997)

	Form of investment	Source of investment
	Large sample (z)	Analyses of variance (F)
WAGE	0.01	0.62
WAGE1[a]	−1.72*	1.88
OPORIN	6.64***	2.95**
HEDU	−2.65***	4.15***
EXR	4.60***	6.83***
EMPLOY	0.002	1.64

Notes
a Excludes the outlier reporting 50 yuan for hourly wage.
b *significant at 10% level, **significant at 5% level, ***significant at 1% level.

Workers' hourly wages may not only be influenced by their educational level, but also by other factors as well. First, there may be important differences in the wage levels by form of investment that are not accounted for by differences in returns to education, but are simply because, say, other things being equal, WFOEs pay higher wages than NWFOEs. For example, the wages in a joint venture may well be held back by the wages that are paid to workers in the Chinese parent firm, while a WFOE would be free from such influences in setting wages and, indeed, because they tend to be completely new firms, they may well want to offer wages with a significant premium in order to entice workers to move to their firms. In addition, firms with different foreign investment sources (CN, EU, JP, US) may well be influenced by the wage standards in their home countries or economies in setting their wages (Liu *et al.*, 2003). For these reasons, we also include the form (FM) and source dummies (EU, JP, US) as explanatory variables in the regression equation.

In addition to these, we also control for a firm's industrial sector (SECTD), size (EMPLOY) and investment strategy (EXR). For example, there may exist certain established wage differentials between industries. There is also a sizeable body of literature showing a positive effect of firm size on wages.[26] Finally, one would expect FIEs that pursue a cost-reduction strategy to be more likely to pay a lower average hourly wage to workers than those pursuing the opposite market-seeking strategy.

We thus regress the natural logarithm of hourly wages (ln(WAGE)) on a selection of variables just noted. Estimation uses the White-heteroskedasticity-consistent OLS technique. The results are given in Table 12.11.[27] Clearly they lend support to our hypothesis that returns to education are greater in WFOEs than in NWFOEs. However, while education is shown to have a positive effect on the average hourly wages of workers in WFOEs, its effect is actually negative in NWFOEs. It is difficult to

Table 12.10 Pearson correlation matrix

	ln(WAGE)	OPORIN	FM	EU	JP	US	SECTD	EMPLOY	HEDU	EXR
ln(WAGE)	1.000									
OPORIN	-0.171**	1.000								
FM	-0.111	0.358***	1.000							
EU	0.196**	-0.149**	0.017	1.000						
JP	0.055	0.026	0.020	-0.100**	1.000					
US	0.110	-0.054	0.081	-0.110**	-0.102**	1.000				
SECTD	0.069	-0.031	-0.073	0.040	0.014	-0.040	1.000			
EMPLOY	0.161**	0.128**	8.61E-05	-0.034	0.015	0.122**	-0.049	1.000		
HEDU	-0.005	-0.184***	-0.158***	0.113***	0.129**	0.068	0.090	0.003	1.000	
EXR	-0.275***	0.371***	0.263***	-0.183***	-0.029	-0.168***	-0.040	0.017	-0.272***	1.000

Notes
a The tests are based on complete observations for each pair of variables in question. ln (WAGE) excludes the outlier reporting 50 yuan per hour.
b *significant at 10%, **significant at 5%, ***significant at 1%.

determine why this is so. It could be that firms with a higher percentage of workers with high-middle school education and above share certain characteristics that depress workers' hourly wages, and this negative influence is being picked up by education. While we have no ways of confirming this or, if true, identifying the characteristics in question, it is interesting to note that in a survey on wages covering over 500,000 workers in 14 leading cities in October 1998, conducted by MOLSS (1998), it was revealed that for workers of certain skill categories and in certain occupations ("elementary skilled" manufacturing and "middle skilled" service workers), those who received college and above-college education were on average actually paid a lower wage than those with only junior-middle school education and below. So our finding of negative returns to education in NWFOEs in Guangdong is by no means an isolated case.

While returns to education are greater in WFOEs than in NWFOEs, it is worth noting that in our sample WFOEs also on average recruited a smaller percentage of workers with high-middle school education or above than NWFOEs (Tables 12.8 and 12.9). Thus it appears that although WFOEs better rewarded education, they also employed the better-educated workers more "economically." Indeed, after controlling for differences in returns to education between WFOEs and NWFOEs, our results show that FM has a negative effect on hourly wages.[28]

Besides the influence of education and form of investment, our results show that source of investment has a statistically significant effect on a firm's hourly wages in the case of EU and JP investment. EU FIEs in particular tend to have a higher average hourly wage as compared with the CN reference group. JP firms also show a weakly significant positive premium. US firms, however, fail to show a significant positive premium. Among the other control variables, firm size clearly shows a significant positive effect while export ratio (EXR) a significant negative effect on firms' hourly wages.

Workers' geographical origin

Our hypothesis in this case is that WFOEs promote a greater geographical movement of workers by hiring a higher proportion of workers from outside Guangdong than NWFOEs. Again, subject to qualifications made at the beginning of this section, we take this to be in support of the view that FDI promotes a greater degree of geographical integration of China's formerly segmented labor market.

That being so, the obvious important explanatory variable to be included in our estimating equation is form of investment (FM). However, in addition to FM, other factors may also affect a firm's decision to hire outside workers. Thus while CN FIEs, being mostly of a Hong Kong background, may have had certain prior ties with the local community in which they make the investment, which may well oblige them to hire more local workers than they otherwise would, non-CN FIEs would be free from such influences. Also, certain policy and institutional barriers to hiring outside workers may exist in some industries but not in others (or they exist but to a lesser degree). Or, equally, outside workers may have certain characteristics that make them more suited to being employed in certain industries and not in others. A firm's investment strategy (EXR) and the educational level it requires of its workers (HEDU) may also affect the extent to which a firm recruits outside workers. For example, if export-oriented FIEs tend to pay lower wages (Table 12.11), and if outside workers are more willing to accept a lower wage (Table 12.10), then one can expect export-oriented firms to hire proportionally more outside workers. Similarly, if the less educated workers outside Guangdong are more likely to migrate to work in Guangdong than the better educated, then outside workers will on average have poorer education than local workers (Table 12.10). In this case, FIEs requiring better educated workers will then be less likely to hire outside workers. Finally, the larger a firm, the less likely it is that the firm's specific labor demands will be met by qualified persons from the local population. In this case a larger firm is likely to hire a higher proportion of outside workers.

In the regression for the percentage of outside workers of a firm (OPORIN), we include all these variables in the estimating equation. Table 12.11 reports the results (Model 2A). FM is shown to exert a highly significant, strong positive effect on OPORIN. However, none of the source dummies is significant. A joint F-test also fails to reject the null that all source dummies have zero coefficients (p-value = 0.642). Among the rest of control variables, the sign of EXR is as expected: more export-oriented firms do tend to recruit a higher proportion of outside workers. EMPLOY has a significant, positive effect on OPORIN. The effects of HEDU and SECTD on OPORIN are negative but statistically insignificant.

A Chow test had rejected the null that there exists no structural difference between two groups of firms, WFOEs and NWFOEs, for the regression of OPORIN, at 5 percent level of significance. For this reason, we also ran separate regressions on the two sub-samples, and the results are likewise given in Table 12.11 (Model 2B). They broadly confirm those from the full-sample regression, with one important further finding, namely, that the positive effect of EXR on OPORIN appears to be driven principally by NWFOEs.

Conclusion

The findings from the Guangdong survey shed valuable light on two important labor market reform indicators: returns to human capital and workers' geographical origin. Using firm-level survey data from Guangdong, we compared the performance of two groups of FIEs, WFOEs, and

Table 12.11 OLS regressions for hourly wages, ln(WAGE), and percentages of workers recruited from outside Guangdong Province (OPORIN)

Variables	Regressions for all samples		Regressions for partitioned samples	
	Model 1 dependent variable is ln(WAGE)	Model 2A dependent variable is OPORIN	Model 2B-WFOE dependent variable is OPORIN	Model 2B-NWFOE dependent variable is OPORIN
Intercept	1.655*** (8.525)	32.946*** (5.336)	51.399*** (3.057)	34.095*** (4.787)
FM	−0.451** (−2.259)	18.998*** (3.607)		
EU	0.615*** (3.443)	−9.484 (−1.477)	23.336 (1.381)	−11.211* (−1.764)
JP	0.339 (1.686)	−1.021 (−0.134)	−7.088 (−0.402)	−0.227 (−0.027)
US	0.209 (0.528)	−6.317 (−0.817)	2.914 (0.204)	−7.459 (−0.762)
SECTD	0.138 (1.001)	−1.986 (−0.427)	15.058 (1.667)	−4.780 (−0.905)
EMPLOY	5.79E-05** (2.112)	0.003** (2.509)	0.006*** (2.716)	0.002** (2.340)
HEDU	−0.004* (−1.937)	−0.076 (−1.099)	−0.070 (−0.486)	−0.094 (−1.178)
FM*HEDU	0.006** (2.175)			
EXR	−0.003** (−2.254)	0.195*** (3.588)	0.119 (0.761)	0.218*** (3.613)
Observations	105	229	52	177
R-squared	0.247	0.209	0.106	0.142
Adj. R-squared	0.176	0.180	−0.036	0.107
Prob. (F-stat.)	0.0010	0.0000	0.632	0.0004

Notes
*significant at 10%.
**significant at 5%.
***significant at 1%.
Figures in parentheses are t statistics.

NWFOEs, in these respects after controlling for source of investment, firms' investment strategy, firm size, and firms' industrial sector. The results show that WFOEs indeed provide positive and greater returns to human capital (measured by the percentage of a firm's workers with high-middle school education and above) than NWFOEs, where the returns are actually negative.[29] WFOEs also hire a much greater proportion (19 percentage points more) of workers from outside Guangdong than NWFOEs, indicating a much greater power by WFOEs in promoting a geographical integration of China's labor market. Other things being equal, firms' investment strategy (proxied by a firm's annual share of export in total sales) and size (total number of employees) also matter to their performance in these respects: The more export-oriented a firm is, the lower the average hourly wage and the greater the percentage of workers from outside Guangdong. Firm size has a positive effect on both hourly wages and the share of workers from outside Guangdong. Source of investment is a significant factor for firms' wage levels (with EU and JP firms paying workers a substantial wage premium compared with CN firms), but not for determining the geographical origins of a firm's workers. US firms do not differ significantly from CN firms in this respect. Finally, industrial sector does not appear to be a statistically significant factor in influencing either hourly wages or the geographical origins of workers.

Our survey data set unfortunately does not enable us to compare the performance of FIEs and non-FIEs directly in the two indicators of labor market reforms. Nevertheless, if, as we assume, the relationship between FDI and China's labor market reform in those respects is monotone, then the results we have obtained concerning the relative performance of WFOEs and NWFOEs may be taken to mean that FIEs generally perform better in those respects than non-FIEs. This lends support to the view that FDI promotes labor market reforms in China.

Two main planks to China's market-oriented labor reforms have been wage reforms (a transition from the former egalitarian wage system to one that relates a worker's wages closely to her performance and human capital), and labor recruitment reforms (removing various previous labor market segmentations). In this chapter we looked at the role of FIEs in promoting labor reforms in both these respects. We argued that FIEs in China have generally "led" the process of labor market reforms. A review of available secondary evidence shows that this is indeed generally true. Our own examination of firm-level survey data from Guangdong has also lent support to the hypothesis.

Notes

1 In this chapter, we use the terms "foreign direct investment" and "foreign-invested enterprises" interchangeably.
2 By "labor regime" we mean the entire system of labor allocation and wage and non-wage remuneration, including the way in which human resources are

managed. Such a system may be predominantly market based, as in most countries in the world today, or command based, as in pre-reform China.

3 We shall omit considering urban collective enterprises (COEs) run by urban street committees, district committees, and so on in pre-reform China when speaking of the urban state sector, unless they are otherwise mentioned.

4 NWFOEs include principally joint ventures (JV), but also cooperative ventures (CV), and other. JVs are FIEs that involve joint equity ownership between a foreign investor and its Chinese partner or partners. CVs are typically FIEs to which a foreign partner contributes funds and production know-how while a Chinese partner or partners contribute land, factory building, and other assets. The foreign and Chinese partners share profits and take responsibilities according to a pre-agreed contractual stipulation.

5 Regrettably, our data set does not contain a controlled group of non-FIEs. However, under the assumption of FDI having a monotonic relationship to our labor reform variables, our findings regarding the comparative performance of WFOEs and NWFOEs in the respects in question can be interpreted to imply that FDI has a positive influence on China's labor reforms in those respects in general.

6 One consequence of the job allocation system was the overstaffing problem of SOEs, which posed major obstacles to SOE reforms subsequently. Since the mid-1990s, large numbers of workers have been "laid off" from the state sector.

7 The only route available for a rural youth to leave their village and to enter the urban state sector was through college education. College graduates from a rural origin were automatically given an urban resident status and became state sector employees.

8 The national wage scale allowed, for the same skill rank, minor variations in wages between major geographical regions to take into account historical differences in living costs, and variations between different occupations to take into account differences in the skills required and in the arduousness of tasks.

9 A further reform area concerns social security and welfare provisions (pension, unemployment and medical insurance, and housing, to only mention the major ones). Before the reform these benefits were provided and administered on an enterprise-by-enterprise basis, which meant that individual workers received these benefits only from their own work unit. Should a worker leave their existing work unit, their entitlement to benefits accredited at their existing work unit would cease, and they would have to obtain these benefits from the new work unit, which might or might not offer the provision. If not, then the fear of losing one's existing benefits would clearly constitute a major disincentive against a worker seeking to leave their existing work unit. An important area of labor reform in China has been to reform its social security and welfare system for the state sector workers so that their benefits are monetized and portable, thereby promoting labor mobility. In our account of labor reforms in China below, however, we shall omit to mention this area of reform.

10 However, from around the mid-1990s, local municipal governments such as in Beijing, Shanghai, Guangzhou, and other cities began to erect a new barrier to geographical labor movements. To tackle the problem of redundant laborers in their own cities, and in the name of improving "labor management," these governments introduced a work permit system targeting outside workers. Only those outside workers with a work permit certificate (in addition to a temporary residence certificate and migrant worker certificate) can legally work in these cities. To encourage more highly educated people and professionals with particular skills to move to these cities, as a rule work permits have been issued on the basis of educational and professional qualifications. Generally speaking, however, those with the proper qualifications have been able to legally enter and work in the cities concerned with ease.

11 See also Zhang (1995), Tso (1998) and Chen (1997).

12 However, see note 10.

13 "Migrant population" in China refers to those who do not have a local *hukou* and local personnel record files (*dang'an*) in the place they work.

14 Non-CN FIEs in China are mainly those whose foreign investment came from the US, Japan, and EU countries; CN FIEs are those whose foreign investment principally came from Hong Kong, Taiwan, Macao, and Southeast Asian countries.

15 The survey covered 11 cities and administrative districts, involving 5,280 enterprises and 2.053 million workers and staff, accounting for 16.3 percent and 43.6 percent of the whole populations of enterprises and of workers and staff in Hebei Province, respectively.

16 Greater wage differentials may be viewed as a negative, rather than positive, development in terms of increased income inequality. However, this needs to be considered against China's historical legacy of a highly egalitarian wage structure. Under a market system, wages would closely reflect a person's productivity and therefore their contribution to their firm. An overly narrowly differentiated set of wages may fail to reflect different contributions workers of different skills and human capital make to their firm. Besides the fact that this has deleterious effects on workers' work incentives, it is not clear whether morally such a system is necessarily superior to one that gives due recognition to differences in people's skills, abilities, and the contributions they make to their firm.

17 The only major institutional obstacle that remains to their doing so is the nonportability of most of their social security and welfare benefits (see note 9). However, reforms in these areas are expected to gradually ease this obstacle as well.

18 A "regular" worker in a state sector work unit is typically one who was hired under the old system, with the right residency qualification and given a guaranteed life-long employment (as long as the enterprise continues to survive).

19 The portable nature of social insurance and monetized (as opposed to in-kind) benefits and housing subsidy in this sector has also given workers added scope for mobility. It is worth noting that the extent to which an FIE in a given city or region can freely recruit employees from outside the city has in recent years been limited by a quota and work permit system akin to that run by *countries* when controlling foreign nationals seeking employment within their boundaries (see also note 10).

20 Whereby the firms from the population data set were first grouped according to investment source, after which firms in each source group were alphabetically ordered, and every k'th firm was then selected in view of the target number of sample firms assigned to each group. The target numbers were 300 for the CN group, and 100 each for EU, JP, and US groups.

21 We solicited the help from students of the Lingnan College, Zhongshan University, who after proper briefing undertook most of the interviews.

22 Our survey covered the hourly wages, geographical origins, and educational levels of both the production workers and management and technical staff. However, in this study we shall only consider the case of *production workers*, leaving aside that of management and technical staff.

Note that under the Chinese educational system, there exists the following stages or levels of education: primary schooling (five–six years), low-middle schooling (three years), high-middle schooling (three years), and university education (three–four years). These represent a typical route of progression for a child. In many cases, however, children stop going to school after primary or low-middle schooling. After primary or low-middle schooling, some may then attend special technical schools, while many progress to high-middle schools. Among those who attend high-middle schools, some may later attend special technical colleges, while others go on to universities.

23 It also needs to be pointed out that our data set does not contain information on non-wage incomes of a worker. However, this omission need not matter if firms are likely to have had the same proportion of non-wage benefits in a worker's total remuneration. According to the information provided by the Bureau of Labor of Guangdong Province, on average these benefits amount to a third of the total labor costs of a firm in Guangdong, or about half of the wage costs. In 1999 on average wage costs accounted for 62.94 percent, social insurance 18.07 percent, welfare benefits 10.25 percent, housing 2.78 percent, training and education 1.26 percent, work place safety 1.05 percent, and other 3.65 percent, of the total labor costs in Guangdong (available at http://www.gzlabour.gov.cn). We have no corresponding information for 1997.

24 The industries are divided into these two groups according to both the average capital intensity and the average management and technical (MT) staff ratio of the industries in question. The average capital intensity of an industry refers to the average of the ratios of total investment to total employment, and the average MT staff ratio of an industry refers to the average of the ratios of the number of MT staff to the total number of employees, of the sample firms of the industry in question. Capital-intensive industries are those with both a high average capital intensity ratio and a high average MT staff ratio. By the standard Chinese industrial classification, there are altogether 22 two-digit manufacturing industries. After further grouping, a cluster analysis yields a rough division of these industries into the two stated groupings. Capital-intensive industries include machinery, mechanical products, metallic and non-metallic products. Labor-intensive ones include food and beverage, pharmaceutical, textile, furniture, electronic products, and chemical products. We thank Angela Wang for sharing the results of her calculation.

25 The mean values for each variable are calculated as simple averages for firms belonging to each group. Other descriptive statistics are calculated accordingly. Two sets of results are given for average hourly wages. The first set does not exclude an "outlier" reporting 50 yuan for average hourly wages; the second set (in parentheses) excludes that outlier. The outlier in question is an overseas Chinese WFOE, with total investment of 200 million yuan and employing 100 workers and staff. Set up in 1993 and with 12 affiliates across China, its main products were wireless and wire telephones. Ninety percent of the workers received high-middle school education or above, and 30 percent were recruited from outside Guangdong. Chinese and expatriate staff received the same pay, something unusual in FIEs in China. Including the outlier, the results are in fact broadly in line with the macro-level wage comparisons in Table 12.2. However, a studentized residual test shows the residual at 5.46, indicating that the firm is truly an outlier.

26 See Brown and Medoff (1989), Velenchik (1995) and Schaffner (1998) for evidence on firm size exerting an independent effect on firms' wages. Explanations for this include unionization, minimum wage compliance, efficiency wages, and other.

27 A Chow test failed to reject the null, at the 5 percent level of significance, that there exists no structural difference between WFOEs and NWFOEs, so that the underlying coefficients for the explanatory variables should be equal in value. Note that because not all interviewed firms answered all our survey questions, and some questions in particular were answered by relatively few firms, the number of complete observations differs between estimations and, in all cases, it falls below the full sample size of 320.

28 A possible reason why hourly wages are lower in WFOEs than in NWFOEs, other things being equal, may well be that in a NWFOE, there exist pressures from the Chinese partner firm for the enterprise to distribute a greater share of "profits" (gross of wages) to workers in the form of higher wages. Such pressures are absent in a WFOE.

29 Note, however, that we did not find WFOEs to pay higher average hourly wage than NWFOEs, even after controlling for various related factors.

References

Brown, C. and Medoff, J. (1989). "The employer size-wage effect," *Journal of Political Economy*, 97(5).

Byron, R.P. and Manaloto, E.Q. (1990). "Returns to education in China," *Economic Development and Cultural Change*, 38.

CSP (China Statistics Press), various issues from 1985 to 2002. *China Statistical Yearbook* and *China Labor Statistical Yearbook*. Beijing, China.

Chen, C.L. (1997). "Comparison of investment behavior of source countries in China," Working Paper No. 97/14, Chinese Economics Research Center, University of Adelaide, Australia.

Dai, Y.C. (1997). *Employment and Income of A Labor Surplus Economy*. Shanghai: Yuandong Press, China.

Du, R.S. (1994). *Reform and Development in Rural China*, Palgrave Macmillan.

Forbs, D. and Linge, G. (1990). *China's Spatial Economy: Recent Development and Reforms*, Hong Kong: Panther Press.

Gelb, A. (1990). "TVP worker's incomes, incentives and attitudes," in W.A. Byrd and L. Qingsong (eds), *China's Rural Industry: Structure, Development, and Reform*. Oxford: Oxford University Press.

Gordon, R.H.. and Li, D.D. (1999). "The effects of wage distortions on the transition: theory and evidence from China," *European Economic Review*, 43.

Gregory, R.G. and Meng, X. (1995). "Wage determination and occupational attainments in the rural industrial sector of China," *Journal of Comparative Economics*, 21.

Knight, J. and Song, L. (1991). "The determinants of urban income inequality in China," *Oxford Bulletin of Economics and Statistics*, 53.

Knight, J., Song, L., and Jia, H. (1999). "Chinese rural migrants in urban enterprises: three perspectives," *The Journal of Development Studies*, 35.

Lai, D.S. (1998). "Human capital, labor market and income distribution," *Economic Research Journal (Jingji Yanjiu)*, Beijing, China.

Lin, C.G. (1993). "Discussing the solutions to the current rural problems," (in Chinese) *Problems of Agricultural Economy*, 2.

Liu, Minquan, Xu, L.D., and Liu, L. (2000). "FDI and linkages: China at the dawn of the WTO Accession," mimeo.

Liu, Minquan, Xu, L.D., and Liu, L. (2003). "Labor standards and FDI in China: some survey findings," in Rana Hasan and Devashish Mitra (eds), *The Impact of Trade on Labor: Issues, Perspectives, and Experiences from Developing Asia*, Holland: Elsevier Science.

Markel, D. (1994). "Finally, a national labor law," *China Business Review*, vol. 21, issue 6, November/December.

Ma, Y. (1999). "Foreign investment in China: opportunities and challenges," Paper presented at OECD/MOFTEC Roundtable on the Environment and Opportunity for FDI in China, Xiamen, China.

Meng, X. (1993). "Determination and discrimination: female wages in China's rural TVP industries." Economics Division Working Papers no. 93/1. Research School of Pacific Studies, Australian National University.

MOLSS (1998). "A survey on wages in 14 cities," Online. Available from: www.molss.gov.cn.

MOLSS (2001). "The labor market wage level of 44 cities in 2000." Online. Available from: www.molss.gov.cn (accessed 10 April 2002)

Roberts, K.D. (2001). "The determinants of job choice by rural labor migrants in Shanghai," *China Economic Review*, 12.

Schaffner, A. Julie (1998). "Premiums to employment in larger establishments: evidence from Peru." *Journal of Development Economics*, vol. 55.

Tso, A. (1998). "Foreign direct investment and China's economic development," *Issues and Studies*, vol. 34, no. 2.

Velenchik, A.D. (1995). "Government intervention, efficiency wages, and the employer-size wage effect in Zimbabwe," Wellesley College Working Paper No. 95–09.

Vernon, R. (1966). "International investment and international trade in the product cycle," *Quarterly Journal of Economics*, vol. 80.

Yang, D.T. (1997). "The effects of institutions on worker mobility and labor market efficiency," in G.J. Wen and D.Q. Xu (eds), *The Reformability of China's State Sector*. New Jersey: World Scientific Publishing Co.

Zhang, Z. (1995). "International trade and foreign direct investment: further evidence from China," *Asia Economic Journal*, vol. 9, no. 21.

Zhao, R., Li, S., and Riskin, C. (1999). *Restudying Income Distribution of Chinese Households* (in Chinese), Beijing: Chinese Financial and Economic Press.

Zhuang, X.M. and Li, Q.Z. (1998). "The situation and analyses of enterprise wages in Zhejiang province." *China Labor*, December, Beijing, China.

Part IV
Concluding remarks

13 Is China the world factory?

Kevin Honglin Zhang

Take an item from the shelves of Wal-Mart or K-Mart and, more likely than not, it will have a "Made in China" label. This is no surprise the China makes 70 percent of the world's toys, 60 percent of its bicycles, 50 percent of its shoes, and 33 percent of its luggage. China also builds half of the world's microwave ovens, one-third of its TV sets and air conditioners, a quarter of its washers, and one-fifth of its refrigerators. China's share in world textiles has risen dramatically since the first day of 2005, when quota and tariff barriers were removed. It is expected that China will take over 60 percent of the global textile market in the coming years, without protectionism in the US and the EU. Therefore many people (for example, Zakaria of *Newsweek* (May 2005) and Shenkar (2005)) view China as the world factory. The evidence cited most frequently is China's export expansion in the past decade. The reality is, however, more complex. A close examination of China's global competitiveness in exports (from the detailed discussion in the preceding 12 chapters of this book) reveals the following points:

- More than half of China's exports are not generated by domestic firms but by foreign-invested enterprise. "Made in China" does not mean "made by China."
- Most of the manufacturing exports are not capital- and technology-intensive but labor-intensive. China is merely a manufacturing center for low-end products.
- Even in exports of labor-intensive products, China's value-added is small. China has a long way to go in building its own brand names and international marketing network.

The conclusion thus is that China is not the world factory, at least not right now. But some questions still remain unanswered: Why is China not currently the world factory? Why has the view of China as the world factory been so popular for years? Can China be the world factory in the near future? This chapter attempts to offer answers to these questions.

258 Kevin H. Zhang

Industrial competitiveness: China's position in the world

"The world factory" was a title first awarded to the UK during the Industrial Revolution, when the country was dominant in world industry. As the US took off in 1870 and surpassed the UK in terms of GDP, the US then became known as the world factory, especially after World War II, when it made up almost half of world GDP. The strong manufacturing performance of Germany and Japan (especially its industrial miracle in the 1970s) won them the title of "world manufacturing centers." The UK's dominance in world industry in the eighteenth century has been widely recognized. The US, Germany, and Japan are still the most powerful economies in the world in almost all aspects, especially in manufacturing technology. Therefore, the requirements for a country to be considered as a world factory depends not only on having a large share of world GDP and the export market, but also on having the highest per capita income and industrial competitiveness.

China's position in world GDP, exports, per capita income, and industrial competitiveness are presented in Tables 13.1–13.4. According to the World Bank (2005), China's GDP in 2003 is ranked 7th in the atlas method based on exchange rates, and is the second largest economy in the world, just after the US, in terms of purchasing-power-parity (PPP method), which many people believe is closer to the truth. However, China is only about 60 percent of the US GDP (Table 13.1), although it is expected that it may be the world's largest economy by 2015, given the growth rate of both nations..

China gained most of the world export share between 1985–2002 (from 1.4 percent to 5.1 percent). By the end of 2004, China became the third

Table 13.1 Market shares of the world top 10 exporters in 2004 and changes over 1985–2002

World export share in 2004			Changes in shares over 1985–2002		
Rank	Country	Share (%)	Rank	Country	Changes (%)
1	Germany	10.0	1	**China**	**3.7**
2	US	9.0	2	US	1.7
3	**China**	**6.5**	3	S. Korea	1.1
4	Japan	6.2	4	Mexico	1.1
5	France	4.9	5	Malaysia	0.8
6	Netherlands	3.9	6	Ireland	0.7
7	Italy	3.8	7	Thailand	0.7
8	UK	3.8	8	Taiwan	0.6
9	Canada	3.5	9	Singapore	0.5
10	Belgium	3.4	10	Spain	0.4

Sources: *World Trade Report 2005* (WTO, 2005); *World Investment Report 2002* (UNCTAD, 2002a).

Table 13.2 China's GDP in the world in 2003 (Atlas method and PPP method)

Rank/country	Total GDP (billions of US$)	Ratio of China to the country	PPP GDP (billions of international dollars)	Ratio of China to the country
1 US	10,949	0.13	10,923	0.59
2 Japan	4,301	0.33	3,568	1.81
3 Germany	2,403	0.59	2,291	2.81
4 UK	1,795	0.79	1,611	4.00
5 France	1,758	0.81	1,654	3.90
6 Italy	1,468	0.97	1,563	4.12
7 China	**1,417**	**1.00**	**6,446**	**1.00**
12 India	601	2.36	3,078	2.09
15 Brazil	492	2.88	1,376	4.69
16 Russia	433	3.27	1,324	4.87

Source: Computed from *World Development Indicators 2005* (World Bank, 2005).

Table 13.3 China's GNI per capita in the world in 2003 (Atlas method and PPP method)

	Atlas method (US$)	Ratio of China to the country	PPP method (international $)	Ratio of China to the country
US	37,870	0.03	37,750	0.13
Japan	34,180	0.03	28,450	0.18
Germany	25,270	0.04	27,610	0.18
Brazil	2,720	0.40	7,510	0.66
Russia	2,610	0.42	8,950	0.56
China	**1,100**	**1.00**	**4,980**	**1.00**
India	540	2.04	2,880	1.73

Source: Computed from *World Development Indicators 2005* (World Bank, 2005).

largest exporting country with 6.5 percent of the world exports (Table 13.2). It is very likely that China will become the number one exporter within a decade, if this rapid growth in exports continues.

What per capita income and competitive industrial performance index (CIPI) indicate is not as positive as GDP and exports. According to the World Bank (2005), gross national income (GNI) per capita for China in 2003 was $1,100 (in the atlas method), ranked as 134th in the world, and is only 3 percent of US GNI per capita ($37,870). The corresponding numbers from the PPP method are 4,980 international dollars, ranked as 119th, and 13 percent of the US. It is safe to say that China is a developing country and it may not catch up with the developed countries in terms of per capital income in the near future.

The most direct and relevant measurement of a country's industrial ability is the competitive industrial performance (CIP) index. The index was constructed by the United Nations Industrial Development Organization (UNIDO), which is based on four indicators: manufacturing value added per capita, manufacturing exports per capita, and the shares of medium- and high-tech products in manufacturing value-added and in manufacturing exports. The first two indicators tell about industrial capability. The other two reflect technological complexity and industrial upgrading.[1] A ranking of 87 economies (selected on the basis on data availability for inter-economy comparison) for 1998 and 1985 by the CIP index was published in *Industrial Development Report 2002/2003* (UNIDO, 2002). Table 13.4 shows the ranking and index values for the top ten countries, China, Brazil, Russia, and India (so called BRIC emerging economies).

The ranking for 1998 reveals a general and expected pattern: industrialized countries congregate near the top, middle-income developing economies (including China) around the middle, low-income developing countries and least developed economies at the bottom. In general, CIP index ranks changed little between 1985 and 1998. But some exceptions exist because leaps in the rankings are nevertheless possible. China changed rank by 24 places (from 61 to 37), being the nation with the largest improvements.

It is interesting to have a closer look at China's position in terms of four indicators, on which the CIP index is constructed (Tables A1–A4 in the Appendix). (a) Manufacturing value-added (MVA): Global MVA grew about 7 percent a year during 1985–1998. Although their share declined,

Table 13.4 Competitive industrial performance index (1985 and 1998)

Country	Rank		Index value	
	1998	*1985*	*1998*	*1985*
Singapore	1	6	0.883	0.587
Switzerland	2	1	0.751	0.808
Ireland	3	15	0.739	0.379
Japan	4	2	0.696	0.725
Germany	5	3	0.632	0.635
US	6	5	0.564	0.599
Sweden	7	4	0.562	0.633
Finland	8	7	0.538	0.494
Belgium	9	8	0.495	0.489
UK	10	12	0.473	0.426
Brazil	33	27	0.149	0.140
China	**37**	**61**	**0.126**	**0.021**
Russia	44		0.077	
India	49	50	0.054	0.034

Source: Computed from *Industrial Development Report 2002/2003* (UNIDO, 2002).

industrialized countries (especially the US, Japan, and Germany) dominate the total. China's share rose by 2 percentage points, from 4.25 percent to 6.31 percent. Still average MVA per capita in industrialized countries was about 17 times that in developing countries compared with about 17 times in 1985. (b) Manufactured exports: From 1985 to 1998, China had raised its share of world manufactured exports by 3.5 percent percentage points (from 0.49 percent to 3.96 percent). But per capita exports from China was still very low ($135 vs. $2035 for the US). Data on MVA and manufactured exports indicate that MVA and exports are highly concentrated in industrialized countries (US, Japan, Germany, France, and UK), though China's share is increasing for both. Manufacturing production is more concentrated than exports. (c) Technological structure of manufacturing value-added and exports: MVA and manufactured exports are becoming more technological-intensive, moving from low-tech and resource-based products to medium- and high-tech products.[2] But China's manufacturing structure remained stable over 1985–1998, with half in high-and medium-tech in total. China made great progress in technological composition of manufacturing exports, with the largest increase in the share of medium- and high-tech exports (from 4 percent to 37 percent).[3]

China's large upward leaps in high- and medium-tech manufactures and exports are associated with participation in integrated global production networks through inward FDI, which sharply raises the share of complex products in exports and MVA (Zhang, 2002). This is not to say that the strategy of entering into high-tech integrated global production systems is the only way to upgrade technology in developing countries. In fact, it may not even be the best and most sustainable way. It introduces new production technologies and raises exports, but it may not develop or deepen local capabilities if China fails to move beyond final assembly of high-tech products. To build genuine technological capabilities in complex activities, China has to do it through a slower, costlier and riskier process of advancing from assembly to real manufacturing, and from there to local design and development. China needs to do much of this without investment by multinational corporations – even restricting foreign entry to encourage the development of deeper capabilities in local enterprises.

Two points are worth mentioning about China's position in world industrial competitiveness. First, manufacturing activity remains heavily concentrated in industrialized countries, though China is increasing its share. But in intensity of industrialization (measured by manufacturing value added per capita) China is still far behind. Second, among developing regions, China is the best industrial performer in most respects, though it lags in manufacturing value added per capita. It has the highest growth rates in manufacturing production and exports. It is far more export oriented than other developing regions. It has a more technologically advanced structure and is rapidly improving all the main drivers of industrial performance.

The preceding discussion suggests that China has not become the world factory, at least not right now, given its industrial competitiveness and low per capita income.

Export competitiveness: China's position in the world

Following the conventional method (Lall, 1998, 2000; UNCTAD, 2002a), we measure a country's export competitiveness by its share in world exports. As shown in Table 13.1, the top ten exporters generate 55 percent of world exports in 2004 and the top 20 account for three-quarters (WTO, 2005). The top ten list in Table 13.1 is dominated by developed economies. China is the only developing country and is in third position. China's strong export growth was underpinned by a strengthening of its export competitiveness in all markets – reflected in an increase of the country's market share by over four percentage points in the past two decades (from 1.4 percent in 1985 to 6.5 percent in 2004). In fact, China is the country that raised the largest market share in the world during the period.

Table 13.5 shows the top ten economies that have gained market share most during 1985–2000, which indicates *dynamic* competitiveness (*static* competitiveness being shown by market shares at a point in time) and reveal the ability of a country to keep up with changing technologies and export patterns.[4] The lists in Table 13.5 contain most dynamic exporters in the world by technology category (resource-based, low-technology, medium-technology and high-technology products).[5] China is the largest winner, leading in all sectors except resource-based manufactures in which it ranks third.

Table 13.6 shows China's share in world export markets by sector over the period 1985–2000. The share of primary products fell slightly, but manufactures gained substantially in the world market share. This increase was even more remarkable in technology-intensive products. By 2000, China generated 8 percent of world exports in manufactures not based on nature resources, compared with less than 2 percent in 1985. About one-fifth of low-tech-good exports were produced by China, which suggests China as the world center for labor-intensive products. It is noted that China has expanded its exports substantially since 2000, especially 2001 when China entered the WTO. Although the relevant data are not available, China's share in manufactures not based on natural resources is believed to rise significantly, given the growth of its total export share by 2.6 percentage points (from 3.9 percent in 2000 to 6.5 percent in 2004).

The structure of China's exports has also changed: in 1985, exports of primary products and resource-based manufactures represented 49 percent of all exports, while in 2002 their share fell to 9 percent. The share of non-resource-based manufactures rose from 50 percent to 91 percent (Table 13.7). The share of high-technology exports jumped from 3 percent in 1985 to 27 percent in 2002, and that for medium-technology exports

Table 13.5 Top 10 export winners in the world by technology category (1985–2000)

Rank	All sectors	Resource-based manufactures	Non-resource-based manufactures	High-technology manufactures	Medium-technology manufactures	Low-technology manufactures
1	**China**	**Ireland**	**China**	**China**	**China**	**China**
2	US	US	Mexico	Malaysia	Mexico	US
3	S. Korea	**China**	Malaysia	Taiwan	US	Mexico
4	Mexico	S. Korea	US	S. Korea	S. Korea	Indonesia
5	Malaysia	India	Thailand	Singapore	Spain	Thailand
6	Ireland	Russia	S. Korea	Mexico	Taiwan	Malaysia
7	Thailand	Thailand	Singapore	Philippines	Malaysia	Canada
8	Taiwan	Indonesia	Philippines	Thailand	Thailand	Turkey
9	Singapore	Israel	Indonesia	Ireland	Hungary	India
10	Spain	Japan	Taiwan	Finland	Indonesia	Poland

Source: *World Investment Report 2002* (UNCTAD, 2002a).

Notes
The ranking is based on percent increment in market share between 1985 and 2000. The data for Russia are 1995–2000.

Table 13.6 China's share in the world export market by sectors (1985–2000) (%)

Sectors	1985	2000	Changes in 1985–2000
Total exports	1.4	3.9	2.7 (4.1 by 2004)
Primary products	2.4	2.3	−0.1
Manufactures based on natural resources	1.1	2.7	1.6
Manufactures not based on natural resources	1.5	7.8	6.3
Low technology	4.5	18.7	14.2
Medium technology	0.4	3.6	3.2
High technology	0.4	6.0	5.6
Others	0.7	1.8	0.9

Sources: *Trade and Development Report 2002* (UNCTAD, 2002b), *World Investment Report 2002* (UNCTAD, 2002a); *World Trade Report 2005* (WTO, 2005).

increased from 8 percent to 20 percent in the same period. Of course, as mentioned before, the large proportion of medium-tech exports and high-tech exports by China reflects relatively simple labor-intensive operations (assembling mainly imported components), rather than complex manufacturing or R&D using substantial local physical and technological inputs, as discussed in Chapter 8.

In summary, China indeed has made great progress in export competitiveness for the past two decades in terms of its world export share. However, China's export boom is inflated in part by its processing trade and foreign-invested enterprises. It also needs to be emphasized that export market shares are hard to gain and hard to sustain. Export market shares may be gained because of temporary advantages such as preferential market access for labor-intensive, low-technology goods. A genuine improvement in export competitiveness can result from the upgrading of human resources or the use of improved technologies.

Potential for China to be the world factory

While the preceding analyses suggest that China is not the world factory yet, the potential for China to be the world factory is quite large. In fact, if one would ask which country could emerge as the new world factory in 20–30 years, the answer for many people would be China. Several advantages that China posses underlie the potential: the current industrial capacity and export competitiveness; its large country size; and its strong centralized government.

In aggregate terms (although not per capita terms), China already has highest industrial capacity and export competitiveness in the developing countries and is in the top place in the world. For example, China is by now the dominant global player in many industries, especially those that

Table 13.7 China's export structure (1985–2002) (%)

Sectors	1985	1990	1995	2000	2002	Changes in 1985–2002
Primary products	35.0	14.6	7.0	4.7	4.1	−30.9
Manufactures based on natural resources	13.6	8.2	7.4	6.9	4.7	−8.9
Manufactures not based on natural resources	50.0	76.2	84.6	87.3	91.2	41.2
Low technology	39.7	53.6	53.5	47.6	44.7	5.0
Medium technology	7.7	15.4	16.9	17.3	19.8	12.1
High technology	2.6	7.2	14.2	22.4	26.7	23.9
Others	1.4	1.0	1.0	1.1	1.0	−0.4
Total exports	100	100	100	100	100	100

Sources: *Trade and Development Report 2002* (UNCTAD, 2002b); *World Investment Report 2002* (UNCTAD, 2002a); *World Trade Report 2005* (WTO, 2005).

are labor intensive (UNCTAD, 2002b; Shenkar, 2005). China-based factories make 70 percent of the world's toys, 60 percent of its bicycles, 50 percent of its shoes, and 33 percent of its luggage. In those product categories, it is often impossible to find a non-Chinese product on store shelves. In some other product categories such as textiles and garments, China's share has risen dramatically since 1 January 2005, when quota and tariff walls were expired.

China's industrial capability in terms of technology is also in good position for upgrading. A huge effort has been made by China to build competitiveness in medium-technology industries. The strategy used in China is to integrate domestic firms into global production chain through FDI. In some ways medium-tech exports show national technological capabilities better than do high-tech exports. The assembly activities of foreign-invested enterprises play a role here too, but less so than in high-tech exports, because strong export performance in medium-tech is often based on deeper local manufacturing. Mobility plays a role as well. Parts and components of high-tech equipment can often be shipped around the world more easily than those of heavy industries. In China medium-tech exports are led by both multinational corporations and domestic firms (Zhang, 2004).

The Chinese government of course is not content with remaining a low-tech, labor-intensive manufacture. In fact China has worked very hard in industrial upgrading. For instance, through attracting and utilizing FDI, China is already active in certain capital- and technology-intensive industries. China builds half of the world's microwave ovens, one-third of its TV sets and air conditioners, a quarter of its washers and mobile phones, and one-fifth of its refrigerators. These products represent the fastest growing segment of its exports as well as its new manufacturing sectors.

China undoubtedly has the advantage of the country size in terms of both population and natural resources. The large country size leads to not only possible huge domestic market, but also the availability of abundant unskilled and skilled labor. The large market provides China with tremendous bargaining power, a trump card that was unavailable to other developing countries.[6] The lure of its domestic market enables China to require technology transfer as a condition for foreign investor entry, capturing unprecedented benefits. For instance, China is the only country in the world where domestic auto makers maintain equity ventures with competing foreign partners, which makes it possible to learn "best practices" from both and end up with potentially more knowledge than either foreign party (UNCTAD, 2002a; Shenkar, 2005). The aim is to create Chinese multinational firms that will hold their own in global markets (like Haier Group in Chapter 4), and replicate the success of Toyota, Sony, and Samsung, but in a shorter time frame.

China's large size also means a vast pool of human resources, including not only an "unlimited" supply of unskilled labor, but also a large and growing number of engineers, scientists, and skilled technicians.[7] The coexistence of cheap labor with increasingly abundant skilled personnel underlies China's strategy of sustaining its dominance in labor-intensive industries even as it enters technology-intensive sectors. Unlike Japan and South Korea, China may not let go of the labor-intensive segment as it moves up the ladder. Instead, it will leverage its dominance in this segment to fund a major push into medium- and high-technology industries.

China's strong centralized government is a big plus in promoting national competitiveness in the global markets. In combination with its large size, a strong government enables China to realize the bargaining power over multinational corporations and also makes it possible for China to allocate resources more efficiently in industrial upgrading. For example, the large scale of improvements in China's infrastructure conditions (highway, railway, and telecommunications) and industrial base and supply network would not be possible without active government intervention.

Conclusion

China's rise through globalization, differs from that of Japan and South Korea, and is not similar to that of the US either. China's real distinction is its huge size and enormous population. China is not the world factory but it has great potential to be so in the near future (20–30 years). China's current position in world GDP, industrial output and competitiveness, and manufacturing exports and competitiveness suggests that it is the global production center for labor-intensive and low-tech products, rather than capital-intensive and high-tech products. However, China seems to be ready to emerge as the world factory in the coming decades. While it will take a long time for China to catch up with the US standard of living, it is possible that China will become the world factory decades before it reaches the US level of per capita income.

The biggest opportunity for China is the potential to develop self-contained, technology-intensive, and large-scale manufactures that combine high quality human capital with low labor and infrastructure costs. With support from its huge domestic markets, China could develop large-scale production and expand its global market share in both low- and high-end industries. Following this process based on rapid upgrading, China could become the world factory through establishing mutually reinforcing links between FDI, exports, and economic growth.

The outcome could be different if China does not follow such the route. It may be used by multinational corporations as an assembly platform for low-value-added exports, the benefits of rising trade and FDI could be extremely limited in terms of technological upgrading and industrialization. Eventually China may be another Brazil or Mexico, developing but not taking-off.

Nobody knows what the outcome will be – only time will tell.

Appendix

Table A1 Manufacturing value-added (1985 and 1998)

Rank	Country/region	1998 Value	1998 World share	1985 Value	1985 World share
1	US	1,432,800	25.42	802,347	32.35
2	Japan	895,425	15.89	396,890	16.00
3	Germany	481,315	8.54	196,622	7.93
4	**China**	**355,540**	**6.31**	**105,698**	**4.26**
5	France	280,223	4.97	114,982	4.64
9	Brazil	151,274	2.68	68,640	2.77
12	Russia	97,357	1.73	–	
15	India	63,860	1.13	33,471	1.35
	World	5,636,100	100.00	2,480,000	100.00
	Developed countries	4,240,800	75.24	2,003,300	80.78
	Developing countries	1,395,300	24.76	476,600	19.22

Source: Computed from *Industrial Development Report 2002/2003* (UNIDO, 2002).

Table A2 Manufacturing exports (1985 and 1998)

Rank	Country/region	1998		1985	
		Value	World share	Value	World share
1	US	550,043	13.00	162,244	13.09
2	Germany	487,273	11.52	165,117	13.32
3	Japan	370,360	8.76	171,785	13.86
4	France	264,005	6.24	83,157	6.71
5	UK	242,113	5.72	73,937	5.97
7	**China**	**167,681**	**3.96**	**6,049**	**0.49**
23	Brazil	38,882	0.92	17,617	1.42
25	Russia	29,659	0.70	–	–
29	India	25,855	0.61	6,209	0.50
	World	4,230,000	100.00	1,239,200	100.00
	Developed countries	3,125,500	73.89	1,045,000	84.33
	Developing countries	1,104,500	26.11	194,000	15.66

Source: Computed from *Industrial Development Report 2002/2003* (UNIDO, 2002).

Table A3 Technological structure of manufacturing value-added (1985 and 1998)

Rank	Country/region	Share of high- and medium-tech industry		Share of low-tech and resource-based industry	
		1998	1985	1998	1985
1	Singapore	80	67	20	33
2	Japan	66	64	34	36
3	Ireland	65	53	35	47
4	Germany	64	64	36	36
5	Switzerland	63	57	37	43
6	US	63	62	37	38
7	UK	62	58	38	42
12	India	59	56	41	44
13	Brazil	58	54	42	46
24	**China**	**51**	**49**	**49**	**51**
34	Russian Federation	41	–	59	–
	World	59	57	41	43
	Developed countries	61	59	39	41
	Developing countries	49	43	51	57

Source: Computed from *Industrial Development Report 2002/2003* (UNIDO, 2002).

Table A4 Technological structure of manufacturing exports (1985 and 1998)

Rank	Country/region	Medium and high-tech exports		Low tech and resource-based export	
		1998	1985	1998	1985
1	Japan	81.1	80.0	14.3	17.7
2	Philippines	74.7	10.5	20.7	42.4
3	Singapore	74.3	39.9	19.9	43.4
4	Mexico	65.5	25.1	22.9	13.1
5	US	65.4	59.4	21.2	19.1
29	**China**	**36.6**	**4.1**	**54.6**	**19.5**
31	Brazil	34.3	23.9	41.7	44.9
40	India	16.6	9.8	61.7	59.6
41	Russian Federation	16.3	–	23.7	–
	World	63.8	57.7	36.2	42.3
	Developed countries	67.8	62.9	32.3	37.1
	Developing countries	53.8	33.5	46.0	66.3

Source: Computed from *Industrial Development Report 2002/2003* (UNIDO, 2002).

Notes

1 According to UNIDO (2002) classification of manufactured products by technology intensity, four types are identified as follows: (i) resource-based manufactures: mainly processed foods, simple wood products, refined petroleum
products, dyes, leather (not leather products), precious stones, and organic
chemicals; (ii) low-tech manufactures: mainly textiles, footwear, other leather
products, toys, simple metal and plastic products, furniture, and glassware; (iii)
medium-tech manufactures: heavy industry products such as automobiles, industrial chemicals, machinery, and relatively standard electrical and electronic
products; (iv) High-tech manufactures: complex electrical and electronic
(including telecommunications) products, aerospace, precision instruments, fine
chemicals, and pharmaceuticals.

2 Medium-tech and high-tech products account for more than 60 percent of global
manufactured exports in 1998, mainly because of rapid growth of high-tech
exports (UNIDO, 2002). Multinational corporations, however, play a key role in
international trade through the integrated global production systems. The relocation of different stages of production based on factor intensity in different
countries results in considerable intra-firm trade. Integrated production systems
are most prominent in information and communication technology industries,
where the high value-to-weight ratio of the product makes it economical to ship
products and components around the world in search of the fine differences in
costs.

3 High-tech exports: China was in 11th place in 1998, compared to not being
among the top 25 exporters in 1985. Medium-tech exports: China was not among
the top 25 in 1985, but in 13th place in 1998. Low-tech exports: China was not
among the top 25 exporters in 1985 but was the global leader in 1998. Yet its
low-tech strengths do not detract from its strong performance in medium- and
high-tech products. Resource-based exports: China was in 12th place in 1998
(not being among the top 25 in 1985) and led in developing countries. Many
developing countries rely heavily on primary exports, but competitiveness in
processed primary products is firmly in the hands of industrialized countries,
many without a large domestic resource base. Again, technology – mainly the
ability to handle large, capital-intensive and complex processing facilities – is of
great importance. So are complex organization (large integrated production
facilities across nations), marketing, and branding.

4 Winners in Table 13.5 do not include large exporters that have not improved
their competitive position during 1985–2000 (e.g. Japan in high-technology
exports), even though they might have the largest market shares over the whole
period.

5 The world export patterns have changed significantly. The changes reflect structural shifts in production caused by new technologies, new demand patterns,
new logistical factors, new ways of organizing and locating production, new policies, and new international trade rules and preferences (UNCTAD, 2002b).

6 China is already the largest market for Boeing's commercial aircraft and American machine tool markers, and its automotive market is the most promising in
the world. China is already Volkswagen's biggest foreign market, ahead of the
US.

7 Another important source of technological, scientific, and managerial knowledge is Hong Kong and Taiwan. A key strength thus is that China is not alone;
rather, it's the hub of a cluster of complementary and increasingly integrated
economies that is Greater China (Zhang, 2004; Shenkar, 2005).

References

Lall, Sanjaya (1998), "Export of manufactures by developing countries: emerging patterns of trade and location," *Oxford Review of Economic Policy*, 14 (2): 54–73.

Lall, Sanjaya (2000), "The technological structure and performance of developing countries manufactured exports," *Oxford Development Studies*, 28 (3): 337–369.

Shenkar, Oded (2005), *The Chinese Century*, University of Pennsylvania: Wharton School Publishing.

United Nations Industrial Development Organization (UNIDO) (2002), *Industrial Development Report 2002/2003*, New York: United Nations.

United Nations Conference on Trade and Development (UNCTAD) (2002a), *World Investment Report 2002*, New York: United Nations.

United Nations Conference on Trade and Development (UNCTAD) (2002b), *Trade and Development Report 2002*, New York: United Nations.

World Bank (2005), *World Development Indicators 2005*, Washington, DC: World Bank.

World Trade Organization (WTO) (2005), *World Trade Report 2005*, Geneva: WTO.

Zakaria, Fareed (2005), "Special report: does the future belong to China?" *Newsweek*, May 9, 2005: page 26–47.

Zhang, Kevin H. (2002), "China as a new power in world trade," in Fung, Pei, and Johnson ed., *China's Access to WTO and Global Economy*, Beijing: Yuhang Publishing House, pp. 32–49.

Zhang, Kevin H. (2004), "Maximizing benefits from FDI and minimizing its costs: what do we learn from China?" in Kehal (ed.), *Foreign Investment in Developing Countries*, Palgrave/Macmillan, pp. 78–91.

Index